THE WORLD ACCORDING TO WASHINGTON – AN ASIAN VIEW

"For those of us in the United States who have been sharply critical of our government's policies, it is refreshing to hear a voice from Asia giving us the point of view of people who have suffered so much from those policies. Patwant Singh's book is grounded in solid history and written with an admirable clarity. I hope it will be widely read."

Howard Zinn, Professor Emeritus, Boston University;
author of *A People's History of the United States*

"It's desperately important in this time of global confrontation that the western nations understand what the rest of the world is really thinking about them; and here is a man with deep understanding of both sides, who writes with elegance and candor."

Anthony Sampson, author of *The Anatomy of Britain, The Arms Bazaar* and *Who Runs This Place? The Anatomy of Britain in the 21st Century*

"A powerful, timely, and urgent book, one that bears witness to the misuse of American power over the past fifty-five years in Asia – power motivated by a reckless desire for political gain. Patwant Singh has written a potent, eloquent and profoundly informed warning."

T. C. McLuhan, author of *The Way of the Earth*

"Most recent studies of US foreign policies are region-specific. Patwant Singh's book addresses the entire Asian continent from China to West Asia. It is no crude anti-American diatribe but a balanced critique; its argument is cogent and draws on a wide variety of sources."

Iftikhar Malik, Professor of International History, Bath Spa University College, author of *Islam and Modernity*

PATWANT SINGH has for over forty years been one of India's leading commentators on international and cultural affairs and the environment. He has broadcast on television and radio in a number of countries, and his articles have appeared in *The New York Times,* Canada's *Globe and Mail,* the UK's *Independent* and elsewhere. From 1957 to 1988 Patwant Singh edited and published the influential magazine *Design,* which covered the full spectrum of the visual arts as well as urban planning and the environment.

Other books by Patwant Singh

India and the Future of Asia
The Struggle for Power in Asia
The Golden Temple
Gurdwaras in India and Around the World
Of Dreams and Demons: An Indian Memoir
The Sikhs
Garland Around My Neck

Patwant Singh

THE WORLD ACCORDING TO WASHINGTON
An Asian View

Common Courage Press Monroe, Maine

© Patwant Singh 2005

The author has asserted the moral right to be identified as the
author of this work

Editor: Antony Wood

Cover design by The Chapman Partnership,
and ARRT Studio, Delhi
photo by Reuters / Mian Khursheed

First published by Understanding Global Issues Ltd
The Runnings, Cheltenham, England
www.global-issues.co.uk

Published in the U.S. by
Common Courage Press
121 Red Barn Road
Monroe, ME 04951
207-525-0900
www.commoncouragepress.com

A CIP catalogue record for this book is available from the publisher

ISBN paperback 1-56751-338-7 ISBN hardback 1-56751-339-5

ISBN-13 paperback 9781567513387
ISBN-13 hardback 9781567513394

Printed in Canada

First printing

To my incomparable Meher

For Phyllis
With
my best wishes.

June 28 '05.

Contents

Acknowledgments

In our chaotic world, in which human achievements and progress are continually beset by acts of aggression and terror, it is difficult to make sense of unfolding events without the help of wise men and women. I am fortunate to have had many share their experiences and insights with me, and respond readily to my unending demands. I am deeply indebted to them for their help and guidance. Many wish to remain unnamed for perfectly understandable reasons, so I am all the happier at least to acknowledge my gratitude to the late Eqbal Ahmad, Elaine Attias, Lina Banerjee, Somendu Banerjee, Amrita Basu, Rasil Basu, Rekha Basu, Satjiv Singh Chahil, Charlie Clements, Tom Dove, John Fraser, Vinod Grover, Dipankar Gupta, Mubashir Hasan, Satish Jain, Shimi Kang, Mark Kesselman, Bernard Lown, Robie Manoff, Teri McLuhan, the late Seymour Melman, K P Prabhakaran Nair, Saeed Naqvi, F Sherwood Rowland, Animesh Roy, the late Edward Said, Syed S Shafi, Ritu Topa, Philippa Vaughan, Geoffrey Ward, Stanley Weiss, Howard Zinn and to those whose magnificent dispatches were of such great help.

I have drawn upon many sources to support my arguments – too many to acknowledge here individually, but details are given in the notes. I have also incorporated occasional passages from my other books and from articles that have previously appeared in Indian newspapers and journals.

The wondrous editorial interventions of Antony Wood, and his meticulous attention to detail, were immensely valuable, and I cannot thank him enough. Equally, my deepest gratitude to my publisher, Greg Bates, for his enthusiasm and his unshakeable faith in this book.

The perseverance and patience of my secretary, Mercy Bahadur, were remarkable throughout the writing of this book, even during the countdown to the merciless deadlines.

Finally, there aren't enough words to thank my beloved Meher for so magnificently rising to every challenge and crisis that faced us, including the time a part of Delhi's cyber system packed up and we were faced with the prospect of losing every word written – or stored – in our computer. She went through those trying days with superb aplomb, and so this book is dedicated to her invaluable support and steadfastness.

Patwant Singh
Delhi, January 2005

Preface

SINCE WORLD WAR II THE UNITED STATES HAS INTERVENED, directly and indirectly, in wars in which millions of Asians have been slaughtered.* Americans did not start all these wars; Asians started some of them themselves. Yet, in a larger sense, the US has the greater responsibility for much of the slaughter during the past century.

American reluctance or outright refusal to participate in international institutions and treaties, from the League of Nations onwards, was an invitation to disaster, and a bad model for humiliated but resurgent nations, such as Germany and Japan in the 1930s, to follow. Also, the overly simplistic ideological wars against 'communism', and the attempts to impose American concepts of 'freedom' and 'democracy', frequently entailed the support of evil regimes and the crushing of political developments much better suited to their times and particular circumstances. And when US firepower became involved the slaughter was far greater than it might have been.

The scope of this book is restricted to the relationship between the US and Asian nations, not because I consider what is happening in Africa and Latin America any less significant but because, as an Asian, I am most familiar with the experience of Asian countries and the confrontation between the US and the developing world seems to me at its starkest in Asia. After the end of World War II, countries descended from ancient civilizations and great cultural traditions – China, Korea, Iran, Vietnam, Cambodia, Laos, Indonesia, Philippines, Afghanistan and Iraq – became killing fields to satisfy US ambitions. Resource-rich Asia and its peoples were and will be easy targets for the weapons of death and destruction that Washington continues to assemble in pursuit of 'The New American Century'.

However, the weaponry a nation possesses does not necessarily confer leadership on it. Effective leadership comes painstakingly, from profound and detailed study of the people to be led – of their habits,

* See note on page 218.

thinking, beliefs, customs, traditions, family and social structures, and all the other aspects that make up the mosaic of societies. An impressive legacy of the British in India is their meticulously compiled Imperial Gazetteer of India, whose many volumes document every detail of the country, its geography and its history. The Gazetteer is the result of a serious effort to understand those who are supposed to be led. Only through these insights could strategies be framed that enabled a handful of British to lead several hundred million people.

Despite the diversity of their media, Westerners in general, and Americans in particular, are often ignorant or misinformed about present-day realities in Asia. Yet it is of crucial importance for them to understand the degree of Asian concern at the alarming implications of the re-election of George W. Bush as President and the reappointment of Dick Cheney as Vice President and Donald Rumsfeld as Defense Secretary. Such understanding is difficult to come by so long as analysis and assessment of unfolding events in Asia is overwhelmingly provided by Western think-tanks, books written by Western 'experts', and advice given to governments is shaped by Western political theories. The condition of Iraq after the invasion of 2003, and the spectacle of a situation badly bungled by a power that believed it had all the answers, illustrates the dangers of such limited thinking.

I have written this book to redress the balance and because I admire America. I have been visiting it regularly for over 40 years. I have long and enduring friendships there, and relish the welcoming warmth I experience each time I visit. I applaud and want to support the courage and convictions of the many Americans who, even though they were outvoted this time, still out number, I am sure, those who approve of reckless US interventions and initiatives abroad. My aim in this book and the epilogue has been to place in perspective the dangers which lie ahead if the euphoria of an apparently decisive electoral victory gives further impetus to Washington's unilateralist follies, and the US continues to try and impose its vision of Pax Americana on an unwilling world.

Patwant Singh
Delhi, January 2005

1

The Long Shadow

The Colonial Process Continued

It is the white race, and it alone – its ideologies and inventions
– which eradicates autonomous civilizations wherever it
spreads, which has upset the ecological balance of the planet,
which now threatens the very existence of life itself.

SUSAN SONTAG[1]

PICK ANY PART OF ASIA – West, South, East or Central Asia – and take
a flight to one or more cities in these regions. In Cairo, Damascus,
Teheran, Delhi, Islamabad, Djakarta, Seoul, Pyongyang, Tokyo or
Tashkent, you will find a premonition of impending disaster in peoples'
minds; a sense of unease at the growing awareness of a distant power's
determination to make the world its economic and political domain. A
power convinced that its huge industrial base, technological skills, lethal
weapons, and a military establishment more sophisticated than any ever
assembled, give it the right to impose its will on others. By 2003 countless
Asians were as uneasy about their future as their predecessors probably
were 400 years ago, when faced with similar uncertainties at the hands
of the European colonists.

The difference between the past and the present era – for those
who have experienced both – is the efficiency of today's killing
machines, which can deliver death with a clinical detachment towards
the innocents killed, the staggering scale of the damage inflicted.
Europe's colonial powers killed too, but in addition to the human
lives lost, damage of a different kind was inflicted as well: they
trampled on their subjects' freedom, pride, rights and sense of
self-worth with equally disastrous results. By making them feel inferior –

racially and genetically – the colonial powers eroded their sense of self-esteem, which in the long run was to prove the most unsettling and damaging result of all. This degrading game, many Asian peoples feel, is about to be played out again.

India's colonial experience, for instance, is still taking its toll. Despite pockets of excellence in the sciences, industry, information technology, agriculture, academic life and literature, its colonial hangover keeps surfacing; a collective inferiority complex of sorts with regard to the West. This is not so in China's case. Even though it was also ravaged by predatory colonialists, it managed to slough off that experience, which is why it stands up to the bullying ways of today's world powers better than India does.

India's and China's initial introduction to the colonial powers came through adventuresome Westerners; men drawn to their shores by the promise of commerce and trade who ended up subjugating them. No wonder Asians are wary of new mantras like globalization and such, which they see as strategies to control their economies; as subtler alternatives to the physical control exercised by the empire-builders of the past. Asia was dominated because of its self-centredness and its indifference to the harsh realities of the world of that time. India's experience at the hands of the British illustrates this; how a country with a unique cultural history could allow itself – through its own weaknesses – to be dominated and demeaned by those who were totally alien to the richness and texture of its own civilization. India allowed itself to be dominated because it drew no lessons from its past humiliations. In the future too, Asian countries will continue to suffer unless they draw on their past experiences to understand the dangers which face them today.

§

The seeds of Britain's Indian Empire were sown in 1585 with the arrival of William Leeds, Ralph Fitch and John Newbury on India's west coast carrying a letter from Queen Elizabeth I in which she requested "liberty and security of voyage" and that the travellers be "honestly intreated and received" so that a "mutual and friendly trafique of merchandise on both sides" could be established. They eventually reached Agra, capital of the Mughal Emperor Akbar. They found Agra "much greater than London … a great resort of merchandise from Persia and out of India and very much merchandise of silk and cloth and of precious stones, both rubies, diamonds and pearls".[2] Fitch's report on his arrival in England eight years later led to the founding of the East India Company, which helped lay the foundations of Britain's Indian Empire. As the Company's trading activities expanded, so did its ambitions, which by the eighteenth century had coalesced into a policy of conquest.

Europe's other colonial powers, aware of the remarkable prospects in India, were not far behind. By 1664 the French had formed La Compagnie des Indes for their trading operations and around 1674 founded their first settlement in Pondicherry. For the next hundred years the British and French fought continuously to prevent each other from wresting control of a decaying empire which had much more to offer than mere trade. The fortunes of the Portuguese – who had arrived in India before the British – were declining, and the Dutch were more interested in the East Indies than India. So the British, victorious over the French in the Carnatic Wars in 1775, but on the rebound from losing their American colonies, were set to realize their imperial ambitions in India.

Their dominance of the subcontinent was neither the result of a far-sighted plan nor a fortuitous event. It came about because of a struggle in which the single-mindedness, scientific bent, cohesiveness and superior military ordnance of the British triumphed over the fragmented rulers of feudal India. Many victories and defeats, savage reprisals and treacherous deals followed each other before the fate of this ancient land was sealed. As more territories kept coming under the Company's control, a system of administration was put in place, large provinces were created, new cities like Bombay, Calcutta and Madras were built, and in 1773 Calcutta was declared the capital of British-controlled India, under a governor-general responsible only to the Company's board of directors in London.

But even then Britain ruled only a part of India, and it could extend its dominion over the entire country only after the death of the legendary Maharaja Ranjit Singh (1780–1839), who had carved the redoubtable northern Sikh kingdom out of Mughal and Afghan territories and had slammed shut the doors of India in the face of Afghan and Central Asian invaders for all time.

The once mighty Mughals were easily overcome by the British because the indulgences and corruption of the imperial court had made a mockery of serious governance, and because its rebellious satraps in the far-flung empire had begun to form their own fiefdoms. The euphoric legacy of the empire built by the victorious Mughals had also faded, and Islam no longer provided the cement to bind its followers together. The Hindus, on the other hand, continued to be fragmented by their rigid caste system which had prevented them from presenting a cohesive and undivided front to Sabuktigin when he and his central Asian horsemen – lured by India's wealth – had first entered Hindustan in AD 986. Following a steady stream of further plunderers from Asia, the Mohammedans began their colonization around AD 1100, and their ascendancy over considerable parts of India lasted till 1858, the year in which the British deposed the last Mughal emperor.

A British historian attributed the rise of Muslim suzerainty over India to the social organization of the Hindus:

> Owing to this, fighting was left to a single caste, the Kshatriyas; the vast majority of the population was untrained in arms and indifferent to the fate of their country. National feeling did not exist, and even the martial clans had little sense of patriotism. In the face of common danger, it is true, they combined for a time, but otherwise they frittered away their strength in endless internecine quarrels ... The hardy Muslim invaders from the north were, man for man, bigger, stronger and better mounted than their opponents ... The Muhammedan religion was a fighting creed ... [and] all Muslims, of whatever race or social position, are equal in the sight of God. Merit was the only test of ability and a slave could rise to the throne of Delhi. In this it contrasted strongly with the endless divisions of caste-ridden Hinduism.[3]

Before the coming of the British, the Mughal Empire had been seriously weakened by internal corruption and extravagance and its rulers' divisive political and religious policies, making British ascendancy over it that much easier. Further factors that weakened it were the founding of the Sikh faith by Guru Nanak (1469–1539) and the rise of Maratha power in the Deccan in Central India under Shivaji (1627–80). The Marathas, Hindus by faith, agriculturists by profession, strong and sturdy of build, and pious by temperament, were cast into a fighting mould by Shivaji, who became a source of inspiration to his people and a cause of much concern to the Mughals.

Sikhism grew out of Nanak's determination to end the suffering caused by the colliding faiths of Hinduism and Islam by bridging their religious divide. Sikhism taught tolerance of other faiths and a concept of equality between every human being. Nanak founded a faith that drew on the basic compassion of Hinduism and the essential brotherhood of Islam – replacing dogma and doctrine by a basic belief in truth.[4]

When Guru Arjan Dev, the fifth of the ten Sikh Gurus, was brutally put to death by the religiously bigoted Mughal Emperor Jahangir in 1606, Sikhism changed from a peaceful movement of reform and reconciliation into the most militant witnessed in India. The rage of the Sikhs at the torture and killing of their saintly and scholarly Guru – who had also compiled their scriptures – set them on a course of implacable opposition to the vagaries of tyrannical and intolerant rulers like Jahangir. Their bitter battles with the Mughals, Afghans and others lasted for over 150 years, until they had ensured the end of their suzerainty over India. In 1699, the tenth and last Guru, Gobind Singh, founded the fellowship of the Khalsa whose distinctive code of personal appearance, dress and conduct set them apart from all others in India. Guru Gobind Singh gave the Sikhs an identity and an ineradicable sense of self-confidence.

Because Sikhism was rooted in the bedrock of its founders' certainties and suffering, it triumphed during the most turbulent years of its existence, in the eighteenth century. Its climax came with the creation of the Sikh Kingdom by the twenty-year-old Maharaja Ranjit Singh in 1801. When the Sikhs lost to the British ten years after Ranjit Singh's death, it was not for want of heroism on the battlefield, but for lack of guile on the part of his heirs in dealing with their adversary's perfidy. There are numerous examples of how the British consolidated their conquest of the Indian subcontinent, but the Sikh experience alone will illustrate the point.

While Ranjit Singh's charismatic personality and his leadership on the battlefield and in statecraft earned him his people's absolute loyalty, his non-Sikh courtiers' volte-face after his death ended his empire. Its betrayal by three key men was masterminded by the British who cannily assessed and employed their treacherous bent to subvert the Sikh Kingdom, the last obstacle in their way to establishing complete suzerainty over India.

The infighting in Ranjit Singh's family after his death enabled Lal Singh to become Prime Minister and Teja Singh Commander-in-Chief of the Sikh army. Gulab Singh, amassing personal wealth in a leaderless Darbar, bided his time. These three, all in the pay of the British, were non-Sikhs. Shortly after Lal Singh and Teja Singh assumed charge of their key positions in November 1845, the British declared war on the Sikh Darbar, a logical move since they now had traitors in place who would deliberately lead the Sikh army to defeat.

In the opening battle of the First Anglo-Sikh War, at Ferozeshahr, the Sikhs broke the British. "Guns were dismounted, and their [British] ammunition was blown into the air; squadrons were checked in mid-careers; battalion after battalion was hurled back with shattered ranks ... Colonels knew not what had become of the regiments they commanded or the army of which they formed a part ... On that memorable night the English were hardly masters of the ground on which they stood."[5] The next morning, however, when Teja Singh arrived on the scene with a reserve Sikh army, instead of annihilating "the wearied and famished English ... [who] saw before them a desperate and, perhaps, useless struggle", he refused to attack the dispirited enemy.[6]

On Christmas Day 1845, Lord Hardinge, the governor–general, "issued a proclamation encouraging desertions from the Sikh ranks, with the assurance of present rewards and future pensions ..."[7] In the last battle of the war, at Sobraon, the Sikhs again broke the British – but at the moment of victory, lost their Commander-in-Chief: "Teja Singh ... fled soon after the first assault ... Lal Singh and his cavalry force were nowhere to be seen. He had taken the road to Lahore".[8] Lal Singh also made it possible for the British to take the road to Lahore, and further compounded his treachery by destroying the boat bridge on the Satluj to prevent Sikhs regrouping on the northern bank.

After their final victory the British imposed an indemnity of a million and a half pounds for war expenses on the Lahore Darbar, which it couldn't pay, so they detached Jammu and Kashmir from the Sikh Kingdom and sold it to Gulab Singh, the non-Sikh prime minister, for a million pounds! "In consideration of the good conduct of Raja Gulab Singh",[9] he was also made an independent sovereign of the newly-carved state. According to the Statement of War Charges prepared by Hardinge, the total expenses incurred by the East India Company came to half a million pounds. This figure was arrived at by deducting from the total cost of two million pounds a million earned by selling Kashmir and another half a million which the Lahore Darbar was made to pay in indemnity. Hardinge noted with satisfaction that "from the financial point of view, the First Sikh War was one of the cheapest ..."[10] The means used to win the Second Anglo-Sikh War (1848–49) were no less sordid than those used in the first, and the curtain finally came down on the proud Sikh Kingdom in 1849.

One of history's ironies is reflected in the similarity between Britain's loss of its American colonies in 1783 and Sikh loss of sovereignty sixty-six years later. Both occurred because of deeply flawed leaderships. Had Britain's leading figures in 1783, Barbara Tuchman has surmised, "been others than they were, there might have been statesmanship instead of folly, with a train of altered consequences reaching to the present".[11] This was true of the Sikhs too. In their case, had their Kingdom's promise not been destroyed by treacherous leaders after Ranjit Singh's death, India's destiny might have been entirely different.

A brutal streak invariably runs through the policies of all occupying powers, and British rule in India was no exception. They, like many others, were willing to go to any extremes in ruthless pursuit of their self-interest, as the following examples will illustrate.

After the 1857 Mutiny had been put down, the two sons and grandson of the deposed Mughal Emperor Bahadur Shah were shot point-blank by a British captain after they had surrendered. "I deliberately shot them one after another ...", he explained later. "I am not cruel, but I confess I did rejoice at the opportunity of ridding the earth of these wretches."[12]

The infamous Amritsar massacre of April 1919 seems to have been aimed at striking terror into the hearts of ordinary men, women and children. At 5.30 pm Brigadier-General Reginald Edward Harry Dyer entered the Jallianwala Bagh (Park) where a large crowd had assembled to hear speeches on two repressive bills introduced by the British government. He ordered his contingent to fire into the crowd. In fifteen minutes they fired 1,650 rounds; estimates of the number killed vary from 379 to 1,000.[13]

The final act of ruthlessness was carried out at Independence on 15 August 1947. By this time the British were desperate to be rid of their largest colony. The subcontinent's division along religious lines was undertaken despite the growing violence between Hindus and Muslims, much of it actually engineered with the idea of justifying partition. Although the British – a handful of whom had ruled the subcontinent through their excellent intelligence network – were fully aware of the communal keg which would explode once partition was effected, they went ahead with it. In the ensuing violence, 600,000 were killed and 14 to 16 million displaced.

The British system of governance in India, as it developed after the fall of the Sikh Kingdom in 1849, took the following form. Administration encompassed executive, judicial, revenue-collection and development functions. The country was carved into provinces, which for better administration were divided into districts. The district officers oversaw the collection of revenues, rents, duties and cesses, a sizeable portion of which went to the treasury, and from there to the British exchequer as charges for administering India. For the development of the country's immense natural resources, metalled roads, canal networks, post and telegraph systems and railways were built. Priority was given to ensuring stable conditions so that peoples' energies could be harnessed to generate wealth for British manufacturers, trading houses, banks and shippers. This was the essential colonial process.

Gradually, the entrepreneurial drive of Indians also made its mark in the form of increasing investment in trade and small-scale industries, and later in banks, insurance companies and other financial institutions. While the British controlled and thus took the lion's share of the colonial economy, it goes to their credit that Indians were not prevented from laying the groundwork for a diversified economy.

It was a Sikh, Baba Ram Singh, who in the 1860s first expressed his opposition to foreign rule, as also to government service, English law-courts, imported goods and mill-made cloth. His emphasis on home-spun cloth, in a symbolic rejection of alien economic control, was the earliest expression of non-cooperation, which Mahatma Gandhi adopted three-quarters of a century later, as the struggle for independence intensified around the indignities of foreign rule and the rulers' arrogance.

Who benefited from India's independence? The erstwhile paramount power. It came out unscathed, and has profited from the lava of hate which has swirled and seethed beneath the surface ever since. As will be seen in Chapter 4, while India and Pakistan continue to cripple themselves with ever-escalating military expenditures, one of their principal arms suppliers, Britain, keeps laughing all the way to the bank.

§

If the British came to trade with India and ended up subjugating it, China's experience with European colonists was even more degrading. Although the Portuguese were the first to arrive in 1516, they were overtaken by other 'white seafarers' like the British and French, who demanded 'as a matter of right' the opportunity to trade with China. After they had forced it to open its doors to foreigners, a macabre twist was given to trade by the enterprising British: they went to war with China over opium. Opium, produced in India, was a lucrative product and they insisted on importing large quantities of it into China, which the incensed Chinese understandably resisted. When China lost the First Opium War (1839–42), the humiliating Treaty of Nanking awarded Hong Kong to Britain; designated Shanghai, Canton, Amoy, Foochow and Ningpo as 'treaty ports' for foreign trade; compelled China to pay for the war and the opium destroyed by the Chinese; and pegged Chinese tariffs at five per cent.

The Second Opium War (1856–58) ended in further humiliations for China: it had to legalize opium imports, cede ten new ports and also the Yangtze River for foreign trade, and give some territory on the mainland to Britain. To top it all, China had "to pay for the cost of her tuition in occidental ways"!

The humiliating treaties – the United States, having signed the Treaty of Wanghia (1844), received more advantages than the British under the Nanking Treaty – stoked China's growing resentments. These were already aggravated by the unsettling effect of cheap foreign goods (particularly textiles), the depraving effects of opium, and the galling privileges the 'most favoured nations' clause accorded to the belligerents, whose missionaries were given the freedom to evangelize, and nationals the right of residence.

It took over a hundred years for these resentments to coalesce into a vibrant nationalism and for a communist government finally to oust all foreigners from China. Although US trade with China had been steadily increasing, attempts to open China's Closed Door were rebuffed. But efforts continued as more was at stake than mere trade. This was summed up in a State Department memorandum by Secretary of State Philander Knox in 1909: "The participation of American capital in investments [in China] will give the voice of the United States more authority in political controversies in that country … the balancing of power in China is essential to peace in the Orient just as it has been necessary in Turkey to keep Europe quiet. Our interests in Asiatic waters require the prevention of the establishment of predominant interests and influences at Peking on the part of other powers". This leitmotiv of US policy is as active today as it was then.

As the contending powers – which now included Japan – continued to manoeuvre over China, some of them signed separate agreements with it. Eventually it was the Nine Power Treaty[14] signed on February 6, 1922 which provided a legal framework to the Open Door policy, to make it acceptable to the international community! This cosy arrangement was ended when the Japanese Army, mindful of its own 'manifest destiny', hit China with force on September 18, 1931. Japan's aggression against China was no accident of history. It was an inevitable outcome of the clashing interests and ambitions of the United States, Britain, Russia and Japan, and the efforts of each to stake its own claims to China's resources and territories. When Japan invaded Manchuria in 1931 the United States was as outraged as the other signatories to the Nine Power Treaty. Yet 70 years later the Bush administration announced its own agenda of pre-emptive strikes, because power is seldom exercised according to a code of conduct. What counts is the extent of power required, and this had now tilted in America's favour.

The historic indignities inflicted on China by the predatory powers varied only in detail, not in the toll they took. If Britain, France, Holland, Belgium and others profited by their colonial drive, Tsarist Russia – and its successor the Soviet Union – did even better at the same game. Not only did the Tsars acquire territories through conquest, intrigue and subversion, so also did the Soviet Union, which used the communist doctrine to penetrate societies in different countries. But first, the Tsarist inroads into Asia.

§

"The absorption by Russia of a considerable portion of the Chinese Empire is only a question of time, unless China succeeds in protecting itself", was the assessment provided to his sovereign by Prime Minister Count Sergei I. Witte in July 1903. Aware of "the eager attention of Europe and America to the vast dormant countries of the Far East", Witte pointed out that "the problem of each country concerned is to obtain as large a share as possible of the outlived Oriental states, especially of the Chinese colossus". His conclusion was to the point. "Russia, both geographically and historically, has the undisputed right to the lion's share of the expected prey".[15] Many of the Tsar's other key advisers also advocated Russian expansion into Asia and the Far East, because "without such domination we are not able either to rule the yellow race or control the inimical influence of our European rivals".[16]

Possibly the most successful of Russia's empire builders, Nikolai Muraviev, was of the view – which he conveyed to the Tsar – that it was perfectly natural for Russia "if not to own all Asia, at any rate to control the whole far Eastern Coast". He also saw enormous benefits in a close alliance "between us and the North American states … ",[17] projecting a compelling concept of a friendly Russia and America dominating the North Pacific and dividing the waters and lands lying between them. With the amalgam of arrogance and deceit that characterized his concept of Russia's goals, he had already written to the Tsar in 1853: "If the defeat of China should entail the fall of her dynasty, this outcome would of course be most favourable to Russia … Our neighbours, Manchuria and Mongolia, would become (in fact, if not in name) our possessions, and Russia would finally acquire all that she could here desire".[18]

Through treaties and other means, the Russians had already annexed enormous stretches of territory in the East, and this had whetted their appetite for more. Their task was made easier by China's wars with France and Britain which had left it weakened. The Taiping Rebellion was further destabilizing it. So the Russians moved in for a share of the spoils in an already beleaguered China. At the signing of the Treaty of Aigun in 1858, a persuasive edge to the negotiations was provided by a cannonade from the Russian gunboats anchored in the River Amur. The message was clear and the treaty was duly signed.

As well as gaining trading and consular rights, the Russians, who had taken over the remote northern reaches by earlier treaties, now acquired the entire territory (185,000 square miles) on the left bank of the Amur all the way downstream to its confluence with the Ussuri. The ownership of the lands east of the Ussuri and up to the Pacific Ocean was to be decided later – or, as events were to show, sooner rather than later.

As the nineteenth century progressed, Russia did much to increase China's agony. Within two weeks of the Aigun Treaty the Treaty of Tientsin, signed on June 14, 1858, opened five Chinese ports to Russia, and the next to be signed provided an even bigger bonanza for the Russians. The Peking Treaty (November 14, 1860) exceeded all previous Russian expectations and demands. In one decisive move the Russians extended their empire to the frontiers of Korea, legalized possession of the port they had already opened on the Pacific, Vladivostok ('Ruler of the East'), acquired the entire Amur basin, and annexed territory east of the Ussuri River. These new areas added 133,000 square miles of territory to Russia. As a bonus the Russians managed to pry loose 350,000 square miles in Central Asia by readjusting the boundary between Sinkiang and Russian Central Asia.

From very tentative and unobtrusive beginnings on the outer fringes of China – much like the arrival of the first four Englishmen in India in 1585 – the Russians could now impose their imperial will on the Manchu court. The move into Asia, initially led by the dregs of Tsarist society, was beginning to pay spectacular dividends. The Russians had added a new dimension to expansionism, mainly through a blend of bluster and deception coupled with an occasional show of force, alternating with secret deals with China's other enemies. No power acquired territory on such a massive scale with so little effort.

The fall of the Uzbek cities of Samarkand and Tashkent had by 1870 given the Russians effective control of most of Central Asia. They now claimed Sinkiang's Ili Valley – a key invasion route into Asia which they had occupied during the revolt of the Sinkiang Moslems against the Manchus. The Chinese were no longer in any doubt of Russia's designs, or the strategy used to further them. Writing of the Ili Valley to his Emperor, the formidable Chinese General Tso Tung-tang asked: "Why should China sacrifice an important area to satisfy Russia's greed? It would be like throwing a bone to a dog to prevent it from biting. But when the bone has been eaten up, the dog would still want to bite. The loss at present is apparent and the trouble in the future will be end-less".[19] Tso's tough reputation helped save Sinkiang and persuaded the Russians to take a more moderate stand. So the less invidious Treaty of St Petersburg (February 24, 1881) superseded the humiliating terms of the Livadia Treaty (1879).

Encouraged by the ease with which they had annexed the legend-ary sultanates of Central Asia – Tashkent in 1864, Samarkand in 1868, Bokhara in 1868, Khiva in 1873 and Kokand in 1876 – the Russians con-tinued their military operations through the 1880s to take their influence all the way to the Pamirs, the future borders of Afghanistan.

The Chinese region they now desired was Manchuria. Fertile and rich in mineral resources, it was the key to their future dominance of the Far East. Russia's chance came with the brief Sino-Japanese war of 1894–95. Japan's stunning victory over China, and the harsh conditions of the Treaty of Shimonoseki (April 17, 1895), again gave Russia the chance to pose as China's friend. To prove it, Russia forced the Japanese – with the help of Germany and France – to vacate Chinese territories they had occupied. That Russia itself coveted them was kept quiet. The Chinese, though apprehensive of Russia's intentions, agreed to sign the contract for the Chinese Eastern Railway on September 8, 1896.

This agreement gave the Russians astounding rights. They were to administer and police the land through which the railway line would be laid, and would impose and enforce laws, regulations and taxes in the area, overriding Chinese sovereignty in its own territory. The railway zone was not a narrow strip running across the face of the land but a wide swathe of right-of-way territory along which towns and cities would be built in due course. The agreement gave Russian penetration of Manchuria a spurious legitimacy. But though it established Russian presence in China, it also alerted the Japanese to the need to pre-empt Manchuria.

Then there was the matter of Korea. While the Russians coveted it for reasons of empire, the Japanese considered it vitally important for their national security. So any outside influence in Korea was incompatible with their strategic interests. In centuries gone by, when the Japanese had tried to establish their influence in Korea, they failed. With the restoration of the Meiji in Japan and the decline of central authority in China, Japan's opportunity came at the end of the nineteenth century. The 'hermit kingdom', isolated for hundreds of years but unable eventually to resist Japanese power, was forced in 1876 to open its ports to Japanese vessels and establish consular relations.

As the Japanese presence in Korea expanded, so did the Koreans' resentment. Within the bewildering web of antagonisms and intrigue between China, Japan and Korea, a strange understanding was reached in 1885: the two neighbouring powers would remove their troops from Korea, which would then invite military advisers from a third country. That third country was Russia.

The Russians rapidly legitimized their presence in Korea. Once in, they energetically exploited their influence in the army and court – in much the same way as they had done in China – and were soon installed at the very centre of power. Just as their pretext with the Chinese had been their desire to 'protect' them from the European powers, so the Russians offered protection to the Koreans from the undesirable Chinese, Japanese and British.

There is a striking similarity between the twentieth-century Soviet strategy of supplying military equipment and instructors to countries they wanted to bring within their orbit – with the ostensible aim of protecting them from the United States – and the tactics the Russians used in China and Korea in the nineteenth century.

Ironically, it was Russia's push to the Pacific and the construction of the Trans-Siberian railway – with its promise of transporting troops, artillery and reinforcements to Japan's very doorstep – that made the Japanese go to war with China. Their aim was twofold: to forestall the completion of the railroad by conquering territory it was to be built on, and to make Korea, under Japanese dominance, a buffer with Russia.

The Japanese struck on August 1, 1894 and in the eight-month war their victories put an end to all pretence of Chinese power in Asia. Japan was the new and dangerous adversary in the way of Russia's drive to the Far East. The decade that followed was a period of connivance, cajolery, coercion and continuing deception, in which alliances were made to deceive allies. Lulled by its sense of destiny, not to mention the ease with which it had extended its empire, Russia was totally unprepared for the decisive defeat by Japan when the two went to war on February 10, 1904. Tsarist expansionism in Asia was halted, not by a combination of European powers but by an Asian power, an island nation, infinitely smaller in size than Russia of the Imperial Tsars.

Significantly, negotiations for peace between Russia and Japan were conducted in the United States at Portsmouth, New Hampshire. America was testing the waters as a new claimant to the spoils that had drawn Europeans to the Asian continent, and the Portsmouth mediation was not only a shrewd move to establish influence there, it was also a trial run for the Asian role the United States would play with considerable benefits for itself in the years ahead.

The old adage for settling international relations was applied at Portsmouth: weaker powers had no right to determine their own fate; it was the prerogative of the stronger powers to do that. So the Treaty of Portsmouth, signed on September 5, 1905, established Japan's "paramount political, military and economic interests" in Korea. Though Russia's extensive timber, trading, mining and industrial concessions in Korea

– in the Tumen River area, Yalu Valley and Hamgyong Province – had by then developed into impressive economic stakes, defeat at the hands of Japan put an end to its Korean aspirations. Through the protocol of July 4, 1910 (one of four Russia signed with Japan), Korea was formally annexed by the Japanese.

Russia's setback was temporary. Within forty years of Portsmouth, as Japan lay in shambles at the end of World War II, the Soviets – successors to the imperial tsars – had occupied Korea north of the 38th Parallel, while the Americans – the honest brokers of Portsmouth – had moved into the South. The game of grab in Korea had not changed, only the players.

§

Soviet expansion started within months of the Revolution. In February 1918, Russian troops entered Turkestan. In April 1920, the Red Army annexed Azerbaijan, and began the Sovietization of yet another border country. The logic underlying the absorption of these two into Greater Russia was disconcertingly forthright: "We cannot do without the petroleum of Azerbaijan or the cotton of Turkestan", said Grigori Yevseyevich Zinoviev, a member of Lenin's Politburo. But he had an engaging way of delivering the coup de grâce. "We take these products, which are necessary for us, not as former exploiters, but as older brothers bearing the torch of civilization".[20] Quite a change from the idealism with which the revolutionaries had viewed the rights of nations forcibly brought under Tsarist rule. "No annexation, no indemnities, and the right of self-determination of peoples"[21] was what Lenin had said at the Petrograd Congress on November 8, 1917, three weeks after the Bolsheviks seized power.

Even as Azerbaijanian aspirations ended for all time, Stalin was saying in 1920: "We are in favour of the secession of India, Arabia, Egypt, Morocco, and other colonies from the Entente, because secession in this case would mean the liberation of those oppressed countries from imperialism and strengthening the position of revolutions. We are against the separation of the border regions from Russia since separation would here involve imperialist servitude for the regions, thus undermining the revolutionary power of Russia and strengthening the position of imperialism!"[22]

Here were the beginnings of a deceptive doctrine which, while simplistic on the surface, was to prove uniquely effective in its impact and results. Seduced by the sight of a peasants' and workers' republic challenging the world's great imperial powers, many thoughtful Asians failed to see the danger of Soviet double-talk. Their admiration for Marxist ideology prevented them from seeing the use to which the Soviets were putting it: the annexation of more territories on the Asian mainland, Mongolia being one of them.

Though their history is now largely lost in the myths of the past, the Mongols under Genghis and Kublai Khan exercised absolute power over an empire which stretched from Korea to eastern Poland, and included China, South Russia, Persia, Afghanistan, Azerbaijan and the Caucasus. Military genius and the hardihood of a warlike people took them – more than seven hundred years ago – from the remote steppes of Mongolia into Europe. The campaigns they fought, their conquests and the splendour of Kublai Khan's court were attributes of a people wholly Asian. There was nothing European in the make-up of the Mongols – the only Asians to dominate large parts of Europe. They bore the imprint of Chinese, Iranian, Indian and Tibetan civilizations. In time, after they had fanned out across the continent and into Europe, the wiles and intrigues that eventually erode all great empires took their toll of the Mongol Empire too.

While there was no Outer or Inner Mongolia when the few Mongol clans rode out of their country to found an empire, the division of the legendary Khans' homeland was forced on the Mongols by Tsarist Russia. As the nineteenth century neared its end, the stage was set with an aggressive and expansionist Russia on one side, and on the other an ambitious Japan. In the centre was a weakened China which had taken control of Mongolia in the seventeenth century. The clashing interests of these rivals eventually led, in 1907, to the dismemberment of Mongolia. France, a European power, provided the formula for the division of an Asian country seven times its size. Those were times when Europeans considered the dominance of Asia their birthright.

The 1907 convention recognized Russian and Japanese 'interests' and carved the country into Outer and Inner Mongolia: the former of special interest to the Tsars, the latter to the Japanese. An opportunity to move in on the spoils came with the Chinese Revolution and the fall of the Manchus in 1911. In October of that year, Outer Mongolia, with the help of Russian arms and encouragement, declared itself independent, and on January 12, 1912 was recognized by Russia.

In the following ten years Imperial Russia, followed by the Soviets, moved towards the annexation of Outer Mongolia by taking it away from Chinese influence and into Russian control. First Mongolian discontent against the Chinese was assiduously fanned, then Mongolian aspirations for a reunified country were subverted, and finally, with China completely ousted, Red Army troops entered the country. The Soviet strategy for reducing Mongolia to a satellite should have been a warning to Asians of how power is exercised by manipulation and subversion.

Even though the Mongolian People's Revolutionary Party, established on Russian soil, had a membership of fewer than a hundred and fifty, it styled itself a provisional government. Within weeks, this 'government' appealed to the Soviet Union for assistance and Moscow gladly obliged. Red Army troops entered Mongolia, a Comintern network was established, the independent state proclaimed ten years earlier was overthrown, and in September 1921 the People's Revolutionary Government was established. Outer Mongolia was now securely in the Soviet camp.

There has been justifiable criticism of American support for juntas in the armed forces of the nations it wishes to subvert. But the way in which the Soviets set up a subservient government in Mongolia, ostensibly in the name of the proletariat, was no less brazen.

§

There was still the matter of the disputed Sakhalin and Kurile islands lying off the Asian coast which both the Russians and the Japanese claimed. Once it became obvious to the imperial powers that the Soviet Union had come to stay, they were not averse to allowing it a share of the spoils, despite their antipathy towards the arriviste Bolsheviks. They did not want the exploitation of Asia to appear too one-sided. It needed the balance which Russia provided. The process of international horsetrading which had begun decades earlier reached its peak with the secret agreement signed at Yalta by the USSR, United States and Britain in February 1945, whereby the Soviets acquired the Sakhalin and Kurile islands. To understand that deal, some knowledge of the islands' history, and the reason why they have been up for grabs so frequently, is necessary.

As the eastward drive of the Tsar's men, in pursuit of Russian imperialism, brought them to the Sea of Japan, they found, just a few miles from the Amur estuary, Sakhalin Island, which the West had once assumed was an extension of the Asian mainland. The Japanese on the other hand – initially out of ignorance, and subsequently as a strategy – insisted it was an extension of Hokkaido, their northernmost island. With some of their people settled in southern Sakhalin, the Japanese looked upon it with proprietary concern. It was not until 1849 that a Russian naval captain, Gennadi Nevelskoy, discovered he could sail around it, and established that it was an island. Not one to let this opportunity pass, Tsar Nicholas I issued an edict in April 1853 ordering the Russians to land on the island, take it over, and "not to tolerate any alien settlements on Sakhalin". The dispute with Japan over the island had begun.

The Kurile Islands now started to be seen as a possible way out of the impasse. This string of islands, largely uninhabited – except for Iturup – with some Japanese settlers at the southernmost end of the chain, had been claimed by the Japanese since the eighteenth century. Yet the Russians had controlled it since 1830. They now offered a solution to this tangled situation: all of the Kuriles to go to Japan in exchange for southern Sakhalin. But it was not until 1875 that an exchange was finally effected. Russia now got all of Sakhalin, and Japan the Kurile chain. This status quo was sustained for the next thirty years until the Russians were routed in the war with Japan. The Treaty of Portsmouth divided Sakhalin along the 50th Parallel and Japan regained control of the southern half.

After several decades of ceaseless struggle over control of Sakhalin and the Kurile islands, the secret Yalta Agreement of 1945 seemed to put an end to the controversy, though arguments over their ownership still continue.

§

At the other end of Asia lies Indonesia, of ancient lineage, and with its own colonial scars – both past and present. The island of Java was home to the very earliest strains of the human race: the bones of 'Java man' (*Pithecanthropus erectus*) were discovered here in 1891. The present-day Indonesians are descended from a negrito race to be found in Africa, southern Asia and Australia, and also from the Malay-Polynesian groups. These diverse people arrived in the Indonesian archipelago centuries before Christ, the dominant religion today being Islam (around ninety per cent), followed by a sprinkling of Buddhism, Hinduism and Christianity.

The Javanese have always had a reputation as a cultivated people, and according to one observer "Java has been civilized longer than England".[23] Their remarkable techniques of rice cultivation, the skill of their craftsmen in gold, copper and bronze, their social organization, and the fact that they lived in towns and cities well before the time of Christ, testify to their composite culture. Indian and Indonesian missions carrying their countries' credentials visited China as early as 166 AD, "at the same time that a representative of Marcus Aurelius arrived in the Celestial Kingdom".[24] Evidence of vigorous trade between Indonesia and China in the first century has surfaced through many excavations, and the country's historic ties with India are highlighted by outstanding works of Hindu and Buddhist art in Java, Sumatra and Celebes.

While the Buddhists, Hindus, Chinese and Muslims arrived in these islands with peaceful intentions, the equanimity of the islanders was short-lived after four Dutch ships dropped anchor off Sumatra's west coast in June 1596. This first visit concluded with a treaty of friendship, to pave the way for trade between the two countries: the same mantra of trade which opened many ancient lands to European traders, and ended in their enslavement.

The Australian diplomat-journalist Bruce Grant has described the ironies inherent in the situation:

> The spectacle of European colonialism is astonishing in retrospect; the arrogance of the 1494 Treaty of Tordesillas with Portugal and Spain, two sides of a small European peninsula, seriously dividing the world into two spheres of interest, is only a little more unreal to contemplate in today's world than the thought of France's vast possessions, or the far flung empire of Britain. But no conquest is more difficult to appreciate than that of the Dutch in tropical Asia. The virtues that made the Netherlands the most ardently-worked plot of land in Europe – thrift, care, cleanliness and attention to detail – were lost in the sprawling plenitude of the East Indies. Holland is about one-quarter the size of Java, or half the size of Tasmania, and the flatness of its skyline, bringing suburbia within reach of everyone's bicycle, was hardly a preparation for pioneering one of the most mountainous and erratic landscapes in the world … The Dutch eventually

did it with sea power, for which they had to thank the industrial revolution and, after the Napoleonic wars, the connivance of the British.[25]

The Dutch visit lasted 350 years. Indonesia is extraordinarily rich in natural resources – oil, tin, rubber and timber. Once they had seen what annexation of this rich archipelago could do for their economy, the Dutch, like the English in India, soon wanted more than mere trade with Indonesia. They wanted to own it. In the 1930s – after they had established their ownership – the Dutch governor–general, Jonkheer de Jonge, provided his perspective of the future: "We have ruled here for three hundred years with the whip and the club, and we shall still be doing it for another three hundred years".[26]

As it transpired, the Republic of Indonesia was proclaimed on August 17, 1945 – less than ten years after de Jonge's boast. But with the Dutch determined to re-establish their sovereignty over it after World War II, the nation had to face very turbulent times before consolidating its control. After much blood-letting during two 'police actions' by the Dutch, Indonesian independence was formally legitimized on November 2, 1949. Its troubles, however, were far from over. While the country was still recovering from its wartime occupation by the Japanese, the subversive activities of the Dutch, and Moscow's divisive moves through Indonesia's growing communist movement, Indonesia's right to make independent decisions was being compromised by the United States. Its immense natural resources qualified Indonesia as a key element in the American oligarchy's aim of remaking the world according to US needs. The following chapter deals with Indonesia's experiences against this backdrop.

§

Even prior to US opposition to Indonesian nationalism, America's subversion of Mohammed Mossadeq's nationalist government in Iran in 1953 had been duly noted by many Asians. The intensely nationalistic Iranian Prime Minister was considered unacceptable not because he was a communist, but because he was prone to place Iran's needs before those of the United States.

American intervention in Iran and Indonesia represented the new reality of the post-colonial age: a resurgent United States – fully cognizant of its industrial, economic and military power – prepared to go to any lengths to achieve its ends: control of the world's oil, gas, mineral and other resources and, if possible, of its political and ideological orientation as well. For quite a while containment of communism was the raison d'être – and the cloak – for many dubious US moves. But when nationalists like Mossadeq and Sukarno were targeted for taking decisions to improve their countries' lot, the US drive for global power became increasingly obvious.

Mossadeq had assumed office with a strong sense of purpose. Iran, a country with a great past, had been reduced to a state of chronic poverty despite its vast oil deposits. Determined to break Britain's stranglehold on Iran's oil resources, Mossadeq nationalized the giant Anglo-Iranian Oil Company within three days of taking office on May 1, 1951. Not unexpectedly, Western oil companies boycotted Iran's nationalized oil, and put pressure on Whitehall and Washington to bring Mossadeq to heel.

US moves now took a direction the British hadn't bargained for. Sensing an opportunity for besting both the British and the nationalists, the United States went to work on turning the crisis to its advantage. It first offered Iran economic assistance, something the British understandably disapproved of. This aid, so Washington said, had a friendly purpose, being intended to help Iran tide over its foreign exchange deficits following the oil boycott. Finding Mossadeq firm on pursuing his own policies, the US administration veered around to the British view, which, in Anthony Eden's words, was quite simply that Mossadeq should go and his place be taken by someone more pliable and sensitive to the strategic and oil interests of the West, and not just of his own country.

Since Mossadeq was obviously not the US's man, his fate was sealed. The CIA, given the go-ahead to get rid of Iran's premier, sent one of its ace operators to engineer the overthrow of the legitimate government. Driving across Iran's borders, Kermit ('Kim') Roosevelt, grandson of President Theodore Roosevelt and the CIA's key agent in the Middle East, established his headquarters in a Teheran basement. Around this time, Brigadier General H. Norman Schwarzkopf, former head of the New Jersey police, also arrived in Teheran. In the 1940s he had helped reorganize the Shah's police, and his contacts with them were excellent. He was also a friend of General Fazollah Zahedi, the man the CIA had picked to succeed Mossadeq.

Events now moved swiftly. While the embattled premier strove to stabilize the situation, the CIA whipped up the fears of those who felt threatened by Mossadeq's policies. These included the Shah, the big landowners, and the army.

With unlimited financial resources, with a staff of five US agents and seven Iranian intelligence operatives, and with the maximum connivance of the US Military Assistance Mission in Iran, Roosevelt now swung into action. Securing the services of street demonstrators, musclemen, mobsters, and disloyal members of the military and police forces, he soon formulated a strategy to destroy Iran's government.

On August 13, 1953, the Shah dismissed Mossadeq and appointed Zahedi as the new Prime Minister. Mossadeq arrested the colonel who brought the dismissal decree. As the premier's supporters took to the streets the Shah and his queen fled the country. With the tide running in Mossadeq's favour and popular enthusiasm at fever pitch, Roosevelt ordered his musclemen into the streets while elements of the army loyal to the Shah cracked down on the government's supporters. The coup was underway. Mossadeq was arrested, Zahedi took over as Prime Minister, the Shah – who had the CIA's chief, Allen Dulles, keep him company during his brief exile in Rome – returned, and hopes of popular rule in Iran ended.

The extent to which the US Military Assistance Mission accredited to Iran helped to subvert that country's nationalist government was made clear by Major-General C. Stewart, director of the mission's programme, in his evidence before the House Foreign Affairs Committee:

> When this crisis came on and the thing was about to collapse, we violated our normal criteria and among other things we did, we provided the army immediately on an emergency basis, blankets, boots, uniforms, electric generators, and medical supplies that permitted and created an atmosphere in which they could support the Shah ... The guns that they had in their hands, the trucks that they rode in, the armored cars that they drove through the streets, the radio communications that permitted their control, were all furnished through the military defense assistance programme ... had it not been for this programme, a government unfriendly to the United States probably would now be in power.[27]

The conduct of the US Mission paid off in terms of benefits flowing from the coup. In the oil agreement signed by a grateful General Zahedi, the monopoly of the British-owned Anglo-Iranian Oil Company was broken, and US companies, such as Gulf and Standard Oil of New

Jersey, received forty per cent interest in the consortium that emerged. The prospects for the future looked good in 1954, and the United States treated its friends well. One of its first acts after the coup was to pay $1.7 million as 'bonuses' to the Iranian army and police.

Kim Roosevelt did not do badly, either. On leaving the CIA, he became Vice-President of Gulf Oil.

General, now Prime Minister, Fazollah Zahedi was a man of many interests who had been arrested by the British during World War II because of his Nazi sympathies. The British agents who went through Zahedi's residence found in his bedroom "a collection of German automatic weapons, silk underwear, some opium, letters from German parachutists operating in the hills, and an illustrated register of Teheran's most exquisite prostitutes".[28]

Though it suited the State Department to label Mossadeq a communist, Washington could hardly be ignorant of the fact that Mossadeq was no communist but a nationalist to the core. He had not come to power on a communist vote, but as the head of a nationalist coalition. The main platform of his National Front was its opposition to the exploitation of Iranian oil by outsiders. The communist Tudeh Party was in fact against him. Mossadeq had, within weeks of taking office, put down a communist demonstration at a cost of over a hundred lives. Even two days before the coup which overthrew him, Mossadeq refused communist support which might have helped him stay in office and thus changed the entire course of the country's history. It is ironic that, in a subsequent Soviet assessment of these events, the decline of the Tudeh Party's impact on Iranian politics was attributed to the fact that it was "fighting on two fronts – against imperialism and against Mossadeq".[29]

In continuing to insist that Mossadeq was a Soviet minion, Washington used the American public's aversion to communism as a cover for its global goals – the establishment of US hegemony in post-colonial Asia, controlling sources of oil and other raw materials for meeting the increasing demands of US industries, creating safe markets for American manufactures – above all, the urge to gain and exercise power, the need of the strong to dominate the weak.

§

Once the former colonial powers could no longer influence events in their erstwhile colonies, interventionism became an increasingly acceptable option in America's foreign policy. Washington intervened if political and social changes legitimately taking place met with its disapproval because they seemed at odds with its interests and beliefs. Intervention was also resorted to when a country nationalized businesses, especially foreign-owned ones. Or if it opted for radical land reforms. Or ignored Washington's disapproval of its actions.

Intervention took many forms: from support for coups, counter-coups and insurrections, manipulation of individuals, leaderships and organizations, and infiltration of parties, professions, media and academic communities to covert and clandestine operations, paramilitary operations and outright wars – not skirmishes, strikes and such, but full-scale wars of attrition with state-of-the-art weapons. What has replaced the colonial age is a different form of dominance backed by the suddenness, unpredictability and scale on which death is delivered – with all the odds favouring the aggressor.

At the end of World War II, America was still a long way from the unilateralism it would flaunt at the dawn of the new millennium, even though some of its actions were disquieting for those who had long admired its advocacy of peoples' rights. The libertarian beliefs of earlier Americans, which inspired others to fight for similar principles in their own countries, have now been overtaken by totalitarian attitudes, and their Jeffersonian ideals by arrogance and belligerence. This is generating global resentments as this once-admired democracy lays waste nations whose leaderships disagree with it.

The purpose of this book is to bring home in time the need for Washington to take heed of the worldwide anger and dismay its ill-advised actions are causing. It would be unwise to ignore them. While Asians, for instance, expect a partnership with the United States – not an inferior relationship – what they are offered instead is the unilateralist approach of the Bush doctrine, with its pre-emptive and punitive strikes, blockading of humanitarian lifelines to 'evil' states, regime-changes, destruction of national economies, and the prospect of more wars. It would seem highly unlikely that in the long run, with such tools of terror and intimidation, Washington can succeed in its goal of global dominance.

Strong-arm methods succeeded in colonial times since the West, which pioneered the industrial age, was ahead of the colonized. It led in technology, firepower, weapons, industrial goods, ships, and much else: it had a scientific outlook, a pragmatic approach to matters of organization, inventiveness and adaptability. But Asians have come a long way since. At the beginning of the twenty-first century, their scientific temper, industrial skills, technological innovativeness and creativity not infrequently can out-match those of their Western counterparts. Their drive is also fuelled by the need to prove their worth to a waiting world because of their past subjugation, and by their disinclination to accept the devious methods employed to subvert and dominate them.

Even as means of delivering death from outer space are being perfected and new weapons developed to degrade the adversary's cities and countryside, it is a fact of today's life that Asians can hit back. If not from outer space, then no less destructively on the ground. The only way of avoiding this is to acknowledge their aspirations to a way of life which will enable them to rediscover their dignity and cultured ways.

2

Between Rhetoric and Reality

Beginnings of US Intervention in Asia

Political language – and with variations this is true of all political parties, from Conservatives to Anarchists, is designed to make lies sound truthful and murder respectable, and to give an appearance of solidity to pure wind.

GEORGE ORWELL[1]

THE BITTER RIVALRY OF THE UNITED STATES AND THE SOVIET UNION savaged Asia in the second half of the twentieth century. The stated purpose of the former was defence of the free world and the right of self-determination for the newly independent states. They would be taught 'the arts of self-government', although the real aim was to dominate their actions and affiliations. The aim of interventionism on the part of both superpowers was to bring as many Asian countries as possible – along with their natural wealth – into their sphere of influence. That the wars fought in pursuit of this aim proved catastrophic for the Asian peoples who were supposed to benefit wasn't of much concern to them. One of the first nations to become the battleground of competing ideologies was Korea. While historians may find it difficult to agree on when the first Americans set foot in Asia, none would dispute their very definite presence in the continent today. American tourists, products, media, multinationals and military bases seem to have become a part of the Asian landscape. Yet the years since World War II have seen a steady decline in the goodwill once entertained for American ideals, intelligence and charm, goodwill that successive American administrations have forfeited by refusing to take the sensibilities of other people into account.

Many Asians no longer see Americans as the standard-bearers of a desirable new order. Their early compassion, concern and generosity towards the less fortunate of the world, qualities unique in history, have been transformed into the cynical and self-interested activities of their political elites and industrial and financial cartels. Successive US governments have cloaked their financial and expansionist dreams in the self-righteous disguise of protectors of the free world. Their actions have not only uprooted traditional societies they had pledged to help, they have also misled the American people.

What started as a form of paternalism after World War II evolved into interventionism. The paternalism was spelt out by Franklin D. Roosevelt at his meeting with Stalin in Teheran on November 28, 1943. The American President "referred to one of his favourite topics, which was the education of the peoples of the Far Eastern colonial areas, such as Indo-China, Burma, Malaya, and the East Indies, in the arts of self-government ..."[2]

He was more specific at their next meeting. At Yalta, he told Stalin on February 7, 1945 that the only true experience the United States had of teaching self-government to people was in the Philippines, and that it had taken fifty years to prepare them for it. He felt that in the case of Korea, the period might be from twenty to thirty years. For Korea, "what we had in mind was a trusteeship composed of a Soviet, an American, and a Chinese representative".[3]

Those were the days of US-Soviet camaraderie when it seemed possible to decide the world's future in an atmosphere of easy informality. The victorious powers saw nothing odd in talking of a tutelage of twenty to thirty years for Korea. Nor did it even appear strange to them that Korean views were given no place in their calculations; the Koreans were not once asked how they felt about their own future. But US-Soviet bonhomie did not last long. Opposing national interests began to strain their relationship, and the Koreans – like other Asian countries in the coming decades – paid a bitter price for the developing confrontation between the two.

Could it possibly be that the independent and self-confident foreign policy of a nuclear-armed North Korea at the start of the twenty-first century is powered in part by the humiliations suffered at the hands of foreign aggressors who bombed, subjugated, and partitioned Korea, fought wars on its soil, and exploited its natural wealth? Anger and rage at indignities and suffering experienced can never be wholly erased.

At the Cairo Conference of 1943, Roosevelt, Churchill and Chiang Kai-shek promised Korea eventual independence after its liberation from Japanese occupation. But the end of World War II brought partition following the broad disposition of the allied forces: the Red Army north of the 38th Parallel and US forces to the South.

Richard J. H. Johnston of *The New York Times* cabled from Seoul at the close of September 1945, the month the Japanese surrendered in Korea: "Today the question on the lips of all thinking Koreans, representing every shade of political opinion, is this: why has our country been divided? Neither the Russians nor the Americans here can answer that. The Koreans' great fear is of what will be inherited by them when the day comes for the removal of Allied controls. Will the country be torn by political strife resulting from the establishment of two opposing ideologies?"[4]

These fears were to prove tragically true. Not only were "Korean hopes for freedom and independence … hung like a ragged scarecrow on barbed wire"[5], but other countries in Asia would also be partitioned to suit the schemes of the Western powers. Korea, an early victim of interventionism, became the battlefield for a proxy war between outside powers. Which is why in August and September 1948 the country was divided into South Korea as America's sphere of influence and communist-led North Korea.

The rationale in support of the Korean War, quite simply stated, was that while US intervention in the affairs of other countries was moral and justified, 'internal aggression' by nationalists or communists was not. So what was the nature of the aggression in Korea to which the United States responded?

Partition of Korea by the superpowers, following the ejection of the Japanese by the Soviet army in 1945, formalised and reinforced the existing hostility between the mainly communist north and the nationalist south, making conflict inevitable. On June 24, 1950, the military forces of the Koreans north of the 38th parallel (in the Russian sphere of influence) crossed the dividing line in an effort to unify their country and fighting broke out between the two sides. Whether the Russians or Americans were guilty of starting the war was not of much consequence to the families of the 300,000 Koreans who lost their lives between June 24, 1950 and July 27, 1953. Both powers were responsible for these deaths.

Washington skilfully got the United Nations to sponsor American intervention, so as to provide an air of respectability to the introduction of foreign troops to South Korea. But instead of creating confidence in the world system, this action was seen by thoughtful observers as a successful exercise in the use of power and money to manipulate votes in the world body, because the pace at which the UN moved was revealing. Within hours of the start of fighting on June 24, the UN Security Council met and approved with minor modifications the draft resolution submitted by the United States. Nine of the fifteen Council members voted in favour and one (Yugoslavia) abstained. The Soviet Union was absent in protest against the presence of Nationalist China's representative on the Council. UN members were told "to render every assistance to the United Nations in the execution of this resolution, and to refrain from giving assistance to the North Korean authorities".[6] No wonder an approving President Truman told a press conference on June 26 that "the government of the United States is pleased with the speed and determination with which the United Nations Security Council acted to order a withdrawal of the invading forces to positions north of the 38th parallel".[7]

With the UN formality out of the way, US combat troops, under General Douglas MacArthur, were ordered in on June 30, 1950: within six days of the start of the fighting on June 24. The air force had already begun intensive bombing of North Korea. In contrast, while the American combat forces grew in months to more than 210,000 men, there were no Soviet troops or advisers with the advancing North Koreans.[8] As for bombing raids, "by the end of the war the United States was exercising almost no target restraint in North Korea and the Communists were doing no bombing in South Korea".[9]

The statistics provided by this panorama of violence were a source of satisfaction to the US administration and military. Within three months of June 1950, all industrial targets in North Korea, except Rashin, had been levelled. Within two weeks of June 1952, when bombing of hydroelectric plants was first authorized, 90 per cent of the power capacity of North Korea was destroyed. Yet not only did the North Koreans' will to resist survive, as in similar circumstances would that of the North Vietnamese in the years ahead, North Korea emerged – as in time would North Vietnam – tougher and more resolute.

It was not American sympathy, moral commitment or support for the people of Korea that made the President order the bombing and later the invasion of North Korea. It was simple self-interest. The United States saw the possible absorption of South Korea by its communist counterpart in the North as a first step in a profound tilt in the balance of power in favour of the Soviets, and this was unacceptable.

Although Truman was squeamish about communists establishing influence in nations close to the United States, he had no compunction in ordering General MacArthur to overrun distant North Korea and take US forces up to the borders of a major Asian power, China. The United States tried hard to make its intervention in Korea look like something other than what it really was: the use of military power to counter the Soviet threat to American hegemony in the Far East. An Asian country provided the setting, and paid a terrible price.

In 2003, fifty-two years after American troops first entered South Korea, 37,000 of them were still based there.

How much goodwill has the United States earned in more than half a century of close engagement with South Korea? Reports at the beginning of 2003 indicated an increasing anti-Americanism with "the highest risk of violence on the streets of South Korean cities".[10] Col. Boylan of the US army, who was attacked and stabbed in Seoul at that time, said: "They [the GIs] are being spat on. They are being cussed at. They are being hit".[11] The resentment, according to some Americans, "verges on hatred", especially among young South Koreans. According to Sally Milne, a British schoolteacher in Seoul: "My friends, American, Canadian, British, New Zealanders and Australian, have all been affected. They have been glared at, spat on, refused seats on the subway and refused service in some stores".[12] For someone on an Asian street it is difficult to distinguish between one Western nationality and another. And therein lies another problem: the rising anti-Americanism in an increasing number of Asian countries that frequently finds expression in indiscriminate anti-Western outbursts.

From its creation, North Korea's nationalistic fervour and drive have helped it develop a formidable arsenal of weapons including missiles, long-range delivery systems, a nuclear capability and a standing army of a million troops – the fourth largest in the world.

Its resentment of the United States has been fuelled by memories of the deadly devastation wrought by it during the Korean War. As if this weren't enough, President Bush has chosen to include North Korea in the states he labels as the "axis of evil", adding for good measure: "I loathe Kim Jong Il".[13]

The moral to look for in these growing tensions is that if the experience of past transgressions can continue to haunt the world for so long, can things get any better through the aggravation of those wrongs by resorting to new aggressions, punitive strikes and such? North Korea's drive to develop a nuclear arsenal has not been fuelled by paranoia, but by US belligerence – past and present. According to a Washington insider: "People talk about North Korea being crazy, but it's not. It's purely rational for a nation with no assets being threatened by the world's major power to develop insurance against attack".[14]

§

Nineteen-fifty was a fateful year for yet another Asian region, Indo-China. Even as full-scale fighting erupted in Korea that year, the seeds of another, far bloodier war were being sown in Vietnam. After the defeat of the Japanese in August 1945, the communist wartime resistance leader Ho Chi Minh, whose forces were in control of most of the country, had quickly declared an independent democratic Republic of Vietnam. The French, however, colonial rulers of Indo-China since the nineteenth century, soon returned to try to restore colonial rule over the whole of the area. Based in the francophile south of Vietnam, they conducted an eight-year war against Ho Chi Minh. In February 1950, following Moscow's recognition of Ho Chi Minh's regime in the north, Washington recognized Bao Dai as president of a French puppet state in the south.

Once again the communist and non-communist powers were establishing spheres of influence in the form of North and South Vietnam. As with Korea, Washington would have no compunctions about the division of another Asian country if it satisfied its interests. Nor about setting the stage for an eventual war between a divided North and South Vietnam.

Washington's attitude to the fighting that broke out between the French and the Vietminh in 1945–46 had already been made clear in a cable sent to the American embassy in Paris by the Secretary of State, George C. Marshall. In it he stressed that the United States should "not lose sight of the fact that Ho Chi Minh has direct communist connections and it should be obvious that we are not interested in seeing colonial empire administrations supplanted by philosophy and political organization directed from and controlled by [the] Kremlin".[15]

The United States, it was obvious, was less concerned with the principle of ending colonial rule and more with replacing it with political systems responsive to its own. Since neither the colonial powers nor the Kremlin – and least of all the nationalists – could be expected to favour Washington's interests, the United States was preparing to look after its own agenda by becoming the dominant power in Asia. Washington's treatment of Ho Chi Minh showed that nationalism had no more appeal for the United States than it had for the French.

The Truman administration's rebuff of Ho Chi Minh at the close of 1945, after his forces had wrested control of Hanoi from the Japanese, is well documented. According to Neil Sheehan in *The Pentagon Papers*, "from October, 1945, until the following February, Ho Chi Minh wrote at least eight letters to President Truman or to the Secretary of State, formally appealing for United States and United Nations intervention against French colonialism". There is no record "that any of the appeals was answered". The conclusion drawn in the Pentagon account is that "non-intervention by the United States on behalf of the Vietnamese was tantamount to acceptance of the French".[16] But the United States went still further. It helped the French re-enter Indo-China.

In 1948 the State Department's Office of Intelligence and Research concluded that there was no evidence that Ho Chi Minh was Moscow's man (the Soviets waited a full five years, until 1950, before according his government diplomatic recognition), yet Washington's attitude remained unchanged. It changed abruptly, however, against him, when Chiang Kai-shek was driven out of China towards the end of 1949. Since there was a perceived threat to America's own post-war ambitions on the Asian mainland now, it did intervene: but against the nationalists, and on the side of colonial France and its figurehead ruler Bao Dai. In due course, the United States was to supplant the French and Bao Dai.

On May 8, 1950, still some weeks away from US military intervention in Korea, Washington announced a grant of $10 million to the French to help them conduct the war more effectively in Indo-China. America's self-appointed role in Asia was becoming clearer.

Meanwhile, "Annamite nationalists spoke of the United States as men speak of a hope they know is forlorn but to which they desperately cling all the same. Could all the fine phrases of the Atlantic Charter, of the United Nations Pact, of President Roosevelt and his successor, really have meant nothing at all?"[17] They were to mean nothing, as the Annamites (the old term for the Vietnamese) were finding out.

The next blow to the Annamites came with the staggering announcement that the Americans had agreed to sell the French $160 million worth of equipment for use in Indo-China. "To the Annamites this looked like American underwriting of the French conquest. The Americans were democrats in words but no help in fact, just as the Russians were communists in words, but no help in fact. 'We apparently stand quite alone', said Ho Chi Minh. 'We shall have to depend on ourselves'."[18] Here was the voice of a clear-headed nationalist, and not of a man directed from and controlled by the Kremlin.

This was a turning point for the United States. Washington not only began to underwrite France's belief in its military and racial superiority, but revealed similar attitudes of its own; thereby destroying the myth, so assiduously created, about liberal and lofty ideals guiding US global actions. In reality, its conduct in world affairs was to be increasingly characterized by double-dealing.

By 1954 America's clandestine and covert actions in Vietnam reached a point where they mocked the treaties, protocols and public pronouncements through which it purported to uphold a civilized world order. Not only was it now paying eighty per cent of the cost of the French war in Indo-China, but even as the conference called to settle the Korean and Indo-Chinese questions met in Geneva in May 1954, and separated the country with a ceasefire line drawn along the 17th parallel, a resolution seeking Congressional authority to commit American troops in Indo-China was also being drafted.

Simultaneously, W. B. Bedell Smith, the US Under-Secretary of State and leader of the American delegation to the Geneva talks, was assuring the Conference that his country intended to refrain from the use of force in deference to the Geneva Agreements, and that the US "would view any renewal of aggression in violation of the aforesaid Agreements with grave concern and as seriously threatening international peace and security".[19]

Here were two faces of the American administration: one sitting at a peace conference supporting the agreements reached by it, the other preparing to contravene them behind the scenes.

Earlier, the National Security Council had urged President Eisenhower to inform Paris that in the event of French acquiescence in a communist takeover of Indo-China, the United States would stop its aid to France. While the French were beginning to look for a face-saving formula which would enable them to pull out of Vietnam, the United States was doing its best to keep them there. If the French Foreign Minister, Georges Bidault, is to be believed, worse still was going on behind the scenes. According to him, around April/May 1954, as the French position at Dien Bien Phu worsened, Dulles twice offered to mount nuclear strikes against the Vietminh at Dien Bien Phu.[20] That neither of these proposals materialized was not due to any lack of interventionist enthusiasm on the part of the American administration but to the President's reluctance to act without Congressional approval.

Undaunted, and still fully determined to oppose Vietnamese nationalism, Washington weighed in with an entirely new set of covert options. These ranged from a proposal by Admiral Badford, Chairman of the Joint Chiefs of Staff, that the US create an "International Volunteer Air Corps" to bomb the Asians, to a French suggestion that the American air force use planes painted with French markings.

But Washington did not wait until the many subterfuges covering full-scale commitment had been worked out. It sanctioned, as early as 1954, the use of sabotage and terrorism against North Vietnam. It was in that year that the United States took the place of the French in Vietnam, who departed after the de facto partition produced by the Geneva agreement. To head its team for clandestine operations in Vietnam, Washington chose Col. Edward G. Lansdale, a CIA agent described in one account as a "legendary intelligence operative". The biographical account appended to *The Pentagon Papers* describes him as the man who advised President Ramon Magsaysay of the Philippines on how to put down the communist-led rebellion.

On June 1, 1954, *at a time when the Geneva Conference was still in session,* Col. Lansdale landed in Saigon. Assisted in his mission by the American establishment in Saigon, and determined to justify Washington's faith in him, the energetic Colonel soon swung into action. In the first year of his covert operations, his team's activities were wide-ranging – from winning over the mistress of the Vietnamese Chief of Staff, General Hinh, to wrecking Hanoi's bus service and sabotaging the North Vietnamese railroads. The CIA's activities expanded from the bizarre to the criminal, with nothing to justify its destructive acts inside Vietnamese territory other than American resentment at the nationalist ideology of North Vietnam. But official Washington was already referring to the North Vietnamese as 'enemies', and its team of subverters set about destroying Vietnamese lives and property with singular cold-bloodedness. It is no coincidence that as a reaction to all this, 1960 saw the formation of the communist resistance movement in South Vietnam, known as the National Liberation Front, and its military arm, the Vietcong.

As is well-known, the nature of American intervention was to shift in February 1965 from subversive, clandestine and coercive activities to an open though undeclared war of unparalleled savageness with massive air bombardments and commitment of ground troops; although from 1950 to 1965 the United States had already flouted every known convention devised to regulate the conduct of nations.

Washington's disinclination to abide by the decisions of the Geneva Conference, even as its representative was giving it his country's fullest support, reveals the deceit the American administration was injecting – and as this book will show, continues to inject to this day – into its international relations. It is now accepted by some Washington analysts that the administration's actions figured prominently in the ultimate breakdown of the Geneva settlement for Indo-China in 1954. What needs highlighting here is that with that breakdown perished all prospects of elections in the two zones of Vietnam.

As at the time of Vietnam, so also in subsequent decades, the United States has preferred strong, well-armed and well-heeled military dictatorships like those in Iran, Indonesia and elsewhere to democracies around the world. Testifying before the Senate Committee on Foreign Relations on February 17, 1966, General Maxwell D. Taylor placed this position in perspective. Speaking approvingly of the government of Prime Minister Ky, a former swashbuckling air force chief and South Vietnam's fifth prime minister in thirteen months, Taylor said:

> This is the first government which is solidly backed by the armed forces; and as long as they are behind this government in the present sense, it is not going to be overturned by some noisy minority as some governments were overturned in the previous years. So I do feel there

are some encouraging indicators of growing stability in the political sense.

At another point in his testimony, he said:

As of today the overall military strength in South Vietnam is approaching seven hundred thousand, the largest military force in being among all of our allies, worldwide.[21]

This from a former Chairman of the Joint Chiefs of Staff, former Ambassador to South Vietnam, Chairman of the Foreign Intelligence Advisory Board, and an influential adviser to both Kennedy and Johnson. It is axiomatic that a powerful state seeking to extend its hegemony over a weaker one finds it easier to work through a small, manageable and willing group. Such groups invariably turn out to be military juntas. The United States has found it easier to bend them to its will than the more cumbersome democratic leaderships accountable and answerable to the broad mass of their people. So it is no accident that it has related better to dictatorships than to democracies.

Since Washington financed and helped establish "the largest military force" among its allies, it is hardly surprising that each of South Vietnam's leaderships, one succeeding the other through a series of coups and counter-coups, was provided by the military establishment. Their qualifications to rule the country were seldom the criterion; what determined their acceptability to the US was the promise of their acquiescence to its wishes.

This was the reality. The statements emanating from Washington were on a loftier plane and less real, like President Johnson's Baltimore speech of April 7, 1965, in which he said the US purpose in South Vietnam was that "the people of South Vietnam be allowed to guide their own country in their own way".

Gruesome contrast to such public pronouncements, showing not simply US dominance of South Vietnam's affairs but also the savagery with which this could be carried out, was provided by the 'strategic hamlets' programme two years later, which aimed at uprooting South Vietnamese peasants and resettling them in hamlets away from areas they had lived in for generations. The logic behind this scheme was that, with the bulk of the Vietnamese population relocated in new and fortified hamlets, the Vietcong would be "cut off from its true base of support – the people". It was a move conceived with chilling detachment, uncomplicated by any concern for the staggering human cost involved. If Vietnamese peasants refused to move from their ancestral homes, their resistance was ruthlessly overcome. "Peasants' homes were often burned after evacuation and their fields wasted in the chemical crop destruction program. No compensation for homes or labor was paid ..."[22] The peasants were told that the move was meant to give them physical security, so that they could make a free choice between the Vietcong and the government ...

American Marine Colonel William R. Corson described the programme as "forced resettlement, physical oppression, coercion, and 'political persuasion' ... " He described a case of population removal in May 1967 in which none of the American officials present "batted an eye over the fact that out of the 13,000 [people moved] only about 100 were males between the ages of sixteen and forty-five".[23]

Over 8,700,000 people, or about two-thirds of the South Vietnamese population, were moved into strategic hamlets in little over a year under this programme. Devised by an Englishman, Sir Robert Thompson, the scheme was enthusiastically endorsed and executed with Washington's full support.

It might be wondered how, in a different international climate, apologists for American actions in Vietnam would react if the United States, not possessing its present preponderant power, found an Asian power stalking its land and resettling, for example, Pennsylvania's population in strategic hamlets in Ohio.

The lesson is not lost on Asians: America got away with the outrage in Vietnam, and in Korea before it, because of its power to sustain intervention in places where it had no right to be – and even less right to plunge them into bloodbaths through the use of sophisticated lethal weaponry. One statistic will suffice to illuminate the scale of the destruction:

> Between 1965 and 1971, US military forces, sometimes in conjunction with the army of South Vietnam, exploded 21 billion pounds of munitions in South Vietnam in a pattern that has come to be known as carpet bombing: 497 pounds of explosives per acre, or 1,215 pounds for every man, woman and child in the country.[24]

What sort of future did those who planned this destruction visualize for a people carpet-bombed for eight years by their 'ally'? How were these people expected to survive in a land defoliated by the extensive quantities of napalm, along with white phosphorus shells, used in

Operations Sherwood Forest and Pink Rose? The effects of this on local climates, animal and plant ecology, and flooding are still, two generations later, to be accurately assessed.

Could racism at various levels of decision-making provide the explanation for the manner in which military power was misused in Vietnam? Could it explain the indiscriminate bombing of North and South Vietnamese alike, and the indifference with which civilian targets were bombed along with the military? Katsuichi Honda, a pro-Western correspondent, writing in the Japanese newspaper *Asahi Shimbun*, described the hunting sprees of helicopter gunship crews who fired at random on villagers in the *liberated zones* of South Vietnam:

> They seemed to fire whimsically and in passing even though they were not being shot at from the ground, nor could they identify the people as NLF. They did it impulsively for fun, using the farmers for targets as if in a hunting mood. They are hunting Asians ...[25]

What explanation – other than contempt for the lives of a different people – can be found for the fact that peasants under the 'pacification programme' were not always warned before air strikes, so that hundreds were killed in cold blood? The reason given was that pacification camps were already full, and no more villagers could be resettled in them.[26]

Much has been written about the technology developed by US industry and research to increase the efficiency and destructive power of American forces in Vietnam. Napalm, vomiting gases, toxic bombs, 'cluster bomb units', bombs guided by TV cameras, 'guava' and 'pineapple' bombs, 'Puff the Magic Dragon', and electronic sensing and detection devices were just some of the items specially developed for Vietnam.

'Puff the Magic Dragon' was a C-47 airplane fitted with three miniguns each firing 18,000 rounds a minute. The effect of this capability was to so saturate the target with bullets that in three seconds a designated area received one bullet to every square foot. Here is an eyewitness account by a Quaker observer in Quang Ngain, in South Vietnam:

> Several of us went to the roof about 3 a.m. The Americans unleashed the terrifying 'Puff the Magic Dragon' ... As I watched it circle overhead last night, silhouetted against the low clouds in the light of the flares, flinging indiscriminate bolts of death earthward, I could vividly visualize the scene below. Men, women, children and animals caught

like rats in a flood. No place to hide, no way to plead their case of innocence to the machine in the sky, no time to prepare for death. The beating the civilians are taking in this war is beyond adequate description.[27]

In contrast is a user's unstinting praise for a new napalm bomb developed by Dow Chemicals, as recorded in an interview the British photographer-writer Philip Jones Griffiths had with an American pilot:

We sure are pleased with those backroom boys at Dow. The original product wasn't so hot – if the gooks were quick they could scrape it off. So the boys started adding polystyrene, now it sticks like shit to a blanket. But then if the gooks jumped under water it stopped burning, so they started adding Willie Peter [WP – white phosphorus] so's to make it burn better. It'll even burn under water now. And just one drop is enough, it'll keep on burning right down to the bone so they die anyway from phosphorus poisoning.[28]

Not all the products were developed for instant killing. It was felt that maiming, and painful wounds difficult to cure, could at times be more effective because of the continuing psychological effect.

An insight into the kind of thinking that shaped US Vietnam policies was provided by Townsend Hoopes, who was Under Secretary of the Air Force at the height of the Vietnam War. Hoopes, considered in the United States to be one of the more humane and enlightened men at the policy-making level, attributed the war's escalation to the Asian's unreasonableness. By not capitulating, and by refusing to avoid pain, death and material destruction, went the Hoopes thesis, the Asian deliberately strains the Christian conscience by forcing it to "carry its strategic logic to the final conclusion, which is genocide".[29]

But that is not all. Townsend Hoopes felt strongly that "ours is a plausible strategy – for those who are rich, who love life and fear pain". Because "happiness, wealth and power are expectations that constitute a dimension far beyond the experience, and probably beyond the emotional comprehension, of the Asian poor", the Asian is willing to "struggle, suffer and die", thus driving the West to genocide, and placing on it a "terrible burden to bear".[30] He implied that this is what happened at Hiroshima and Nagasaki, and asserted that in "unprecedented mobility and massive firepower,

American forces had discovered the military answer to endless Asian manpower ...".[31]

While Pentagon officials were viewing with optimism their solution to the problem of Asian manpower, President Johnson was telling the world at a Lincoln Day dinner in 1965 that "history and our own achievements have thrust upon us the principal responsibility for the protection of freedom on earth".

§

Washington's solution to the irksome problem of 'endless Asian manpower' was enthusiastically applied to Laos and Cambodia as well. The dance of death choreographed for Indo-China – with the count of people killed exceeding six million – took in these two neutral countries which had little to do with America's war in Vietnam. Their principal guilt was their geographical location. Both, being contiguous to Vietnam, were savagely bombed by the US military, who believed that the Vietcong – under relentless American ground and air attacks in Vietnam – had sanctuaries across the border. Even though this allegation has been disputed by several American and other observers, it mattered little to the United States. It considered Cambodia and Laos fair game.

Christopher Hitchens, in *The Trial of Henry Kissinger* (2001), provides a sobering insight into the mindset of Washington's decision-makers which, while highlighting the way decisions were taken by the Nixon administration, unwittingly underscores the similarity between the statements and actions of President Bush and those of Nixon and Kissinger.

Hitchens reveals Kissinger's personal obsession with destroying the allies of North Vietnam: a pre-echo of the obsessive concern of Bush and his advisers with the 'axis of evil' states, particularly Iraq; or as James Carroll of the *Boston Globe* (October 1, 2002) put it, the "myopic fixation on unproven fears about the capabilities and intentions of Iraq, Iran and North Korea". Bemused by the notion of 'hot pursuit', Kissinger also thought of using thermonuclear weapons to obliterate the access route from China into North Vietnam.[32]

Here again an uncanny parallel can be drawn between Kissinger's thinking and the Bush administration's 30 years later. Commenting on the Nuclear Posture Review submitted to Congress on January 8, 2002, William M. Arkin reported in the *Los Angeles Times* (March 10, 2002) that "The Bush administration, in a secret policy review completed early this year, has ordered the Pentagon to draft contingency plans for the use of nuclear weapons against at least seven countries, naming not only Russia and the 'axis of evil' – Iraq, Iran and North Korea – but also China, Libya and Syria".

Back to Cambodia. It was eventually decided to drop Kissinger's various other options and to settle in favour of punitive measures against Cambodia and Laos for allegedly aiding the North Vietnamese.

> Even before the actual territorial invasion of Cambodia, for example, and very soon after the accession [in January 1969] of Nixon and Kissinger to power a programme of heavy bombardment of the country was prepared and executed in secret. One might with some revulsion call it a 'menu' of bombardment since the code names for the raids were 'Breakfast', 'Lunch', 'Snack', 'Dinner', 'Supper' and 'Dessert'. The raids were flown by B-52 bombers which, it is important to note at the outset, fly at an altitude too high to be observed from the ground, and carry immense tonnages of high explosive: they give no warning of approach and are incapable of accuracy or discrimination because of both their altitude and the mass of their bombs.[33]

Discrimination between military and civilian targets, and between women and children and resistance fighters, was of little consequence to US decision-makers where Asian lives were concerned. This was chillingly brought home again when the same class showed no moral qualms during the genocidal bombings of Afghanistan in 2002, and in Iraq during the Coalition's invasion of March 2003. The extent and scale of the bombing of Afghanistan, in addition to ravaging its people, damaged its future by destroying centuries-old tunnels, aqueducts, aquifers and reservoirs built into the mountains to store water and other supplies in a country which alternates between droughts and heavy snows. All this was done "to get Osama bin Laden dead or alive", just as the Iraqi people were terrorized from the air for weeks on end in order to get Saddam Hussein "dead or alive". Then there are the large number of cluster bombs – which decimate living beings over a wide area – still lying around unexploded, waiting to seal the fate of innocent Afghan men, women and children in the coming years, as will also be the case in Iraq.

The independent investigator Fred Branfman confirmed some distressing facts about such bombing missions over Indo-China. Given "the speed and height of the planes", he was troubled that no checks were run on the missions to ascertain whether civilian or military targets were being hit. So he asked a bombing officer on duty "if pilots ever made contact before dropping their enormous loads of ordnance; oh yes, he was assured, they did. Worried about hitting the innocent? Oh no – merely concerned about the whereabouts of CIA 'ground teams' infiltrated into the area!"[34] Though Branfman's report was carried in Jack Anderson's syndicated column and in the *Atlantic Monthly*, the administration never questioned its authenticity or followed up its statements.

The expanded and intensified bombing campaigns took an estimated 600,000 civilian lives in Cambodia and 350,000 in Laos. (These are not the highest estimates.) Figures for refugees are several multiples of these. In addition, the widespread use of toxic chemical defoliants created a massive health crisis which naturally fell most heavily on children, nursing mothers, the aged and the already infirm.[35] The same categories of innocents became victims of the sanctions against Iraq after the 1991 Gulf War.

Branfman's investigations were unwittingly prescient. The Bush administration virtually re-enacted in Iraq – although on a considerably lesser scale – the programme that destroyed Laos and Cambodia in the 1970s. And may destroy other states in Asia, profoundly affecting the lives of millions of innocent Asians.

The bombings and invasion of neutral Laos and Cambodia, without a formal declaration of war, were described in detail by William Shawcross in his book *Sideshow: Kissinger, Nixon and the Destruction of Cambodia* (1979). His book, he said, was an attempt "to examine the Nixon administration's uses of power ... [and] to demonstrate how decisions made in Washington affected the lives of one particular and distant people ... [and] the consequences that other countries face when the world's most powerful nation and, in my opinion, the world's most vital democracy, is governed as it was after Richard Nixon and Henry Kissinger moved into the White House in January, 1969".[36]

Shawcross highlights in particular the extent to which Washington was at pains to keep the savaging of Cambodia and Laos a secret. This whimsically waged war on the side was illegal and outside the limits of civilized international conventions. So it had to be cloaked in secrecy, with this stipulation coming from the very top. When the request for sanctioning strikes in Cambodia was put to the President, "Nixon and

Kissinger were adamant that if it were done, it had to be done in total secrecy. Normal 'Top Secret' reporting channels were not enough. Later General Wheeler [Chairman of the Joint Chiefs of Staff] recalled that the President said – 'not just once, but either to me or in my presence at least half a dozen times' – that nothing whatsoever about the proposal must ever be disclosed".[37]

How would the secret be kept from the press? Wheeler had the answer. In a cable to General Creighton Abrams, Commander of the US Forces in Vietnam, he advised: "In the event press inquiries are received following the execution of the Breakfast Plan as to whether or not US B-52s have struck in Cambodia, US spokesman will confirm that B-52s did strike on routine missions adjacent to the Cambodian border but state that he has no details and will look into this question. Should the press persist in its inquiries or in the event of a Cambodian protest concerning US strikes in Cambodia, US spokesman will neither confirm nor deny reports of attacks on Cambodia but state it will be investigated".[38]

As a footnote to the above, when *The New York Times* briefly reported Wheeler's request for Presidential sanction of the strikes on March 26, 1969, "Ronald Ziegler, the White House Press Secretary, was quoted as giving a 'qualified denial' to the reports. 'He said that to his knowledge no request had reached the President's desk'".[39]

The bombings had already started on March 18. It seems clear that after the Afghan and Iraq campaigns, further countries on Washington's hate list will be targeted – less for 'harbouring' terrorists and more for countering the US agenda of global dominance. That instead of ridding the world of terrorism, the indiscriminate use of military power will create more vengeful terrorists is, of course, for saner persons in Washington to tell their President and his advisers. But such advisers seem to be few and far between today, although saner voices did exist in Washington once. President Eisenhower used his moral authority and US economic power to end British, French and Israeli occupation of Egypt after the 1956 Suez War.

He also blocked French moves to attack neighbouring Tunisia, which was aggravating France's troubles with Algeria. Britain too was roundly condemned for attacking a Yemeni town that was supposedly helping rebels in the British colony of Aden. Even some of Kissinger's staff resigned in protest against the invasion of Cambodia. But the moral focus shifted between the Eisenhower and Nixon administrations. Subversion

– or occupation – of sovereign nations was seen as a right by the Nixon presidency, whose destruction of Cambodia ranks as a major crime by any civilized standard.

Exactly a year after the bombing of Cambodia began, Prince Sihanouk, its head of state, was deposed (on March 18, 1970), and the very next day his deposition was approved by Washington. On April 30, brushing aside the principled precedent Eisenhower had set against French and British adventurism, Nixon announced that American and Vietnamese troops had crossed into the country.

The presidential rhetoric used to justify the invasion was vintage Washington: "We live in an age of anarchy. We see mindless attacks on all the great institutions which have been created by free civilizations in the last five hundred years ... small nations all over the world find themselves under attack from within and without ... If, when the chips are down, the world's most powerful nation, the United States of America, acts like a pitiful, helpless giant, the forces of totalitarianism and anarchy will threaten free nations and free institutions throughout the world".[40]

Kissinger provided a more convincing and colourful footnote to this after the invasion. When asked to comment on whether extending the war into Cambodia did not violate the Nixon Doctrine which disapproved of American involvement in Asian countries, he said: "We wrote the goddam doctrine, we can change it".[41]

The civil war that took such a gruesome toll of Cambodia was another outcome of Washington's interventionist role in Cambodia, whose longtime ruler Prince Norodum Sihanouk had displeased it by being too friendly with China. A peeved Washington encouraged the overthrow of Sihanouk in 1970 by the pro-American prime minister Lon Nol. In the words of Samantha Power in her Pulitzer Prize-winning book *A Problem from Hell: America and the Age of Genocide* (2003), "The United States had backed a loser. Lon Nol was pro-American, but like many US-sponsored dictators of the period, he was also corrupt, repressive, and incompetent".[42]

Inevitably, resistance against him by the Khmer Rouge, a group of radical Cambodian communist revolutionaries, gained ground and in 1970 turned into a savage genocidal war. Beginning in the same year, US ground forces launched their invasion of Cambodia, which lasted five years until Lon Nol's own overthrow in 1975.

Under the leadership of Saloth Sar, who preferred to call himself Pol Pot, the Khmer Rouge killed over two million out of seven million Cambodians as well as inflicting the most depraved and unbelievable atrocities on its own people. Pol Pot was overthrown in 1979, ironically enough, by Hanoi's armed forces.

The end result of taking hostilities into Cambodia was over ten years of one of the most brutal civil wars in which unspeakable atrocities were committed, a staggering number of people killed and millions made homeless. According to one observer at the time: "In Cambodia, a former island of peace … no one smiles today. Now the land is soaked with blood and tears … Cambodia is hell on earth". This, some fifteen years after President Johnson had stated that the aim of US policy towards Indo-China was to allow its people "to guide their own country in their own way".

§

Laos fared no better. Its pounding by the United States Air Force was even more merciless than Cambodia's. The offensive against Laos too was kept a secret, as this country – with half of Cambodia's population – had little to do with America's war in Vietnam. Of course, friendly media prepared the ground through frequent references to North Vietnamese supply lines, sanctuaries and such. But since the 1962 Geneva accords prohibited foreign troops in Laos, the need for secrecy was even greater. Washington in any case had found an ingenious way of getting around this prohibition. It gave the CIA "the job of conducting a 'secret' war" in Laos, and for years the agency conducted a covert, full-scale war there with a private army, L'Armée Clandestine, of more than 35,000 troops assembled, armed, trained and paid for by the United States. To support it "CIA-hired pilots flew bombing and supply missions in the agency's own planes", and later, when "L'Armée Clandestine became less effective after long years of war, the agency recruited and financed over 17,000 Thai mercenaries for its war of attrition …".[43]

The US air force dropped three million tons of bombs on Laos (one ton per head), forced 700,000 peasants to abandon their land, and left plenty of unexploded ordnance to wreck havoc for decades to come.[44] Difficult though it is to comprehend the chilling statistic of *one ton of bombs per head*, it is possible to understand it given the mentality of those who dropped the bombs. The testimony of Fred Branfman is once again revealing. "The speed and height of the planes [he was told by Jerome Brown, a former targeting officer for the United States embassy in the Laotian capital of Vientiane] meant that targets were virtually indistinguishable from the air. Pilots would often decide to drop bombs where craters already existed, and chose villages as targets because they could be more readily identified than alleged Pathet Lao guerrillas hiding in the jungle."[45]

The facts uncovered by Branfman, which were published by *Harpers* magazine and which he passed on to other media as well, were found irksome by the American establishment. And so:

> Under pressure from the US embassy, the Laotian authorities had Branfman deported back to the United States, which was probably, from their point of view, a mistake. He was able to make a dramatic appearance on Capitol Hill on April 22, 1971, at a hearing held by Senator Edward Kennedy's Senate Subcommittee on Refugees. His antagonist was the State Department's envoy William Sullivan, a former ambassador to Laos. Branfman accused him in front of the cameras of helping to conceal evidence that Laotian society was being mutilated by ferocious aerial bombardment.[46]

Aside from death by bombing, the damage done to the Laotians' land and future livelihood was also reported by Linda and Murray Hiebert, two volunteer workers of the Mennonite missionaries who spent five years in Laos and Vietnam. They found "that irrigation networks have collapsed and that paddy fields are pockmarked with bomb craters". Others reported that because of the number of buffaloes killed in the firepower unleashed on the Laotians, farmers had "to harness themselves to till their fields". In one area alone, where "before the war the population of the district owned 83,000 buffaloes to provide draught power and meat, when peace came there were only 250 buffaloes".[47] To add to the impending spectre of food shortages and starvation, "unexploded bombs buried in the ground hamper food production".[48] Still others wrote that the savage bombings had "turned more than half the total area of Laos into a land of charred ruins".[49]

By this stage, Washington's covert activities in sovereign Asian states were no longer confined to removing leaderships whose political and social attitudes did not serve US interests. Individuals were no longer the target; entire populations of 'rogue' states were. Instead of surreptitious deals to overthrow those who refused to accept Washington's dictates, large-scale, round-the-clock carpet-bombing of every man, woman and child of those countries became the new currency of terror. America's air force, army and arsenal of lethal weapons were the instruments of that terror, on-hand and ever-ready to unleash their firepower.

This is the other face of terrorism. Since it has been anointed as a holy crusade to defend the principles of democracy, justice and freedom, few see it as terror. Yet it is no different from the ruthless killing of innocents in New York's twin towers. The same callous disregard for human life accompanies both.

§

The change of direction in American policies, from inspired, just and mostly humane beginnings to a headstrong, aggressive and acquisitive role in world affairs, can largely be attributed to World War II. As the United States developed its industrial potential to meet the insatiable needs of a world at war, it laid the foundations of a power which few others could match. The war was the catalyst which helped the United States develop its military, industrial and economic muscle.

The realization of its growing strength reaffirmed its faith in the nineteenth-century ideal of Manifest Destiny, a belief in America's right to extend its power by trampling, if necessary, on the freedoms and choices of others. It derived its strength from its own power base, having within its borders vast reserves of natural and human resources combined with political unity and enormous size. It was not dependent – like the European colonialists – on distant colonies for its raw materials and manpower. To scale with its own size, America eventually aspired to influence the politics, policies and priorities of other nations in order to ensure its global dominance.

The blueprint of the American imperium has been in the making since the 1960s and 1970s, when the US's drive to control the world's strategic resources was an early indicator of its global ambitions. These resources were not only necessary to meet its own enormous needs, but their control meant it could deny them to those it disapproved of. The question as to America's right to such resources was immaterial, more important was the need to establish US hegemony around the world, and thus its control over them. Since this could be done only through military power, in America's vision of the future, raw power was what counted, and today still counts, not the niggardly details of ownership rights, international protocols and such.

Which makes it easier to understand America's interest in resource-rich Indonesia and the methods it used to facilitate the exploitation of that country's oil, tin, rubber and timber wealth by American cartels. The two hurdles which had to be first cleared were Indonesia's mercurial nationalist leader Sukarno and the Dutch who wanted to regain their colony after World War II. Neither had reckoned with American ingenuity.

To understand the Indonesian story, it is necessary to go back to the time the country achieved its independence. The republic that emerged from the trauma of Dutch rule, the Japanese occupation, and finally the armed struggle with the colonialists who tried to re-establish their empire after World War II, was an Indonesia tempered by conflict, rid of the exploitative policies of the Netherlands, and inspired by the prospect of freedom. This is the context of Sukarno's rule, even if the often lurid colours he has been painted in may to some extent be justified.

Sukarno was president of a country pivotal to the future of South-East Asia. Indonesia's population amounted to half that of the entire area and it possessed incredible natural resources which made it potentially one of the richest nations on earth. The pattern was all too familiar, as was the aftermath. Sukarno was destined to meet the same fate as Mossadeq of Iran. He was outspoken in his criticism of attempts to make a mockery of the aspirations of newly independent nations which had emerged from the shambles of World War II:

> Colonialism and imperialism are living realities in our world. Their sentiment of superiority, of arrogance towards us who were once their colonial subjects is thrust down our throats … Their political, economic or military interference is always with us, sometimes subtly, often insultingly. At every move we make for economic reconstruction … they exploit their technological superiority to manipulate conditions in order that our nations can be kept eternally subservient to their selfish interests.[50]

His outlook had been shaped by the racial discrimination he had experienced at the hands of the colonial powers and by his outrage at seeing his country's resources make vast profits for outsiders while Indonesians lived in terrible poverty. He was equally resentful of US attempts to dominate the political and economic decisions of Asian countries after their liberation from colonial rule. At the close of the 1950s, this volatile and intensely nationalistic man set his country on a course which would place its resources beyond the reach of American cartels. But that also meant that the noose around him would start tightening.

Sukarno's first move to set things right was in 1956 when he repudiated Indonesia's huge public debt to the Dutch, which it had been made to shoulder when power was transferred in 1949. It was a galling burden, forced on the Indonesians as the price of freedom – it was designed to compensate the Dutch for the cost incurred in fighting the fledgling republic.

Sukarno took his next step – the takeover and nationalization of all Dutch firms – at the end of 1957. It followed in the wake of Indonesia's anger at the UN's refusal to play a mediatory role in the dispute with the Netherlands over the question of sovereignty in West Irian (Western New Guinea). Mass demonstrations against Dutch control of the Indonesian economy were swiftly followed by government action. It started with the cancellation of KLM's landing rights, followed rapidly by the takeover of the Dutch shipping line KPM, Dutch banks, estates, and other businesses. These moves brought to an end one of the more exploitative economic structures imposed by a colonial power on a captive people. This uneven economic relationship – which continued into the post-independence years – placed Indonesia among the world's least industrialized nations, leaving it almost entirely dependent on the export of raw materials and with even the export trade controlled by the Dutch.

Sukarno could be erratic, brash and reckless – as in his extraordinary confrontation with newly founded Malaysia in 1963, which he opposed as "neo-colonialism", taking military measures which proved unpopular with the Indonesian army. However, those who have experienced exploitation, economic dependence and perversion of civilized social norms can understand what it does to people. While the resentment of the Dutch, who found themselves deprived of access to the economy they had dominated for years, is understandable, it scarcely follows that Sukarno's changing of the status quo was bad for Indonesia. Or that he was not a true nationalist. What economic advantage could Indonesia get by allowing the Dutch to continue their stranglehold on its economy?

A counter-offensive to Sukarno's actions against "free enterprise" was not long in coming. In February 1958, a rebellion by segments of the conservative Western-influenced Indonesian elites took place in Sumatra, where much of Indonesia's oil was produced at the time. It was led by Sjafruddin Prawiranegara, a one-time governor of the Bank of Indonesia, supported by two former premiers, Mohammad Natsir and Burhanuddin Harahap. Also involved was Sumitro Djojohadikusumo, a former minister of trade, industry and finance who had fled Djakarta in 1956. Military support came from a handful of dissident officers.

What were America's stakes in this rebellion? Despite the Dutch monopoly of major Indonesian enterprises, America's Stanvac and Caltex had established a substantial interest in Indonesian oil production in the years following World War II. By 1957, they had helped to double the pre-war production figure of 7.9 million metric tons. The nationalization of Netherland's assets in that year took care of the Royal Dutch, their only main competitor on the scene. American interest in Indonesia was therefore high, especially in oil-rich Sumatra. Djakarta's nationalization moves, while no doubt jarring, had in no way threatened US interests. The undercutting of the Dutch had, in fact, improved the US position, in much the same way as the ousting of the British had established American influence in Iran.

Why then did the United States supply the Sumatran rebels with arms, equipment, planes and personnel? Why did the CIA support them? What brought elements of the Seventh Fleet to the Sumatran coast at the time of the rebellion?

Washington was hedging its bets. It was not going to let an opportunity slip in Sumatra, even though it would have preferred to bring the whole of Indonesia under US hegemony. After all, the revolt might well snowball into something significant for US interests. There was enthusiasm in the CIA and the State Department for supporting these dissident elements. Even if Sukarno survived, so they reasoned, Sumatra, Indonesia's major oil producer, might secede, and private American and Dutch holdings would then be safeguarded.

Acting on intelligence reports of imminent troop landings in Sumatra by marines of the Seventh Fleet, which had been sighted off the coast, elements of the Indonesian armed forces landed in Sumatra on March 12, 1958. It was a timely move aimed at pre-empting armed intervention by American troops on the pretext of protecting the lives of foreign citizens in Sumatra. A foreign intervention with considerable potential for long-term mischief was prevented by Djakarta's quick action.

The threat of American intervention was not only from the Seventh Fleet. The CIA's involvement was far more significant. According to Victor Marchetti, who spent 14 years as a high-ranking officer in the agency, "the CIA gave direct assistance to rebel groups located on the island of Sumatra. Agency B-26s even carried out bombing missions in support of the insurgents. On May 18, 1958, the Indonesians shot down one of these B-26s and captured the pilot, an American named Allen Pope. Although United States government officials claimed that Pope was a 'soldier of fortune', he was in fact an employee of a CIA-owned proprietary company, Civil Air Transport".[51] At a news conference in Djakarta on May 27, the authorities produced captured documents and identification papers to establish his links with the CIA.

High-level statements out of Washington at the very time the CIA had been ordered to provide logistical and personnel support to the rebels are revealing. They show how mis-statements made by those at the very top were used to cover up the attempted subversion of a sovereign state.

Testifying before Congress in March 1958, the American Secretary of State, John Foster Dulles, said: "We are pursuing what I trust is a correct course from the point of view of international law … and are not intervening in the internal affairs of this country". A few days later, on April 1, he reiterated that because the United States viewed the trouble in Sumatra as an internal matter, "I would not want to say anything which might be looked upon as a departure from that high standard". Later in the same month he declared: "It did not seem wise to the United States to be in the position of supplying arms to either side … it is still our view that the situation there is primarily an internal one and we intend to conform scrupulously to the principles of international law that apply to such a situation".[52] President Eisenhower went on record a few days later to say that while "soldiers of fortune" were probably involved in the affair, "our policy is one of careful neutrality and proper deportment all the way through, so as not to be taking sides where it is none of our business".[53]

Djakarta soon put the rebellion down and Washington now played its other card. Having been disappointed in the hope that a secessionist move would come out of the Sumatra revolt, it changed its policy from dismembering Indonesia and hiving off its most productive and oil-rich parts to building up pro-American elements in the army in preparation for seizing any opportunity that might present itself for more economic advantages.

Five days after Pope's capture, Washington sold a million dollars' worth of arms and 37,000 tons of rice to the Djakarta government. It also produced twelve Globemaster aircraft for stamping out the last of the Sumatran rebellion.

When Kennedy succeeded Eisenhower in the White House, he quickly saw that the best way of strengthening American influence in Indonesia was through the Indonesian army. As Arthur Schlesinger put it in his *One Thousand Days*, Kennedy "was anxious to strengthen the anti-communist forces, especially the army, in order to make sure that, if anything happened to Sukarno, the powerful Indonesian Communist Party would not inherit the country".

After the abortive revolt, the irrepressible Sukarno launched his programme of "Guided Democracy", which was to be "intrinsically Indonesian", and not imitative of the political forms of the West. As well as strengthening his own position, he moved Indonesia closer both to the Soviets and to China. The Soviet premier, Nikita Khrushchev, visited Indonesia in early 1960. Next came a treaty with Peking and a succession of meetings with Chou En-lai and other Chinese ministers which suggested that Sukarno was taking his country closer to Peking than to Moscow, although his relations with the Kremlin had resulted in large purchases of arms from the Soviets.

Sukarno proceeded to upset Washington still further by recognizing not only North Korea and North Vietnam, but also the National Liberation Front in South Vietnam, and by mocking the concept of US aid. At a meeting attended by the US Ambassador he said, "To hell with your aid". The question now being asked was: how far was he prepared to go?

In 1965 almost all the businesses in Indonesia that were still foreign-owned were nationalized, except for the American oil companies, but even their operations came under government supervision. Finally, the takeover of their local sales was decreed. The time to deal with Sukarno had come. The United States could put up with any amount of leftist rhetoric, but when its businesses were threatened with concrete losses it took swift action. Sukarno soon fell from power in circumstances which have never been satisfactorily explained.

Six generals were murdered on September 30. This was subsequently referred to as a "Communist coup" by those who staged the Army's counter-coup a day later. It was a strangely uncoordinated and inept affair. Did Sukarno play any part in it or know about it? His presence at the air force base where the bodies were found, his lack of concern at the killings, and his absence from the funeral have been quoted as evidence against him.

One of the key figures in these shadowy events was known as 'Sjam' (Kamaruzaman bin Ahmed Mabaidah), head of a special bureau of the Indonesian Communist Party for infiltrating the armed forces. He was behind the 'Movement of September 30', but there have been suggestions that he was in fact a double or triple agent, and that his real role was to provide an excuse for the clean sweep that followed: the army's counter-coup. It was launched by General Suharto on the day after the murders, and eliminated first Sukarno's supporters in the armed forces, and eventually Sukarno himself.

Kathy Kaldane, an American investigative journalist, exposed the degree to which Americans had secretly collaborated in the 1965–66 massacres which enabled Suharto to seize the presidency. "They [US officials] systematically compiled comprehensive lists of communist operatives. As many as 5,000 names were furnished to the Indonesian army, and the Americans later checked off the names of those who had been killed or captured." Robert J. Martens, political officer in the US embassy in Djakarta, told her: "They probably killed a lot of people and I probably have a lot of blood on my hands, but that's not all bad. There's a time when you have to strike hard at a decisive moment".[54]

If we consider who profited most from these confused events, there is no doubt that the long-term benefit went to the Indonesian army, the US government and, above all, of course, the huge oil and other cartels. After all, "the displeasure of the big oil companies has also preceded a number of internal coups, from Iran in 1953 (where it is now known the CIA was implicated), to Brazil (1964), Ghana (1966) and Greece (1967). It should not surprise us that these oil giants should supply a powerful input into US foreign policy, facilitated by their intimate links with relevant branches of the bureaucracy, particularly the CIA".[55]

The outcome of President Kennedy's determination "to strengthen the anti-communist forces, especially the army" could not have been better for the oil giants, nor indeed for all foreign enterprises. Within a month of succeeding Sukarno, on March 11, 1966, General Suharto's government officially reversed the policy towards private enterprise and foreign investments. In December of that year, foreign-owned companies were denationalized and restored to their former owners.

Even more significant was the outcome of the conference held less than a year later in Geneva, in November 1967. Sponsored by Time-Life Corporation, the invitees "in the course of three days, designed the corporate takeover of Indonesia". Attended by some of the "most powerful capitalists in the world, the likes of David Rockefeller", the corporate giants at the conference included "the major oil companies and banks, General Motors, Imperial Chemical Industries, British Leyland, British American Tobacco, American Express, Siemens, Goodyear, The International Paper Corporation, US Steel".[56]

This is how Indonesia's resources were carved up by the corporate giants in Geneva: the copper in West Papua went to the Freeport Company (Henry Kissinger was on the board) and its nickel to an American and European consortium; the tropical forests of Sumatra, West Papua and Kalimantan went to a group of American, Japanese and French companies; and the giant Alcoa Company got the largest share in Indonesia's bauxite.[57] The ever-helpful Suharto hurriedly passed a Foreign Investment Law so that those who obtained his nation's natural resources did not have to pay any taxes for the first five years. He was even more accommodating in acquiescing in the control of his economy passing into the hands of the Inter-Governmental Group on Indonesia. The United States, Australia, Canada and Europe controlled the IGGI, with the key role played by the International Monetary Fund and the World Bank.

Kennedy's foresight had paid off.

The increase in oil production was spectacular – from a daily output of 300,000 metric tons a day in 1946 to two million barrels a day in 1981. To this day, though Japan imports a substantial proportion of its oil from Indonesia, the beneficiaries are not the Indonesians but American oil companies that control their oil. This has profound political and economic significance, for whoever controls Indonesia's oil controls its economy. The United States controls both.

The pattern is similar with other Indonesian resources. To take only one example, the production of timber, unlike oil, requires no particular technological sophistication. Yet here too there has been massive foreign investment, with the United States very much in the lead. Timber exports increased from only $10 million in 1966 to $160 million a year five years later. For foreign companies this brought an annual return of 40 to 50 per cent on their investment. For Indonesia it meant the rapid destruction of its extraordinary timber wealth and also its ecological balance.

Long after Sukarno's removal, despite efforts to give the impression of an economic miracle, the country remains one of the least industrialized in the world. In the food sector, where it was once almost self-sufficient in rice, its imports now account for nearly one-quarter of the total world trade in rice. Oil and rubber account for around 60 per cent of its exports, timber, tin and coffee for 20 per cent, and assorted raw materials for the rest. All are controlled by outside investors. The outlook for the Indonesian economy is, to say the least, bleak.

3

American Internationalism: The Right to do Wrong

The New Imperium: Shock and Awe

A little group of wilful men representing no opinion but their
own, have rendered the great Government of the United States
helpless and contemptible.

WOODROW WILSON[1]

I N THE PREFACE TO HIS BOOK *The Trial of Socrates* (1989), the distinguished
American intellectual I. F. Stone hoped it would show the "way to
a liberating synthesis of Marx and Jefferson". It was a hope worthy
of him, but in reality the sum total of what the Marxist and Republican
ideals both expressed over the years was a cynical contempt for the
"utopian and liberationist" beliefs that breathed life into those ideals. In
Asia the imperial ambitions of the United States and USSR converged
to make a mockery of the idealists' noble goals: freedom, common
humanity, moral clarity and just governance. The people of Asia ended
up paying a bitter price for the betrayal of those cherished beliefs. They
paid with their lives. And in staggering numbers.

A self-evident truth in the exercise of power is that strong states seeking to dominate weaker ones are seldom squeamish about how they do
it. Nor are they too fastidious about their democratic pretensions.

As was noted in Chapter 2, the United States prefers to bend military
juntas to its will rather than cumbersome democratic leaderships answerable to a broad mass of people. Thus Washington has all too frequently
used its dollars, arms, aid, intelligence agencies and media to help
pliable and corrupt leaderships and stage-manage coups d'état. In almost
every Asian country degraded by the United States in this way, the killing

of countless innocents was overseen by military dictatorships installed by Washington in order to serve America's needs – General Zahedi in Iran, Air Marshal Ky in Vietnam, General Suharto in Indonesia.

When Field Marshal Mohammad Ayub Khan seized power in Pakistan on October 7, 1958, the Americans found him more to their taste than Pandit Nehru, since they were less interested in India's democratic governance and more in the military dictator's willingness to join the South-East Asia Treaty Organization (SEATO) in 1954 and the Central Treaty Organization (CENTO) after that. Pakistan's take for overthrowing a democratic government was $1.5 billion in American military assistance and $2.5 billion in economic aid.

So much for freedom and just governance. As for common humanity, or moral clarity, it is worth recalling that while Washington was justifying its bombing and invasion of North Korea because of *its sympathy and support for the people of Korea*, one of General Douglas MacArthur's air force officers was boasting that "When the Fifth Air Force gets to work on them there will not be a North Korean left in North Korea".[2] Shortly after this, US Air Force General Curtis LeMay said of the Vietnamese: "We're going to bomb them back into the Stone Age".[3] These wars fought in Asia by the United States were not meant to be humane, they were waged to extend American military power in Asia. And with a severity never seen before.

§

The script for what is to come has been broadly revealed by Harlan Ullman, a 'defense intellectual' at the White House and Pentagon, and it has credibility. Ullman is nothing if not inventive. He applies his creative mind to discovering novel ways of eliminating fellow-humans, like attacking the neurological system with electromagnetic waves, "to control the will and perception of adversaries, by applying a regime of shock and awe. It is about affecting behavior". Ullman enthusiastically elaborates on his vision of the future. The United States should, he urges, "deter and overpower an adversary through the adversary's perception and fear of his vulnerability and our own invincibility … This ability to impose massive shock and awe, in essence to be able to 'turn the light on and off' of an adversary as we choose, will so overload the perception, knowledge and understanding of that adversary that there will be no choice except to cease and desist or risk complete and total destruction".[4]

This former head of extended planning at the US's National War College is not averse to using conventional weapons. His suggestions for the massive use of cruise missiles formed "the basis for the Pentagon's war plan" (the 2003 war against Iraq). It proposed that the United States "smash Baghdad with up to 800 cruise missiles in the first two days of the war. That's about one every four minutes, day and night, for 48 hours. The missiles will hit far more than just military targets. They will destroy everything that makes life in Baghdad liveable. 'We want them to quit. We want them not to fight', Ullman told CBS reporter David Marin. So 'you take the city down. You get rid of their power, water. In 2, 3, 4, 5, days they are physically, emotionally and psychologically exhausted'".[5] When the war against Iraq was launched on March 20, 2003, it actually took US forces three weeks to take Baghdad.

Ullman draws inspiration, and confidence in the efficacy of his plan, from the experience of Hiroshima in 1945: "You have this simultaneous effect, rather like the nuclear power weapons at Hiroshima, not taking days or weeks but minutes ... Super tools and weapons – information-age equivalents of the atomic bomb – have to be invented", he wrote in *The Economic Times*. "As the atomic bombs dropped on Hiroshima and Nagasaki finally convinced the Japanese Emperor and High Command that even suicidal resistance was futile, these tools must be directed towards a similar outcome."[6]

§

So Washington is no place to look for humanity or moral clarity, since lies are routinely peddled there as divinely inspired truths. They can, however, be found in men and women of conscience all across America who are courageously questioning the destruction of their society's moral underpinnings and liberating beliefs. These dissenting voices, if they can muster enough support, could restore to their country's govern-ance the moral focus that successive administrations have lost. There are many examples of principled dissent. The speech in the US Senate on February 12, 2003 by Senator Robert Byrd, a Democrat from West Virginia, was one of them: "I truly must question the judgement of any president who can say that a massive unprovoked military attack on a nation [Iraq] which is over 50 per cent children is 'in the highest moral traditions of our country'".

Another statement rejecting Washington's wayward policies was signed before the invasion of Iraq by over 55,000 Americans. The signatories to *A Statement of Conscience: Not in Our Name* included writers, artists, actors, directors, producers, playwrights, academics, legislators and others. Repudiating the Bush administration's wayward policies, their statement pointed out that:

> In our name, the Bush administration, with near unanimity from Congress, not only attacked Afghanistan but arrogated to itself and its allies the right to rain down military force anywhere and anytime … What kind of world will this become if the US government has a blank check to drop commandos, assassins, and bombs wherever it wants? … We are confronting a new openly imperial policy towards the world and a domestic policy that manufactures and manipulates fear to curtail rights … President Bush has declared: "You're either with us or against us". Here is our answer: We refuse to allow you to speak for all the American people. We will not give up our right to question. We will not hand over our consciences in return for a hollow promise of safety. We say NOT IN OUR NAME. We refuse to be party to these wars and we repudiate any inference that they are being waged in our name or for our welfare. We extend a hand to those around the world suffering from these policies; we will show our solidarity in word and deed …[7]

In an article in *The Progressive*,[8] Howard Zinn, historian and author of *A People's History of the United States* and one of the signatories to *A Statement of Conscience*, urged his fellow-Americans to say "no" to the demands of a manipulative "government which came to power by a political coup, not by popular will", and which would shed blood for oil and big business. He asked for a resounding "no" on several counts: "No blood for oil, no blood for Bush, no blood for Rumsfeld or Cheney or Powell. No blood for political ambition, for grandiose designs of empire". He said that calls "for the impeachment of George Bush should multiply", because the "constitutional requirement 'high crimes and misdemeanors' certainly applies to sending our young halfway around the world to kill and be killed in a war of aggression against a people who have not attacked us".

In an equally forthright indictment of the Bush administration and some of its key men like presidential adviser Richard Perle and Deputy Defense Secretary Paul Wolfowitz, Edward Said, author of *Orientalism* and *Culture and Imperialism*, asked:

Isn't it outrageous that people of such a dubious caliber actually go on blathering about bringing democracy, modernization, and liberalization to the Middle East? It is particularly galling that Perle, about as unqualified a person as it is imaginable to be on any subject touching on democracy and justice, should have been an election adviser to Netanyahu's extreme right-wing government during the period 1996–99, in which he counselled the renegade Israeli to scrap any and all peace attempts, to annex the West Bank and Gaza, and try to get rid of as many Palestinians as possible. This man now talks about bringing democracy to West Asia.[9]

In a way rather different from what I. F. Stone may have had in mind, the growing people's movement in the United States is more likely than the nation's leaders to restore early American ideals of democracy. Quite naturally the question being debated around the world is: can the American people's will deflect the administration from its military adventurism and the evangelical zeal with which it is polarizing the world along religious and racial lines, and turning the clock back to the time of the crusades?

Put another way, will the imperial interests of the United States continue to – or be allowed to – place the world's more vulnerable nations on call to serve American needs and dictates? This is what happened in the case of Afghanistan – a prime example of how the American imperium will work. That this remote and land-locked country, with its craggy peaks, impassable mountain passes and tough tribesmen should have found a key place in the calculus of US interests was predictable enough. The war waged on Afghanistan was not a war on terror, it was to secure that country for oil and gas pipelines from the Central Asian republics – with their staggering deposits of these resources – to ports on the Arabian Sea. Had punishment of the al-Qaida terrorists been the prime aim of the Afghanistan War there would have been more heard of Osama bin Laden and the Taliban.

§

But the odds against restoring a moral focus to America, and deflecting it from its heady goal of Pax Americana, are high. American big business, with its determination to straddle the world, is unlikely to make way for humanitarian concerns and international decencies. Especially as US multinationals have seldom reached so deep into the heart of an administration as they have in the Bush presidency. That the business of America is business is convincingly proved by the Bush family's own extensive holdings in the oil industry, along with those of the president's key officials.

The example of Vice President Dick Cheney will demonstrate the point. As Secretary of Defense to the elder President Bush, he oversaw the Gulf War, watching, with satisfaction, no doubt, the destruction of Iraq's oil industry, infrastructure, and much else. The satisfaction was not on account of a particularly sadistic streak in him, simply the love of profit. On leaving government, the Secretary of Defense joined the oil giant Halliburton as its CEO. The CEO then secured his company contracts worth hundreds of millions of dollars to help rebuild the destruction he had wrought in Iraq in the first place, in a war which Saudi Arabia and Kuwait financed, the brunt of which was borne by Iraqis, and profits running into hundreds of millions from which were made by US corporations.

The Gulf War seemed to have whetted Mr Cheney's appetite. When the younger Bush won the nomination, Cheney boarded his wagon as Vice President. The leave-taking from Halliburton was not too sad; his separation benefits came to $34 million. As an American columnist put it: "This burn-and-build approach to business guarantees that there will be a market for Halliburton's services as long as it has a friend in high places to periodically carpet bomb a country for it".[10] Halliburton was, of course, just one amongst many US companies which benefited from the country's actions in Iraq.

Some idea of how far the tentacles of American corporations reach can be had from the hundreds of billions spent on the military. The wealth that keeps flowing into the coffers of defence contractors like Boeing, Lockheed Martin, Hewlett-Packard, Dow Chemicals, Hughes Electronics, Bechtel, Union Carbide and numerous others, provides powerful backing for those who want to see America at war. Many wars, in fact, since more wars mean more profits. Not just from procurement of a wide array of weapons and support equipment, but also from rebuilding cities, ports, roads, bridges, docks, industrial installations, power-generating plants, water supply facilities, and much else. Leaving these other avenues of profit aside, the United States, with its annual defence spending alone coming close to $400 billion, spends *more than the combined military spending of the next 25 nations.*

The real question, however, is: what does the United States hope to achieve with this outlay?

The answer lies in two documents which have captivated President Bush to the extent that the goals set by them and the recommendations they make now form the core of his government's policies. The first, 'Project for the New American Century', was prepared in September 2000 by an ardent group of empire loyalists who believed that the time had come for the United States to get "its chance at a global empire". The report pointed out that "At no time in history has the international security order been as conducive to American interests and ideals". What the term "security order" – which could be interpreted in any number of ways – boils down to is: being the only superpower left to impose its writ on the world, the United States couldn't be more securely or advantageously placed to give shape to its dream of empire.

In Pax Americana, according to this report, the US military will be expected to perform "constabulary duties" as the policeman of the world providing, in addition, "American political leadership rather than that of the United Nations". To ensure America meets these responsibilities and discourages any country from daring to challenge it, "the report advocates a much larger military presence spread over more of the globe, in addition to the roughly 130 nations in which US troops are already deployed". It argues for "permanent military bases in the Middle East, in Southeast Europe, in Latin America and in Southeast Asia, where no such bases now exist".[11]

So what the United States aims at becoming, with its ever-increasing defence budgets, is planetary policeman, sole political arbiter of the world, the only forum for airing international disputes, a court of last appeal for grievances of six billion people around the globe. In effect the New Rome. Although – it is early times as yet – there is an identity crisis of sorts among the New Romans. For instance, Donald Kagan, professor of classical Greek history at Yale, and co-chairman of the September 2000 New American Century project, draws his inspiration from Hollywood, rather than the Caesars. "You saw the movie *High Noon*?" he asks. "We're Gary Cooper".[12]

This latter-day Cooper is in good company, for among those who helped compile the above project report are many who now occupy key positions in the Bush administration: aside from Dick Cheney and Donald Rumsfeld, there are, at the time of writing: Richard Perle of the Defense Policy Board and one of Bush's 'thinkers'; I. Lewis Libby, Chief of Staff to Vice President Dick Cheney; Paul Wolfowitz, Deputy Defense Secretary under Defense Secretary Donald Rumsfeld ("those two symbols of vacant power and overweening arrogance", as Edward Said described them); while Eliot Cohen and Devon Cross as members of the Defense Policy Board advise Rumsfeld. Steven Cambone heads the Pentagon's Office of Programme, Analysis and Evaluation, while Dov Zakheim is the Defense Department's comptroller. John Bolton is Under Secretary of State.

A handful of people make far-reaching recommendations to the President who then places them in powerful positions to implement those recommendations. Their plan in this case aims at changing a republican state into an imperial oligarchy.

The second document that provides further insights into the US agenda for the future is the Bush administration's National Security Strategy document released on September 20, 2002. This paper, which each administration prepares, spells out its strategy for the country's defence, and this particular one mirrors the ideas of the New American Century group. It reaffirms the heady possibilities the global environment presents to the Bush administration, with the opportunity to establish "permanent US military and economic domination of every region on the globe, unfettered by international treaty or concern". In an exquisite twist to the term "internationalism", the National Security Strategy document "speaks in blunt terms of what it calls 'American internationalism', of ignoring international opinion if that suits US interests".[13]

There is much more of such material couched in the arrogant language of naked power, leaving little doubt that the decencies once observed in the conduct of international relations could soon become a thing of the past. In addition to which America's military power will now incorporate nuclear capability in its conventional weapons systems to enforce America's writ – wherever and whenever necessary. Willingness to deploy the ultimate source of mass genocide in the form of theatre nuclear weapons in future wars indicates the extent to which rules are being rewritten by a neo-imperial America bent on tearing up all existing rulebooks through which nations were until comparatively recently endeavouring to establish a just world order.

Among the international treaties drawn up either on America's initiative or with its active involvement have been the Nuclear Non-

Proliferation Treaty, the Anti-Ballistic Missile (ABM) Treaty, the Kyoto Protocol on Greenhouse Gases and Global Warming, and the Treaty to Establish a Permanent International Criminal Court for War Crimes. Each of these has been repudiated by the Bush administration.

§

As if to drive home his contempt for such treaty-constraints, Bush personally singled out nuclear disarmament for scathing comment. James Carroll of the *Boston Globe* placed such treaties and the entire non-proliferation process in perspective by observing that even though the idea had sustained international hope,

> Bush renounced the ideal of eventual nuclear disarmament, by renouncing any "intention of allowing any foreign power to catch up with the huge [military] lead the United States has opened since the fall of the Soviet Union more than a decade ago". American military supremacy, based on nukes, is forever. And so, therefore, is the inherently destabilizing gulf between nuclear have and have-nots ... "We will not hesitate to act alone", Bush declares, promising to extend American sway by "convincing or compelling states to accept their sovereign responsibilities". The United States has become a ludicrous self-contradiction: a dictator state dictating democracy.[14]

Ludicrousness alone would be no problem. But Washington's intention of developing nuclear weapons for use in conventional wars presents a more sinister scenario. Its implications are still to be comprehended: not only in terms of the numbers killed outright but those who will die lingering deaths through radiation, and the gradual and painful disintegration of the human body in a nuclear-contaminated environment full of deadly toxins. Many of these aspects are apparently covered in the still-classified Nuclear Posture Review (NPR), a Congressionally-mandated re-examination of US nuclear policy, which the White House submitted to Congress in early 2002.

The review reverses the long-held belief that nuclear deterrence is an option of last resort. It no longer will be. The NPR, by all accounts, covers "every conceivable circumstance in which a president might wish to use nuclear weapons...". To help him make his life and death decisions, "Defense Department strategists [seek to] promote tactical and so-called adaptive nuclear capabilities to deal with contingencies where large scale nuclear arsenals are not demanded. They seek a host of new weapons and support systems, including conventional military and cyber warfare capabilities integrated with nuclear warfare. The end product is a now-familiar post-Afghanistan model – with nuclear capability added. It combines precision weapons, long-range strikes, and special and covert operations".[15]

The likely deployment of nuclear weapons in every future theatre of war the United States opens is just one aspect covered by the NPR. Another, even more irresponsible and harebrained, is the branding of six countries by President Bush – Iraq, Iran, North Korea, Cuba, Libya and Syria – as the "axis of evil". They are designated for the full treatment – for "large scale nuclear" attacks – in the Pentagon's contingency plans.

Couldn't this list of six be increased to a dozen or more, depending on the mood of the man in the White House? Wouldn't the integration of nuclear with conventional weapons encourage other nuclear powers to remove the barriers which have separated the two from the outset of the atomic age? Wouldn't a headstrong President want to 'take out' such countries too? How does the United States reconcile its goal of limiting nuclear proliferation – by compelling aspiring nuclear states to give up their nuclear programmes – with its own decision to adapt nuclear technology for developing a whole new generation of deadly weapons for both pre-emptive strikes and conventional warfare? Couldn't the technology for developing such weapons be adapted by terrorists too? Why this wilful crossing of the nuclear threshold, since no power at present threatens American hegemony?

On pre-emptive strikes, Philip Bobbitt, author of *The Shield of Achilles* (2002), says that since the old policy of deterrence could work only against known enemies, like the former Soviet Union, and not against terrorists with no known location, "it is no good relying on deterrence as the sole element to prevent an attack on you".[16] Thus the need for pre-emptive strikes. But this is precisely the flaw in the argument. The epochal shift in the United States' weapons policy, its crossing of the nuclear threshold, the extension of its military power around the globe, and its brazen unilateralism, have very little to do with containing terrorism. That was, and is, a convenient pretext. What they have to do with is the use of coercive power for compelling acquiescence to American dictates.

There is another flaw in Bobbitt's justification for the strategy of pre-emption in the so-called war on terrorism. Since, according to him, America's "intelligence budget alone is greater than the combined defense budgets of Iran, Iraq, Syria, North Korea and Libya", couldn't Washington's many interlocking intelligence agencies locate and deal with its terrorist adversaries in time? Does it need to devastate a whole country and inflict untold 'collateral damage' on its people – as it did in Afghanistan? Especially in view of the fact that "Given the advances in electronics and information technologies in the past ... the NPR also stresses improved satellites and intelligence, communications, and more robust high-bandwidth decision-making systems".[17]

Since America has the technology and resources to track down terrorists, what Washington wants to achieve through its pre-emptive strikes was more forthrightly spelt out by Harlan Ullman: "to control the will and perception of adversaries, by applying a regime of shock and awe. It is about affecting behavior". It is worth remembering that in this context "adversaries" does not mean terrorists, but entire populations of countries the United States wishes to bring under its suzerainty. Empires are not built by the squeamish or by bleeding hearts.

When would the United States want to use tactical nuclear weapons? The review seems to suggest that this, to a great extent, will be left to the discretion of the military and the Pentagon's nuclear strategists. A breed which at the best of times is not very fastidious about the ethical and moral implications of lives extinguished by its weapons. "The NPR says they 'could be employed against targets able to withstand nonnuclear attack', or in retaliation for the use of nuclear, biological, or chemical weapons, or 'in the event of surprising military developments'."[18] Any excess, of course, can always be justified in the name of a "surprising military development".

§

It will be in place at this stage to recall a remarkable American's single-minded stand against nuclear proliferation, and how he mobilized medical opinion worldwide against the mounting nuclear threat. Dr Bernard Lown's implacable opposition to those who wanted to develop nuclear arsenals was rooted in his acute awareness of the stark fact that "medicine, which in past wars mitigated misery and saved lives, has nothing to offer following a nuclear war", since in such a war doctors too would be incinerated along with the rest.

This conviction, shared by Dr Evgueni Chazov of the Soviet Union, resulted in an amazing collaboration – amazing because it took place during the Cold War. The efforts of these two led to the founding of the International Physicians for the Prevention of Nuclear War, and within five years of that – after the IPPNW had rallied physicians from over 40 countries – Bernard Lown and Evgueni Chazov were awarded the 1985 Nobel Peace Prize. It was richly deserved, because the IPPNW not only educated a large worldwide public on the nature of nuclear war, but the political clout of its vast constituency contributed to slowing the nuclear arms race. This was made possible by its specific agenda: that both superpowers agree to disarmament initiatives, with the cessation of nuclear testing as the first trust-building measure. The acceptance and implementation of several initiatives testify to the success of its efforts.

At the award-giving ceremony in Oslo on December 10, 1985, Egil Aarvik, Chairman of the Norwegian Nobel Committee, observed: "This year's prize is more concerned with the problem of disarmament, but it is also at a deeper level concerned with human rights – perhaps even the most fundamental human right of them all – the right to live. The right to a life and a future for us all, for our children and for our grandchildren. Yes, it is concerned with the unborn generations' right to inherit that earth which we today tend on their behalf".[19]

In his acceptance speech, Bernard Lown placed the physician's view in perspective:

> We physicians protest the outrage of holding the entire world hostage. We protest the moral obscenity that each of us is being continually targeted for extinction. We protest the ongoing increase in overkill. We protest the expansion of the arms race to space. We protest the diversion of scarce resources from aching human needs. Dialogue without deeds brings the calamity ever closer, as snail-paced diplomacy is outdistanced by missile-propelled technology. We physicians demand deeds which will lead to the abolition of all nuclear weaponry.[20]

The White House submitted the Nuclear Posture Review to Congress seventeen years after these Nobel Prize-winners criticized the moral obscenity of targeting human beings for extinction. The Bush administration's cynical response to those who believe in a compassionate and caring world comes through clearly in its 2000 and 2001 policy documents and the NPR.

This US administration is not the first to show its indifference to human life. Even as countless Americans have insisted on people's right to life, successive US administrations have treated that right with contempt. Especially the right of distant populations of another colour and different beliefs. There is no other explanation for the millions brutally killed in Korea, Vietnam, Cambodia and Laos. The racial bias in those genocidal wars needs highlighting since Western media are unlikely to remind the world of how Western societies have savaged innocent men, women and children in Asia and elsewhere. The highlighting is also necessary because the number of liberal Americans in the first years of the third millennium who are willing to oppose Washington's wayward policies is growing.

This public sentiment is reflected in a personal letter from Bernard Lown who comments on the newest developments in US defence policy:

> It is painful to witness our reinvention of the Cold War now labeled the war on terrorism. Aside from the obscene immorality of the new policies, the Bush administration's actions besmirch the good name of our country, enlarge the sense of outrage against America's disregard of international law, and unleash forces with unintended and dreadful consequences. The inexorable logic of the current military posture of integrating nuclear with conventional weapons removes the firewall that has from the very outset of the atomic age separated the two. It gives sanction to every country, that is able, to go nuclear.[21]

His concern reaches beyond the strategic and psychological purpose of using nuclear power to coerce nuclear have-nots. The world's scientific temper having changed from the time the European powers established their empires, the definition of the term 'proliferation' has also changed from the time it was first used. Proliferation now guarantees, as Bernard Lown puts it, that

> Sooner or later nuclear devices will become the indispensable murderous instruments of terrorists. The USA has porous boundaries. As we have failed against drugs flooding this country so will we fail to interdict the entry of nuclear material. Instead of attacking the Twin Towers, had the al Qaida gang resorted to some nuclear mayhem, it would take years rather than months to clear the radioactive debris to

make Manhattan once again habitable. Americans had better begin to speak out in moral outrage before the lights go out.[22]

If Lown and his fellow-physicians were able to mobilize doctors and global public opinion against the nuclear threat more than twenty years ago, an even greater sense of urgency is needed now to face the unfolding scenario presented by the threat of integrating nuclear elements with conventional military systems. The lay public is largely unaware of the nature of this threat. Iraq's traumatic experience after the Gulf War should be an eye-opener, and that war took place a decade before the decision to deploy nuclear weapons in the field was taken. The Gulf War, in fact, was viewed as an opportunity by the United States – and to an extent the UK – to use bombs, rockets, munitions and shells made out of lethal nuclear substances like depleted uranium (DU).

§

Depleted uranium (DU) is the left-over material after nuclear bombs have been made from fissionable types of uranium. In the words of the US Army Environmental Policy Institute, "Depleted uranium is a radioactive waste, and as such, should be deposited in a licensed repository".[23] But instead of being deposited in expensive-to-build repositories, it has been frequently given free to weapons manufacturers – since disposing of this radioactive waste according to prescribed norms would have proved immensely costly – so that they could use it "as core and coating for bullets, missiles and tanks".[24]

Thus, in spite of its deadly long-term radioactive properties, munitions made from DU were used in the Gulf War. Countless Iraqis and hundreds of American soldiers have paid the price for this chilling unconcern for their lives.

Scientists on both sides of the Atlantic agree that aside from the particularly gruesome manner in which it destroys human lives, the use of DU results in a health and environmental catastrophe of breathtaking scale. The American nuclear scientist Leonard Dietz believes that because of the use of DU in projectiles, "the Gulf War was the most toxic war in the history of mankind". The US Army estimates that about 14,000 such high calibre shells were fired during the Gulf War. According to the German investigator Siegwart-Horst Gunther, "Estimates by the British Atomic Energy Authority say about 40 tons of this type of ammunition are scattered in the border regions between Iraq, Kuwait and Saudi Arabia. Other experts assume that there is probably 300 tons of it. Not more than 10 per cent of these projectiles have been detected".[25]

The big question thus is: what hazards does such used, radioactive DU ammunition lying around pose for the populations of the areas around it? And what threat do the hundreds of tons of DU dust particles in the Iraqi and Kuwaiti air pose to human life? The Pentagon has confirmed the presence of 320 tonnes of DU dust in Iraq alone, and some estimates put the figure at 900 tonnes.[26] *DU remains radioactive for 4.5 billion years.*

Illnesses linked to DU exposure range from all kinds of cancers, leukemias and other malignancies to birth deformities, kidney, respiratory and urinary problems, chronic fatigue, memory loss, muscular spasms, vision problems, damage to other organs, and genetic manifestations. These and many more illnesses have been documented in detail by courageous doctors, reporters, investigative journalists, and others who have visited Iraq since the Gulf War and published their findings in horrifying detail.

Dr Charlie Clements, a Vietnam veteran himself, with an impressive record of outstanding work on issues of war, human rights and humanitarian needs of refugees, narrates what he saw in Iraq in a personal letter: "UNICEF estimates that 500,000 more children died in Iraq in the decade following the Gulf War than died in the previous decade. These children are part of the 'collateral damage' from the last war". And what if another war broke out? "Pregnant women, malnourished children, and the elderly will be the first to succumb." Commenting on the extent to which this visit angered him, he wrote, "I have worked in many war zones before and I have been with civilians as they were bombed by US-supplied aircraft, but I don't think I've experienced anything on the magnitude of the catastrophe that we have now visited on Iraq".[27]

While honest figures of civilian men, women and children killed, maimed or mangled for life will take time to compile, they will be horrific because of the savagery with which the highly populated city of Baghdad was bombed for weeks in 2003. And it was not the only city to be given the full treatment. So to claim that during these bombings 'collateral damage' was kept to a minimum is an outright lie. Some idea of the toll – both immediate and long-term – the bombings took can be had from Chalmers Johnson's thought-provoking report (discussed in

Chapter 5) in which he deals with the effects of the two Gulf Wars on the Iraqi people and American veterans.

What 'collateral damage' has meant in stark human terms can also be judged from the following eye-witness accounts of Iraq's travails after the Gulf War.

Writing of what she saw in Iraq after the 1991 Gulf War, Felicity Arbuthnot, a UK-based journalist who has covered the impact of DU in great detail and was chosen by Amnesty International as humanitarian journalist of the year, observed, "Death stalks children of Basra from the moment of birth. The unimaginable can be found: babies with twisted limbs, or without any limbs, eyes or brain – or even without a head". The Iraqi pediatrician Dr Jenan Hussein told Arbuthnot, "If you are not prone to fainting, I will show you a baby born just an hour ago". The little infant "had no eyes, nose, tongue, esophagus, or genitalia. The impossibly twisted legs were joined by a thick web of flesh". She made clear that "we see many similar cases".[28]

Dr Hussein has completed a thesis in which she compares Iraq's experience of cancers and birth deformities with those that followed the bombings of Hiroshima. "I have studied what happened in Hiroshima. It is almost exactly the same here; we have an increased percentage of congenital malformation, an increase of malignancy, leukaemia, brain tumours; the same."[29]

Susan Taylor Martin, writing in *St Petersburg Times*, has reported equally numbing encounters with the living-dead to which man's inhumanity has reduced fellow-men. "It is a heart-breaking Cyclopean eye. Or no face at all, just a gaping hole where the nose should be … some with tails, two hands, no brains or such terrible malformities they barely appeared human."[30]

Iraq has recorded a 70 per cent rise of cancers, leukaemias and malignancies since 1991 which are directly linked to DU. All reports from different parts of Iraq point to one disconcerting fact on which Iraqi doctors are agreed: something strange has been happening since the 1991 Gulf War. Not only have the numbers of those stricken with various types of malignant cancers soared (262 per cent jump nationwide), as well as those born with birth defects (five times as many), but according to Dr Hussein "the numbers will go up more and more. The trend may continue forever. DU is radioactive and Basra is saturated with DU. This is a crime. What crime have our children done to deserve this?"[31]

In order to avoid being labelled criminal, every government, organization and alliance which has used DU has lied through its teeth to deny
the charge. When a team of UN scientists "demanded to know from Nato
the location of DU bombings in Kosovo [where Nato had the gall to use it
long after DU's deadly toll in Iraq stood revealed], Nato refused to tell them
… From the very start of the alliance bombing campaign against Serbia,
Nato had lied about depleted uranium. Just as the American and British
governments still lie about its effect in southern Iraq during the 1991 Gulf
War. United States and British tanks had fired hundreds of rounds – thousands in the case of the Americans – at Iraqi vehicles, using shells whose
depleted uranium punches through heavy armour, and then releases an
irradiated aerosol spray".[32]

If lying is bad, even more so is preventing investigation into the use of
DU in Iraq and elsewhere. Still worse – in fact, nothing short of a crime
against humanity – is when countries allow their arms industries to use
DU for military ordnance. Yet that is precisely what the United States
and UK have been doing.

Pointing a finger at Aerojet and Honeywell among others, Gunther
disclosed in 2000 that not only were these two American corporations
engaged in mass production of DU ammunitions, but such ammunition
was being mass-produced in Britain and France. "It is likely that it is
being exported to other Nato countries as well as to Australia, Japan
and New Zealand."[33]

He also confirmed that even in Europe, to avoid paying the high costs
of storing it, DU "is passed on to interested parties, sometimes even free
of charge". Obviously, this largesse ends up in military hardware in some
unfortunate developing country over which the West – most likely the
United States – wishes to assert its dominance. The havoc wreaked on
human beings in Iraq by DU after the Gulf War has been noted in the
preceding pages, but even more serious is what lies in store from it in
the years ahead.

Toxic substances in these lethal projectiles – many of which lie deep
in the ground – contaminate the water and food crops. Thus not only
have people ingested toxic substances, but so also have animals, and
these substances have seeped into the soil. Gunther, again, reported that
after the 1991 Gulf War "Bedouins from Kuwait battlefields, which US
soldiers used as training grounds, reported that hundreds of dead camels,
sheep and birds lie in the desert. Examinations made by an American

veterinarian, a specialist in infectious diseases, showed that the animals had died neither from bullets nor from disease. Some carcasses were covered with insects, but the insects were also dead".[34]

A British company turned down an offer to remove the ammunition lying scattered about. Because of the contamination risk its staff would be exposed to.

This attitude on the part of a commercial firm is to an extent understandable. But it is reprehensible on the part of the United Nations. John Pilger, a renowned London-based investigative journalist who was in Iraq in early 2003 filming the documentary *Paying the Price: Killing the Children of Iraq*, noted that "Under the economic embargo imposed by the United Nations Security Council, now in its 14th year, Iraq is denied equipment and expertise to decontaminate its battlefields from the 1991 Gulf War". He further disclosed that Professor Doug Rokke, US Army physicist responsible for "cleaning up" Kuwait, told him he had witnessed "Iraqi officials pleading with American and British officials to ease the embargo, if only to allow decontaminating and cancer assessment equipment to be imported. 'They described the deaths and horrific deformities, and they were rebuffed,' he said. 'It was pathetic.'"[35]

After the 1991 war these critical items were not the only imports denied to Iraq by the United Nations Sanctions Committee, which, incidentally, is dominated by the Americans and fully backed by the British. Other requests Washington has vetoed or delayed have been for vital medical equipment, chemotherapy drugs, baby food and even painkillers.

Following his return to London, Pilger discussed his findings with Professor Karol Sikora, who as chief of the cancer programme of WHO had written in the *British Medical Journal*: "Requested radiotherapy equipment, chemotherapy drugs and analgesics are consistently blocked by United States and British advisers [to the Sanctions Committee]. There seems to be a rather ludicrous notion that such agents could be converted into chemical and other weapons".[36] Sikora further told Pilger that "Nearly all these drugs are available in every British hospital. They are very standard. When I came back from Iraq last year, with a group of experts I drew up a list of 17 drugs that are deemed essential for cancer treatment. We informed the UN that there was no possibility of converting these drugs into chemical warfare agents. We heard nothing more".[37]

This is just one of countless examples of the bizarre extent to which callousness towards human suffering is shown by victors who justify the savaging of entire populations by the most brutal means while professing 'care and concern for the people'. As the distinguished Indian journalist P. Sainath puts it, "A people have to be bombed and butchered into accepting humanitarian aid".[38] Which, of course, is only given to the 'deserving', and which Iraq didn't seem to deserve after the Gulf War.

John Pilger recounts his conversation with an Iraqi doctor who was particularly upset because nitrous oxide had been banned as a possible "weapons dual use" drug by the UN Sanctions Committee. This life-saving drug is commonly used to stop bleeding in caesarean sections. "I can see no logic in banning it", said the frustrated doctor. "I am not an armaments expert, but the amounts used would be so small that, even if you collected all the drugs supply for the whole nation and pooled it, it is difficult to see how you could make any chemical warfare device out of it."[39]

At least three senior officials of the UN have taken the unprecedented step of resigning from their positions on ethical grounds. The stand Denis Halliday, Hans Von Sponeck and Jutta Burghardt took needs to be admired, especially at a time when men and women of conscience have preferred to compromise rather than stand up to the unprincipled ways of the present US leadership.

Denis Halliday resigned in 1998 as the UN's Humanitarian Co-ordinator for Iraq, after 34 years with the United Nations, because he found "the policy of economic sanctions totally bankrupt. We are in the process of destroying an entire society. It is as simple as that ... Five thousand children are dying every month ... I don't want to administer a programme that results in figures like these ... I had been instructed to implement a policy that satisfies the definition of genocide: a deliberate policy that has effectively killed well over a million individuals, children and adults ... the Security Council is now out of control, for its actions here undermine its own Charter, and the declaration of Human Rights and the Geneva Convention".[40]

Two years later, in February 2000, his successor, Hans Von Sponeck, also resigned as Humanitarian Co-ordinator in Baghdad. Clearly he took his 'humanitarian' concerns more seriously than those who sat on the United Nations Sanctions Committee. "How long", was his question, "should the civilian population of Iraq be exposed to such punishment for something they have never done?"[41]

Within two days of Von Sponeck's resignation, Jutta Burghardt, head of the World Food Programme in Iraq, also resigned because she was unable to tolerate any longer what was being done to the Iraqi people. Each was convinced – on the basis of first-hand evidence – of the West's culpability in mass deaths of innocent people in Iraq. One statistic is enough to indict the Sanctions Committee: it had until October 2001 ordered 1,010 contracts for humanitarian supplies worth $3.85 billion – the figure now stands at more than $5 billion – to be kept on hold. And seven words uttered by Madeleine Albright, President Clinton's representative at the United Nations, are sufficient indictment of the Clinton and George Bush Sr's administrations. When asked if the lives of 500,000 Iraqi children were a price worth paying for enforcing the sanctions, she replied, "We think the price is worth it".

§

A thread that runs through the Bush administration's National Security Strategy is this definition of American Internationalism: "ignoring international opinion if that suits US interests". It certainly cannot be faulted for its forthrightness. Nor for its arrogance or grotesque sense of infallibility, for these are the perks of a superpower. But it can be faulted for its presumptousness; for assuming a gullible world will go on accepting the administration's claim to moral ideals and international decencies. The world has had ample opportunity for being less gullible about US pretensions.

In time, the horrors of the Nazi years may well be compared to the Americans' use of technology to take more Asian lives than the Germans took of Jewish. Both these genocides show an icy indifference to human life on the part of leaderships unable to see people of another faith or colour as husbands, wives, children, brothers, sweethearts or loved relations. They were seen as sub-humans – to be exterminated without emotion. How else can the lack of human feeling in these mass killings be explained?

The warped mindsets of men like Townsend Hoopes during the Vietnam War and the admirers of US military technology used in Indo-China provide only a partial glimpse into the thinking of these leaderships. Another interesting explanation for what immunizes societies to genocide, and makes them produce more efficient machines for mass murders, is provided by Robert Jay Lifton in his book *The Nazi Doctor* (1986). This professor of psychiatry here investigates the psychology of genocide, and while his principal aim is to analyse why Germany's medical profession willingly collaborated in the Nazi death camps, he provides broader insights into the psychological makeup of those who make such crimes possible. In the Nazi sequence of killings, for instance, the transition from face-to-face shooting of victims to technologically advanced gas chambers removed the element of empathy, of reacting to victims as fellow human beings. The victims became distanced and impersonal – mere statistics.

As the methodologies of killing improved, the challenge of technology became greater. It became the main focus in the task of inventing better killing machines. The Nazis thus reached a point in which "ethics played no part", technology having helped create its own environment in which what mattered was performance, how efficiently the task in hand could be accomplished. This provided a sense of normality, since the millions who would be murdered in cold blood would be pushed beyond the conscious periphery of those excited by the more immediate technological possibilities and challenges before them.

Even if this explanation is given some credence, though it is difficult to accept that above-average minds can distance themselves so completely from human sensitivities, what possible justification can there be for the UN Sanctions Committee's inhumanity in blocking vital life-saving drugs and equipment from reaching a ravaged Iraq after the 1991 war? The indifference with which hundreds and thousands of mostly women and children were left to die proves that theories on human behaviour can never fully plumb the depths of the human mind. The members of the UN Sanctions Committee were not scientists or physicists insulated from ground realities; they were bureaucrats and political appointees, well aware of what they were doing.

Once again Pilger provides damning evidence of UN complicity in the massacre of innocents. When he talked to Kofi Annan, the UN Secretary-General, and asked him, "What do you say to the parents of the children who are dying [as a result of the blockade of Iraq]?" and reminded him that "the UN was set up to help people, not harm them", Annan's reply was, "Please do not judge us by what has happened in Iraq".[42] Why not?

Pilger also talked to Peter Van Walsum, Chairman of the Sanctions Committee.

P: Do you believe that people have human rights no matter where they live and under what system?

W: Yes.

P: Doesn't that mean that the sanctions you are imposing are violating the human rights of millions of people?

W: It's also documented the Iraqi regime has committed very serious human rights breaches.

P: There is no doubt about that. But what's the difference in principle between human rights violations committed by the regime and those caused by your committee?

W: It's a very complex issue.

P: What do you say to those who describe sanctions that have caused so many deaths as 'weapons of mass destruction' as lethal as chemical weapons?

W: I don't think that's a fair comparison.

P: Aren't the deaths of half a million children mass destruction?

W: I don't think that's a very fair question.

P: How much power does the United States exercise over your committee?

W: We operate by consensus.

P: And what if the Americans object?

W: We don't operate.[43]

§

If the Nazis were successful in transmuting "their most murderous actions into technological problems", the Americans have gone further than any nation ever did in integrating their technological skills into the creation of deadly killing machines through a permanent war economy. The staple industries of the US economy are those producing a vast array of military equipment. Meanwhile, other industries producing consumer and capital goods are closing down in the United States, and the goods they once produced are being outsourced to countries like China, Korea, Taiwan and Mexico. But for industries catering to military needs, lavish government spending is the rule.

Seymour Melman, a man of impressive scholarship I talked to at length when he was Professor of Industrial Engineering at Columbia University, and who has consistently campaigned against the militarization of American society over the years, recently pointed out: "Now, at the start of the twenty-first century, every major aspect of American life is being shaped by our Permanent War Economy ... as a war-focused White House and a compliant Congress ... appropriate astronomical sums of money for the military".

He gave some telling examples. President Bush's 2004 military budget "would include funding new military bases around the world and the manufacture of a host of weapons of astonishing complexity and costliness ... Thus the newest major aircraft programme – the Joint Strike Fighter – is expected to cost as much as $750 billion, a historically unmatched price. The new nuclear attack submarines, each longer than a football field, are now priced at $2.4 billion each. Look at the maps published in our newspapers of new foreign military bases built for American forces – each of them magnificently equipped for an unstated but long duration".[44]

The Bush administration's obsessively increasing expenditure on the military at the expense of American society's liberal, generous and humane traditions is gravely imperilling global stability and wrecking the world's goodwill. The concern of Asians, which this book reflects, is with improving their own quality of life, and they are deeply troubled by the upheavals a trigger-happy President and his acolytes, with their dreams of empire, are causing in Asia.

Anyone blessed with brains can see – which men bemused by power appear unable to – that vast numbers of Asians today are gripped by an excitement generated by expectations and hopes, by their determination to succeed. Most of them are unwilling to accept the dictates of alien powers, or an inferior relationship with the West. But like all human beings they too have their old regional rivalries to contend with, their need for raw materials, their territorial ambitions, their sense of destiny, and much else. If their efforts to enter the modern world are obstructed by new and wholly destructive influences from a cynical and manipulative US administration, not only will their hopes and aspirations be frustrated, but their anger and frustrations will do incalculable harm to long-term US interests.

The Bush administration's war on Iraq, together with the spurious justifications provided for it, its belittling of the United Nations, and its contempt both for international opinion and its own protesting millions who demonstrated against its brazen aggression, have eroded US credibility. Instead of setting civilized norms for international relations, the United States has shown people worldwide the degree to which its leaders can tell barefaced lies.

The most blatant were told by the President in his televised speech on March 17, 2003, on the eve of launching his unprovoked war on Iraq. Behind his accusation that Iraq had "aided, trained and harboured terrorists, including operations of al-Qaida", and that the existence of such links was sufficient justification for going to war with Iraq, lay the outrageous pressure put by his administration on the CIA to write intelligence reports emphasizing links between Saddam Hussein's government and al-Qaida.

James Risen of *The New York Times* exposed this deception a few days after the President's address. "The danger is clear", the President had said in his televised speech. "Using chemical, biological or, one day, nuclear weapons obtained with the help of Iraq, the terrorists could fulfill their stated ambitions and kill thousands or hundreds of thousands of innocent people in our country, or any other." In support of his efforts to portray Iraq as a nuclear menace, he had earlier stated in his State of the Union address that "Saddam Hussein recently sought significant quantities of uranium from Africa". The President had made his statement in the full knowledge that information about the uranium deal with Niger came from forged documents which the CIA had rejected. But "analysts at the agency [CIA]", Risen reported, "said they had felt pressured to make their intelligence on Iraq conform to Bush administration policies".[45] Eighty-five-year-old Democratic Senator Robert Byrd also rose in the Senate on March 19 to point out that "The case this administration tries to make to justify its fixation with war is tainted by charges of falsified documents and circumstantial evidence".

California Democratic Congressman Henry Waxman was blunt in questioning the President on this:

> The most persuasive argument in favor of the March 2003 war was to prevent Iraq from developing nuclear weapons … it has become incontrovertibly clear that a key piece of evidence … was a forgery. On March 7, the Director General of the International Atomic Energy

Agency, Mohamed El Baradei, reported that the evidence that Iraq sought nuclear materials from Niger was "not authentic" ... Even more troubling, however, the CIA, which has been aware of this information since 2001, has never regarded the evidence as reliable. The implications of this fact are profound: it means that a key part of the case you have been building against Iraq is evidence that your own intelligence experts at the Central Intelligence Agency do not believe is credible. It is hard to imagine how this situation could have developed. The two most obvious explanations – knowing deception or unfathomable incompetence – both have immediate and serious implications.[46]

Further, the President said to the Iraqi people in the same televised speech: "If we must begin a military campaign, it will be directed against the lawless men who rule your country and not against you ... we will help you to build a new Iraq that is prosperous and free". It is hard to see how he could have expected his Iraqi audience to believe in his intentions of non-aggression against themselves when in the twelve years between the end of the 1991 Gulf War and the start of the new invasion, the United States had caused the deaths of half a million Iraqi children by enforcing UN sanctions and the effects of its use of weapons made of DU during the Gulf War had caused countless other deaths.

No less shameful a lie was the President's assurance that the military campaign would be directed against 'lawless men', and not the people of Iraq. Missiles launched from hundreds of miles away on densely populated cities cannot differentiate between 'lawless' and law-abiding people. If two US Tomahawk cruise missiles could land in Turkey instead of Iraq, or an American Patriot missile bring down a Royal Air Force Tornado jet and very likely some helicopters as well, or 'friendly fire' kill the first nine British soldiers who fell in the invasion, how could anyone believe presidential claims about how accurate and precise the bombing raids on Baghdad were, or who they were directed against? It is impossible to accept that every effort was made to avoid killing innocent Iraqi men, women and children in those pulverizing raids.

Leaving aside empirical evidence of civilian casualties in the March-April War, there cannot be a more damaging exposé of the Bush administration's real intentions than the treatment proposed for Baghdad by Harlan Ullman, the White House and Pentagon official whose mental orientation was discussed earlier in this chapter. Ullman's recommendation was quite clear. "The missiles will hit far more than just military targets. They will destroy everything that makes life in Baghdad liveable", he is reported to have said. According to him, "One way to 'shock and awe' [apparently he invented the phrase] Saddam, is to remind him that the US has 'certain weapons' that can destroy deeply buried facilities. That's a not-even-thinly-veiled reference to the newest kind of nuclear weapons … ".[47] It is against the backdrop of this thinking within the White House that the President extended his public assurance to the Iraqis and expected the world to believe it! Ullman's case proves that even more dangerous than the President's lies is the advice he gets from his close advisers, like Defense Secretary Donald Rumsfeld, whose own circle of weird advisers includes such men as Ullman and Richard Perle. On the morning of September 12, 2001, the very day after the twin towers tragedy, Rumsfeld wanted a retaliatory US attack on Iraq![48] Without a shred of evidence available at that stage to link anyone with the destruction of the twin towers, a ranking member of the Bush cabinet was ready to go to war with Iraq. With such influences at work on a US President, the prospects for world peace seem remote.

A few words about Richard Perle, whom Maureen Dowd of *The New York Times* described as The Prince of Darkness. The man is unreal. He believes there should be "no stages" in America's war on terror. "This is total war. We are fighting a variety of enemies. There are lots of them out there. All this talk about first we are going to do Afghanistan, then we will do Iraq … this is entirely the wrong way to go about it. If we just let our vision of the world go forth, and we embrace it entirely and we don't try to piece together clever diplomacy but just wage a total war … our children will sing great songs about us years from now."[49] Either that or there will be no children left to sing.

§

The improprieties of 'American internationalism' do not end there. The idea of a constitutionally governed nation's president asking its armed forces to produce a suspect "dead or alive" is a raw, unreasoned response to a tragedy. And proof of the guilt of the suspect – Osama bin Laden – is still awaited. Yet even though the President mocked the internationally accepted concept of justice – that an accused is innocent unless proved guilty in a fair and open trial – according to a poll, only three per cent of Americans felt Mr Bush's reaction to the attacks was too strong. Eighty-eight per cent thought it was very good. In fairness to Mr Bush, his predecessor President Clinton also confirmed with some effrontery that he had already sanctioned Osama bin Laden's killing – because intelligence reports had indicated his involvement with the bombing of US embassies in Kenya and Tanzania – and the administration had approached a group in Afghanistan for the job. But the hit could not be carried out for lack of the necessary intelligence to do it!

Osama bin Laden aside, US administrations have in the past ordered the assassination of heads of state, including Muammar Gaddafi, Fidel Castro and Saddam Hussein. All escaped, but the Libyan leader's infant daughter was killed in an air strike ordered to kill him. Either because of a change of heart or for whatever other reason, an executive order during the presidency of Ronald Reagan in 1981 stated: "No person employed by or acting on behalf of the United States government shall engage in or conspire to engage in assassination". Small comfort. Because news reports suggest the order can be circumvented in different ways, one of them being to get third parties to do the killing. Such a job, according to *The Washington Post*, was assigned to Pakistan in 1999; its aim was to capture or kill Osama bin Laden. The CIA trained and equipped 60 Pakistani commandos for the assignment, but the military coup in Pakistan ended this initiative.

These ongoing covert actions rebut Mr Bush's professions of justice, decencies and such, for example in his address to a joint session of Congress on September 20, 2001 in which he rightly condemned terrorists for making "no distinction among military and civilians, including women and children". However, when he said: "By aiding and abetting murder, the Taliban regime is committing murder", alongside this would also have to be placed: Washington's attempts to murder foreign leaders whose ideology and independent ways it has found irksome; its funding, arming and training of terrorists in Nicaragua in the 1980s who killed over 30,000 civilians; its support for a corrupt military regime in El Salvador, which resulted in the killing of thousands of families; the assassination of Archbishop Romero, a peace advocate; as well as US actions in Chile, Laos, Cambodia, Vietnam and Iraq.

Mr Bush felt the September 11 terrorist attacks took place because "they hate what we see right here in this chamber – a democratically elected government. Their leaders are self-appointed. They hate our freedoms – our freedom of religion, our freedom of speech, our freedom to vote and assemble, and disagree with each other ... by abandoning every value except the will to power – they follow in the path of fascism and Nazism, and totalitarianism".[50]

There are possibly more people in the world who have admired, rather than hated, the freedoms Americans used to enjoy in their country. Many aspired to a life there because of the opportunities it offered to those with initiative, intelligence, entrepreneurial drive and capacity for hard work. Many more have admired American generosity during the calamities people everywhere have faced.

But after September 11 this dream has soured, as US xenophobes have turned against fellow-citizens of different appearance and colour. If people in much of the world now hate the United States, they do so because it is averse to letting others experience the freedoms it has. It enjoys democratically elected governments itself but supports dictatorships abroad; it helps these come to power and tries to keep them in power. Though Islam is the religion of choice of over a billion people it is often demonized by US leaders unless US dictates are accepted. People of many countries hate the mayhem successive American leaderships have caused around the world. The latest Iraq war will not inspire greater love for America but more hate. A president less prone to lying would tell his countrymen that.

Mr Bush charged those he sees as rogue states with "abandoning every value except the will to power". The evidence as to who is most driven by "the will to power" – to global power – has long been before us.

No dreams of global power can succeed so long as a stark central reality of our times continues to be ignored. This was recently placed in perspective by Dr Mubashir Hasan, one of the founders of the Pakistan People's Party and a man respected for his moral authority: "It is no longer possible to sustain a violence-free world order", he said, "when one-fifth of people live in vulgar abundance, while four-fifths struggle in abysmal poverty for mere scraps to survive".[51]

The United States, with just five per cent of the world's population, consumes more than 25 per cent of the earth's resources, including oil. Eventually, it is not a handful of power-hungry men in their ivory towers, but the mass of discontented people around the world, no matter of which country or region, whose frustrations are likely to explode and influence the future world order – the military power, financial resources and technological lead of the US notwithstanding. Unless statesmanship of a higher order than hitherto is shown by more responsible world leaders in dealing with their peoples' discontents.

4

New Tools of Dominance

Economic Instruments of Global Strategy

In the councils of government, we must guard against the
acquisition of unwarranted influence, whether sought or
unsought, by the military-industrial complex. The potential for
the disastrous rise of misplaced power exists and will persist.

DWIGHT D. EISENHOWER[1]

A N ENDURING PARADOX OF OUR TIMES is that while vast numbers of the
earth's people are struggling to survive, their leaders spend staggering sums of money on costly weapons of war, instead of on critical social
sectors like education, health and housing, or on clean drinking water,
sewage systems, electrification and public transport. While people long
for their new-born to survive the scourge of infant mortality, to educate
their children, live in decent houses, and have medical facilities when
they need them, their leaders pour national wealth into militarizing their
countries.

Another irony is that while the US is generous in dispensing lessons in democracy and civilized behaviour to the world, its own
actions reveal the hollowness of its lofty pretensions. One notable
example of this was indicated by *The New York Times* on June 24,
2003 when it mentioned "repeated American warnings to Iran not to
interfere in Iraq's internal affairs". George Orwell would have been
hard put to imagine the effrontery of these warnings coming from a
power which at that very moment was in full military occupation of
Iraq and was sitting atop its vital resources.

A closer look at the militarization of the world under the US's
sponsorship since World War II will reveal the contradictions between

noble intentions and sordid realities still further. As the Stockholm International Peace Research Institute pointed out more than 20 years ago: "The basic economic consequence of the militarized world in which we live is a waste of the world's limited resources. If the resources of raw materials, productive capacity, and above all human skills and ingenuity which are now engaged in the world war industry were directed to civil … economic ends, the effect on the living standard of the average world citizen would be profound".[2]

This tragic play of perverted priorities is largely due to a collusion between some corrupt Asian leaders and the West's industrialized, weapons-producing powers. With the foreign policies of many Western nations closely linked to their arms industries, led by the US, whose rising levels of production necessitate increasing exports of military hardware, their priorities are twofold: to boost the demands of existing markets and to create new ones. As neither is possible without periodic aggravation of tensions around the world, the creation of conflicts becomes an integral – though unstated – part of policy, since conflicts lead to escalating defence budgets of developing countries.

Senator William Proxmire did not mince words while placing the matter in its proper perspective almost a quarter-century ago: "Arms trafficking has become a new international currency – a profitable expanding business in the world. Under the justification that business is good for our balance of payments, or if we do not sell weapons someone else will … The arms merchants and their government spokesmen are turning the world into a vast armed camp. While it may be true that some weapons are for show and some are for deterrence and some are for national pride, the only responsible long-term conclusion is that most are for war".[3] The tragedy of our times is that far fewer voices like Proxmire's are now raised by America's law-makers against the increasing waywardness of its administrations.

Arms-producing nations continue deftly to manipulate regional rivalries to keep tensions high and precipitate wars. Many political moves since the end of World War II, such as partitioning former dependencies to create new and warring states, e.g. India and Pakistan, the two Koreas, and most countries of West Asia, have led to spectacular arms sales. Asian rivalries have been assiduously encouraged since they contribute substantially to the revenues of arms-producing nations. The urge to acquire better and more lethal weapons takes on a keener edge when tensions are high.

It is nobody's case that arms-producing powers force unwilling nations to arm against their wishes. But neither can it be said that the accelerating arms race in several Asian regions was, or is, accidental. More than one factor has contributed to it, including the politics of sub-version and containment during the Cold War. In those days Washington and Moscow, fully aware that aside from profits there were many other benefits of the arms game, created a weapons culture which helped them extend their ideological and political influence through interven-tions and support to insurrections. All of which required arms. Which, of course, the two gladly supplied. The Cold War at least provided some space for manoeuvre to those who preferred to remain unaligned between the two, even if it did not prevent Asia from becoming the bat-tleground of countless wars after World War II as the United States and Soviets struggled to establish their spheres of influence.

The end of the Soviet Union ended the scope for manoeuvre, with the United States emerging as the sole superpower. But it was a different United States. Driven by the desire for global hegemony, it was now obsessed with framing its new foreign policy around its military power. While the most sophisticated weapons were developed to further its own aims, a large number have been sold to nations it has edged into wars. Wars which have decimated their populations, economies and political institutions, but been of immense help to American defence industries.

The Iran-Iraq War exemplified the cynicism with which the arms trade is conducted. The United States not only supplied Saddam Hussein with chemical weapons, biological agents including anthrax, and other vital ingredients for chemical warfare, but also cluster bombs for halting Iran's human-wave assaults. The person deputed by the Reagan administration to fly to Baghdad and sell Hussein these weapons for exterminating the Iranians was Donald Rumsfeld, the man who wanted to attack Iraq the day after the twin towers tragedy.

Iraq is one in a long list of countries the United States helped to arm for political gain and profit after World War II. It is not the only one to have done so. Europe's arms-producers have been equally active. In addition to profits the arms trade has the added attraction of enabling suppliers to influence global events. It places the industrialized powers in a uniquely advantageous position from which to manipulate the politics of nations, thus making a mockery of their efforts to shape their own destinies. Among the leading European arms-producing countries – Britain, France, Holland, Germany and Italy – marketing thrust can sometimes be greatly helped by knowledge of the organizational structure and psychology of their former subject nations. A definite asset in all respects – including fomenting trouble. Obviously the advantages enjoyed by the European arms-producers could not possibly be to the liking of the United States – though appearances of solidarity had to be maintained. So the Reagan years saw a new impetus to America's defence industries. "The Reagan administration clearly intends to increase sales", wrote one commentator,

> but to whom? The buyers' choice between the United States and the Soviet Union, always political, is unlikely to be affected by aggressive marketing. Unless total sales increased, a larger American share of the market would come at our allies' expense … France, Britain, West Germany and many smaller countries have large, modern arms industries that they consider vital to their national security and economic well-being. All insist that they must export arms to keep their weapon industries viable … Europeans have turned to developing countries for sales largely because of American dominance of what was supposed to be a two-way trade with the North Atlantic Treaty Organization. Increased American competition would undoubtedly lead them to seek new Third-World customers.[4]

The Americans have been very successful in finding customers in the newly-emerging nations. Their aggressive salesmanship, financial resources and global reach, combined with a willingness to extend 'aid' for buying arms, have produced excellent results. As has the absence of qualms at the human cost involved in developing new markets. The millions killed in Asia by the US military, or the armies of the juntas it supports and arms, are proof of it. The killings served a dual purpose: they helped Washington develop a stranglehold on its spheres of influence (although Vietnam is a question mark), while providing opportunities to 'blood' and 'combat prove' new weapons on the battlefield.

Where moral qualms are concerned, Britain's political leaders are even less troubled by them. As the world's second largest arms exporters – the United States being the first – they refuse to be sidetracked by such 'non-issues' as human costs, double standards or ethical concerns.

Nothing illustrates this more convincingly than these words of Winston Churchill: "I do not understand this squeamishness about the use of gas. I am strongly in favour of using poison gas against uncivilized tribes".[5] At another point he explained that his personal enthusiasm for it was because its moral effect would be good, and it would spread lively terror. He was expressing his views on the use of poison gas against the Iraqis after World War I, when he was Secretary for War and Air. Churchill also added that the use of gas was a "scientific expedient" which should not be prevented "by the prejudices of those who do not think clearly".[6] Back to Orwell!

Now for business. Morality, of course, has nothing to do with business, and British arms policy towards India in 2002 shows how mundane considerations like ethical concerns and such can be easily brushed aside. It makes no difference, incidentally, which party is in power; there is little to choose between the policies of Labour (Old or New) and those of the Conservatives. Both are of a piece.

The brazen-faced double-talk of Britain's New Labour government was highlighted by the business-like manner in which it went about selling missiles, rockets, torpedoes, howitzers, combat vessels and military aircraft to India and Pakistan during the heightened tensions between the two in the summer of 2002. With their armies facing each other in combat-readiness along the border, with British ministers including Tony Blair and Jack Straw flying in and out of New Delhi and Islamabad to exert a 'calming influence', with Britain asking its nationals to leave the two countries because of the impending war, the British government was briskly granting licences for export of military equipment to the two nations on the brink of war.

Commenting on the impropriety of this in the House of Commons on June 19, 2002, Menzies Campbell, foreign affairs spokesman of the Liberal Democrats, said: "What on earth is the British government doing granting arms licences as recently as last month [May 2002] when a million soldiers were facing each other across the line of control with the overhanging spectre of a nuclear exchange? The government policy towards arms exports to India and Pakistan has lacked coherence and appears to be in breach of its own published criteria".[7]

The criteria for arms exports which Campbell was referring to specify that "The government will not issue an export licence if there is a clear risk that the intended recipient would use the proposed export aggressively against another country or assert by force a territorial claim ... the government will take into account the existence or likelihood of armed conflict between the recipient and another country".[8]

Earlier, MPs were assured by Foreign Secretary Jack Straw that "On the issue of arms sales [to India and Pakistan] I may be wrong but I do not recall approving a single arms control licence in the past two months".[9] Well, he was wrong. The next day *The Guardian* reported that "Export licences covering more than 200 categories and specific types of equipment were issued from December to May [2002]".[10] More pointedly, "figures showed that the Department of Trade and Industry issued 39 export licences to India and 4 to Pakistan between 1 May and 20 May this year [2002] alone".[11] Straw was unfazed. "We are not a pacifist country", he said, "and I do not believe that we would make the world a safer place by Britain not being involved in ... responsible defence exports".[12] If the government were serious about peacemaking, it has been pointed out, it might be expected to "place conflict prevention above the interests of UK defence exporters".[13]

At about the same time as the India-Pakistan confrontation during the summer of 2002, Jack Straw was defending "plans to change UK arms guidelines to allow military aircraft components to be sold for US fighter planes destined for Israel ... Opponents believe there is a risk that the F-16s fitted with the British-built 'heads up' displays could be used against the Palestinians".[14] Straw denied that the rules were being changed under pressure from the United States. But only the very naïve would take his denials seriously. Nor did it bother the British government much that the Israelis might use the same planes to strafe the hapless Palestinians since the moral calculus, as we have seen, has little to do with arms exports.

Even less so when job security in the weapons industries is weighed against the deaths of those the arms will kill. According to Robert Linfield, speaking for British defence manufacturers, a third of the country's working population is dependent on the arms industry, that is, around nine million people.

If the victims of sophisticated arms are marginalized people of different coloration and creeds, morality becomes even less important. This ingrained indifference to the tragedies of distant peoples was numbingly brought home, once again by New Labour, in the arms aid extended to General Suharto, the Indonesian dictator. "In New Labour's first year in office", John Pilger recently commented, "Britain was the biggest weapons supplier to Indonesia, with Blair approving eleven arms deals with Indonesia under cover of the Official Secrets Act ... During one twelve-month period, almost £1 billion of ECGD [Export Credit Guarantee Department of the Department of Trade and Industry] money financed the sale of Hawk fighter-bombers to Indonesia. The unknowing British tax-payers paid up; the arms industry reaped its profits; and the Hawks were used to bomb villages in the mountains of East Timor".[15] Suharto's blood-letting – by which he seized power and which continued long after – increases the horror of this. Even the CIA reported that those "massacres rank as one of the worst mass murders of the 20th century".[16] The CIA should know. Suharto came to power with Washington's aid, encouragement and support, and it watched approvingly as its new protégé massacred close to a million of his countrymen during his thirty-year rule.

The American system greatly facilitates large-scale arms sales and support to those like Suharto by enabling suppliers and builders of bombers, missiles and military hardware to move in and out of top government jobs. This is best illustrated by the example of former Secretary of State Alexander Haig. In the words of James Fallows: "Until the beginning of the Reagan administration the President of United Technologies was Alexander Haig – former four-star general, former Supreme Allied Commander of NATO forces, Reagan's Secretary of State, and perhaps the single most dramatic example of the traffic between defense contractors and the government ... United Technologies, which makes helicopters and jet engines, among other things, received [contracts worth] $2,553,600,000 [in one year, 1978. It ranked third amongst US defence contractors]".[17]

The first two defence contractors at this time were General Dynamics, manufacturer of F-16 and F-111 airplanes, Tomahawk cruise missiles and nuclear submarines, with its Pentagon contracts in the same year totalling $3,492,100,000, and McDonnell Douglas, producer of F-15 and F-18A fighters and Harpoon missiles, with contracts totalling $3,229,200,000. Then came companies manufacturing nuclear warheads, Minuteman nuclear missiles, large transport planes, B-52 bombers, F-14 fighter planes, jet engines, Sidewinder, Patriot and Hawk missiles, 'Smart' missiles like the Falcon and Phoenix, cruise missiles, and ships of every size, shape and description. This is just a very small listing of what defence contractors produce.

When he was at the State Department, Haig no longer had to call on his former colleagues for business. As Secretary of State, he was in a position to orchestrate it all, and if there were differences between him and the Secretary of Defense, Casper W. Weinberger, they were not of principle – just of ego and the conflict of personalities, and of who pulled more weight with the President.

Ronald Reagan is probably the fountainhead of George Bush's inspiration since one of Reagan's advisory panels emphasized that "no area of the world is beyond the scope of American influence", and that the United States must possess "sufficient military strength to cope with any level of violence"[18] anywhere. This doctrine is significant in that while in the years following the Vietnam war, US military expenditures had begun to decline, Ronald Reagan's use of the military card to win his 1980 election marked the beginnings of an expansionary phase in America's and the world's militarization.

This single, obsessive aim of exercising global influence dominates the thinking of the Bush administration. Many of its key men have held positions of responsibility under previous Republican presidents. And they have diligently planted their delusions of infinite power in the mind of the White House's present occupant. Of his two closest associates, Vice President Dick Cheney has been a member of all Republican administrations since Nixon's, when he was Deputy White House Counsel under Rumsfeld. He replaced Rumsfeld as Chief of Staff under President Ford. Under George Bush Sr, Cheney was Defense Secretary during the invasion of Panama and the Gulf War.

As President Ford's Secretary of Defense and then his Chief of Staff, Donald Rumsfeld "was able, almost single-handedly, to kill the Salt II treaty with the Soviet Union. He has consistently opposed any arms control, calling the ABM treaty 'ancient history' during his 2001 confirmation hearings. A longtime supporter of 'Star Wars' defense schemes, Rumsfeld oversaw a 1998 commission that measured the ballistic missile threat to the United States".[19]

With figures like these holding the highest offices in the administration, America is being led, as John Le Carré puts it, into another "of its periods of historical madness" – into military adventures on the lines of the 2003 war on Iraq. If past US policies have proved catastrophic for Asia, the future looks even more grim; and it will be no less disastrous for the United States. Joseph Wilson, American chargé d'affaires in Baghdad during the 1991 war, has pointed this out:

> American pre-eminence in the Gulf is necessary but not sufficient for the hawks. Nothing short of conquest, occupation and imposition of handpicked leaders on a vanquished population will suffice. Iraq is the linchpin for this broader assault on the region. The new imperialists will not rest until governments that ape our worldview are implanted throughout the region. Our global leadership will be undermined as fear gives way to resentment and strategies to weaken our stranglehold. American business men already complain about hostility when overseas, and Arabs speak openly of boycotting American products. Foreign capital is fleeing American stocks and bonds; the United States is no longer a friendly destination for international investors. For a borrow-and-spend administration, as this one is, the effects on our economic growth will be felt for a long time to come. Essential trust has been seriously damaged and will be difficult to repair.[20]

Wilson is right. And while the empire-builders of the past had big ambitions, America's today are much bigger. For that reason, the risks Wilson underscores must be judged in the context of America's interests worldwide, not just in the Arab states. What he doesn't elaborate on, however, is the extraordinary ability of America's defence industries to influence senators, congressmen, media, and key men in the administration, including, at times, the choice of who should occupy the White House. As indeed they have influenced the choice of George W. Bush. That being the case, defence contractors are unlikely to allow Washington to be easily diverted from its goal of world dominance. The prospect it holds of unending wars and violence which can keep the weapons suppliers' cash registers ringing is too seductive.

The need to keep the world on edge and increase the demand for more and better weapons will, as in the past, rate a high priority in the coming years, and this particularly since international arms sales have recently showed a marked decline: from $32.5 billion in 2000 to $21.3 billion in 2001 – the lowest level in eight years. The drop is even more dramatic compared to the 1997 figure of $46.9 billion. The factors which contributed to the fall in arms sales were mostly economic, ranging from a drop in orders from East Asia, due to the 1997–98 economic crises there, to a reduction in sales to Europe of US systems because

of a reorganization of European military priorities and the general jolt
the global economy received after the technology setback in the 1990s.
West Asian orders also declined after the Gulf War.[21]

What this indicates is the need to stir the pot. And who could be
better at it than the Bush administration with its restive hawks, unreformed imperialists, and eager flag-bearers of the new American
Internationalism. To retain its share of 50 per cent of global arms sales
(the UK and Russia ranking second and third) – which it has maintained
for close to ten years – the United States, as also other arms manufacturing countries, needs more wars and conflicts to keep the order
books filled. Defence industries are much too vital to the economies
of weapons-producing powers to be left for long without the oxygen of
orders. Which explains, in part, why Tony Blair has so willingly placed
himself at the beck and call of the White House. And why Bush and
his consigliere Rumsfeld were panting for a war with Syria or Iran even
while the invasion of Iraq was still not fully secured.

It also helps explain why France, after opposing America's invasion
of Iraq, lost no time in making overtures to Washington once the war's
outcome was clear. President Jacques Chirac was not about to jeopardize France's weapons and other exports in an oil-rich region which the
United States was rapidly bringing under its influence. To the realistic
French, realpolitik was all-important. Just two examples will show the
extent to which spheres of influence count in arms sales. The first is from
West Asia and the second from the other end of Asia.

For several years Saudi Arabia has been the world's leading importer
of military-related equipment, though the value of its imports in 2000
and 2001 fell from the peak period of the second half of the 1990s when
post-Gulf War deliveries were at their highest. Which is understandable,
because wars help persuade others in the neighbourhood to stock up
their weapons. The suppliers are more than willing to help in every
possible way. Anthony Sampson's description of the arms trade written
a quarter of a century ago remains as true as ever today:

> The important arms salesmen of today are government servants,
> honoured or knighted for their services to exports; the major arms
> exports to the Middle East are achieved not by gun-running or by
> quick bargains in Manchester or Paris, but by long drawn-out negotia-
> tions between civil servants in Washington or London, endorsed by
> Presidents and cabinets. The setting of a modern arms deal is not an

old hulk unloading crates at night at a deserted wharf, but an Arab prince being welcomed in London or Paris by a guard of honour and by the Minister of Defence.[22]

While Saudi Arabia was the world's biggest importer of military equipment between 1994 and 2001, the next largest was Taiwan – although its imports were much lower in value than Saudi Arabia's. While other countries showed a downward trend in their outlays on military equipment between the years 2000 and 2001, South Korea announced a record defence budget of $14.1 billion for 2002 (a 16–17 per cent rise over 2001). Its plans for weapons purchases included fighter jets, missiles, attack helicopters and naval vessels. The South Korean government awarded Boeing the $4.5 billion contract for the purchases of 40 F-15K aircraft, ordered a study of its intention to purchase 48 Raytheon Patriot air-defence missile systems under the SAM-X programme, and further, had the purchase of 36 attack helicopters, Boeing's AH-64D Apache Longbow and Bell's AH-1Z Super Cobra under review.[23]

What is interesting is that in the 2001 list of the world's leading arms suppliers, the two Asian countries listed are China and South Korea. The former ranks fifth, the latter eleventh. The ten leading recipients of arms deliveries in their order of ranking the same year were: Saudi Arabia ($4,800 million), China ($2,200 million), Taiwan ($1,200 million), South Korea ($900 million), Egypt ($700 million), Israel ($600 million), India ($500 million), Kuwait ($400 million), Pakistan ($200 million), Sri Lanka ($200 million).

The volume and value of arms sales in Asia are clear proof – if any proof were still needed – of how helpful Asian conflicts have been for arms-producing countries. The preceding pages have given only a passing idea of the extent to which the arms race drains the resources of developing nations, and of the arms-producers' role in this thriving trade. Corrupt leaderships of recipient countries, in collusion with arms-suppliers, also play a pivotal part. The lure of kickbacks and other incidental benefits is one obvious contributory factor. Another, more subtle and as disgraceful, has to do with the mystical and menacing aura of weapons. Arms derive their mystique from the illusion of power and the surge of self-confidence they impart to otherwise insecure leaderships carrying a hangover from their colonial subjugation. The arsenals of arms, men in uniform, naval fleets and air formations dazzle them as symbols of grandeur and seeming invincibility – giving them a sense of heightened self-esteem, a euphoric high obtained at the cost of their people's most basic needs. For this no one else can be blamed but corruption – both material and of the mind – within these countries.

§

Industrialized nations recognized the political and economic advantages of foreign aid early on. Economic assistance enabled emerging countries to arm themselves, and affluent nations to become more affluent since a boost to the purchasing power of the buyer meant more business for the seller. It was calculated at the end of the 1960s that over 80 per cent of the US's foreign aid programme was spent on US products.[24]

President Kennedy was quite clear about it:

> Too little attention has been paid to the part which an early exposure to American goods, American skills, and American ways of doing things can play in forming the tastes and desires of new emerging nations – or to the fact that, even when our aid ends, the desire and need for our products continue, and trade relations last far beyond the termination of our assistance.[25]

The New York Times later provided another perspective on 'aid': "… for the purposes of balance of payments, the United States is really getting two dollars back for every one lent – one immediately with purchase of American goods and another when the loan is repaid".[26]

Estimates of how much of foreign aid is spent on procurement of military hardware vary. What is certain, however, is that nations with over-stretched economies could never have invested in arms and other imports – on the scale they did, and still do – without large helpings of foreign aid. No objective study seems to exist on whether donors or recipients profited more from massive arms sales over the second half of the twentieth century. Certainly those developing countries with huge military establishments and arsenals of arms to match have not benefited from the outlays on them, while the arms suppliers certainly have. Robert S. McNamara, when Secretary of Defense, revealed a particularly significant aspect of military assistance – training of foreign military personnel. In his testimony to a Congressional Committee, he said: "Probably the greatest return on our military assistance investment comes from the training of selected officers and key specialists at our military schools in the United States … I need not dwell upon the value of having in positions of leadership men who have first-hand knowledge of how Americans do things and how they think. It is beyond price to us to make friends of such men".[27] Honestly spoken!

Undoubtedly foreign aid – whether economic or humanitarian – has helped countries build their badly needed infrastructure, start industrial projects, develop management, technical and scientific skills, and create new vistas of opportunity and self-sufficiency. Humanitarian aid has helped in times of distress and alleviated human suffering caused by natural calamities. But aid has a dark side to it too. New Delhi learnt as early as 1950–51 how the politics of aid – even humanitarian aid – work.

In that year 60 per cent of US food aid to India was cut off because of Jawaharlal Nehru's criticism of American intervention in Korea. Not only did the Prime Minister and India's UN delegate criticize MacArthur's crossing of the 38th Parallel, but they also called for Communist China's admission to the UN. Matters worsened when "India's reaction to the US's resumption of the air war in Korea in the summer of 1952 was sharply critical … Congressional reaction was to discount the administration's arguments for expanding aid to India, and to reduce it instead. If India showed neither understanding nor sympathy towards America's international problems, what was the value to the United States of showing sympathy … to India's domestic problems?"[28]

Politics and not humanitarianism was, and still is, the touchstone of most aid policies, even in times of famine. In 1966, the spectre of a serious famine in India coincided with negotiations between the Indian government and some American oil companies interested in building fertilizer plants in India. Food shipments, which India understandably awaited with considerable anxiety at the time, were held up until concessions for the companies had been extracted by Washington. Those of India's people who were starving could wait, but not the multinational majors.

According to Kenneth Keating, the American ambassador to India in the 1970s, US aid stems from the belief "that the world will be a more peaceful place if each and every nation can provide social justice and economic progress for its people". A noble aim which cannot be faulted. So why does Washington underwrite so many military juntas around the world? The truth is that aid is influenced less by this laudable aim and more by the desire to create conditions helpful to America's vital interests. If these are better served by military juntas, so be it. The term 'aid' can be misleading, often conveying the impression it is some sort of largesse; a give-away to nations in need. This is far from the case. The recipients pay for all the assistance they receive. Whatever the way in which repayments are made, aid does not come free. As noted earlier, around 80 per cent of US aid could end up back in the United States, spent on US products.

§

It would be entirely unrealistic to discuss American economic assistance without taking into account the power and influence of US corporations and financial institutions at every level of their country's government and society – especially since private invest-ments and loans have largely replaced aid. "It's no longer possible to tell where the corporate world ends and government begins", as one recent commentator put it.[29] The influence of multinational corporations and banks reaches into the innermost corridors of power, and into every segment of American life.

It also reaches into the lives of countless Asians and their govern-ments, and often in brutal ways. The influence of multinationals on Asian countries drains their peoples' lives, disparages their rights, diminishes their self-esteem, denudes their forests, depletes their natural resources, destroys their ecology, mocks their aspirations, and pushes them back into the era of servitude. Once again Indonesia, which mir-rors these degradations, is worth studying, but before that, it will be instructive to look at what two Americans of standing have had to say on the subject.

"There are two ways of conquering a foreign nation. One is to gain control of its people by force of arms, the other is to gain control of its economy by financial means", is how Secretary of State John Foster Dulles put it.[30] George F. Kennan, head of the State Department's Policy Planning Staff, was even more specific. "We have 50 per cent of the world's wealth but only 6.3 per cent of its population. In this situation, our real job in the coming period ... is to maintain this position of dispar-ity. To do so, we have to dispense with all sentimentality ... we should cease thinking about human rights, the raising of living standards and democratization".[31]

The thinking behind both these statements makes it easier to understand Indonesia's experience of the multinationals once they had carved
up the country at the Geneva Conference following Sukarno's overthrow
(see Chapter 2). More revealing – and horrifying – is what came of the
conferees' pledge "to create a new climate in which private enterprise
and developing countries work together … for the greater profit of the
free world".[32] How did Indonesia fare after the Geneva Conference of
November 1967 entitled *To Aid in the Rebuilding of a Nation*, presided
over by James Linen, president of Time Inc.? John Pilger, who visited
the country over thirty years after what he calls the "corporate takeover of Indonesia", gives this account of what he saw in his book *The
New Rulers of the World*: "Jakarta is ringed by vast, guarded, relatively
modern compounds, known as export processing zones, or EPZs.
These enclose hundreds of factories that make products for foreign
companies … from the high-street designer look of Gap to the Nike,
Adidas and Reebok trainers that sell in London's Oxford Street for up
to £100 a pair. In these factories are thousands of workers earning the
equivalent of seventy-two pence a day, about a dollar".[33]

The conditions under which these workers live, and spend most of
their lives, are described thus:

> Clinging to the factories, like the debris of a great storm, are the
> labour camps where these workers live … like the majority of
> humanity who are not touched by the delights of McDonald's and
> Starbucks … who cannot afford to eat enough protein … these are
> globalisation's unpeople. They live with open, overflowing sewers
> and unsafe water; up to half their wages goes on drinkable water …
> past their homes run stinking canals … the result is an urban environ-
> mental disaster that breeds mosquitoes; today, a plague of them in the
> camps has brought a virulent form of dengue fever, known as 'back-
> break fever' …[34]

This is the stark reality of Indonesia and its people; unfeelingly
exploited citizens of a country with an incredible wealth of natural
resources. Potentially one of the richest nations on earth, it is targeted
for that very reason by multinationals backed to the hilt by their government and its military. The formula of global exploitation now in
place is quite simple: if you covet someone's possessions, take them.
If the owners object, bomb them. But get a hand-picked native of
the country to do the dirty work for you, like silencing people who

demand their rights. Rights? What rights can the vanquished have? Or vassal states? In Chapter 2 some of the multinationals which fed on the spectacular feast served up by a captive Indonesia are listed – with timber companies making an annual return of 40 to 50 per cent on their investment. The state of the economy of this country, rich in resources, historical traditions and cultural mix, can be simply summarized: it had a total national indebtedness of $262 billion in 2001.

In 2003, the new feast being savoured by the multinationals was Iraq. While the detritus of war was still being cleared, and the last rites of those who had perished in the savage bombings were still being carried out, Washington was handing out the spoils of war. It was called 'reconstruction': a word with a certain resonance, conveying a sense of purpose – a worthy resolve to rebuild what had been wantonly destroyed. But who benefits from this generosity? They are many, but just a few names will tell the story: that the war was not only about oil, but also about rebuilding ports, docks, power grids, water works, communication networks, roads, bridges and public buildings, in addition to repairing and modernizing oil installations. And of course, the country that fought the war gets the spoils.

The man who knows most about this is Dick Cheney. His smooth transition from President Bush Sr's cabinet as Defense Secretary to CEO of the oil major Halliburton to the Vice President's office under the younger President Bush was mentioned in the previous chapter. Halliburton again signed up contracts worth hundreds of millions of dollars after the Iraq war. According to *The New York Times*, these could go up to $7 billion.

Close on the heals of this ranking oil company comes the construction giant Bechtel, with reconstruction contracts in post-war Iraq which could add up to a few billion more. "On its board is George Schultz", Bill Moyers has recently noted, "who ran Bechtel before he became President Reagan's Secretary of State. One of Bechtel's senior vice presidents is a former general who serves on the Defense Policy Board along with other hawks like Richard Perle and James Woolsey who wanted war with Iraq and got it. They advise the Pentagon and then turn around and make money out of their defense contracts".[35]

The system makes things easy for them. George Schultz, in addition to the other hats he wears, was chairman, during the countdown to war, of the board advising the Committee for the Liberation of Iraq – a group close to the White House. He was a passionate advocate of war with Iraq, and committed, among other things, "to work, beyond the liberation of Iraq, for the reconstruction of its economy".[36] This 'iron web' of relationships among powerful individuals inside and outside government is noteworthy for the extreme finesse with which they skirt conflicts of interest and avoid the danger of public scrutiny; men with influence over decisions of war and peace, whose businesses stand to benefit from war.

The members of the Defense Policy Board are chosen by an under secretary of defense and approved by the Defense Secretary, at present writing Donald Rumsfeld. A Washington watchdog group disclosed that out of 30 board members, at least nine have connections with corporations whose defence contracts exceeded $76 billion in 2001 and 2002. The goals of these people, according to Bob Herbert of *The New York Times*, "may or may not coincide with the best inter-ests of the American people. I think of the divergence of interests, for example, between the grunts who are actually fighting this war, who have been eating sand and spilling their blood in the desert, and the power brokers who fought like crazy to make the war happen and are profiting from it every step of the way".[37]

The list of multinationals which are profiting from Iraq's devasta-tion and destruction is long and keeps growing. Quite early on, the US Agency for International Development (USAID) asked US multinationals to bid for a wide variety of goods and services, including airports.

A few words about Andrew Natsios, head of USAID, will be in place in view of his connection with Bechtel, whose record in managing the largest public works project in the United States has come under much criticism. This project, 'Big Dig', the building of a highway under Boston, was estimated in 1985 to cost $3.5 billion. Natsios was chief executive of the Massachusetts Turnpike Authority, the agency responsible for Big Dig, from 2000 to 2001. According to Senator Robert Havern, Chairman of the Massachusetts Joint Transportation Committee, the biggest cost overruns – from $10.8 billion to $14.7 billion – took place in Natsios's time. According to *The Observer*, "Havern says: 'This is the biggest works project in the history of America, and it is the largest cost overrun of any project'. He thought some of the fault would be Bechtel's, and was surprised it was under consideration for Iraq. 'I cannot believe that he

[Natsios] would not, with the knowledge he has from here, be very skeptical.' "[38]

No reassuring endorsement of a man who was going to be largely responsible for overseeing the expenditure of hundreds of millions of dollars of Iraqi money on Iraq's reconstruction.

Writing in unambiguous terms about this "liquidation sale" of post-Saddam Iraq, Naomi Klein deplores the fact that the Iraqi people had no say in what was being done to their nation's assets. "Without any real democratic process, what is being planned is not reparations, reconstruction or rehabilitation. It is robbery: mass theft disguised as charity; privatization without representation". Her concluding remarks are even more to the point:

> A people, starved and sickened by sanctions, then pulverized by war, is going to emerge from this trauma to find that their country has been sold out from under them. They will also discover that their newfound 'freedom' – for which so many of their loved ones perished – comes pre-shackled with irreversible economic decisions that were made in boardrooms while the bombs were still falling. They will then be told to vote for their new leaders, and welcomed to the wonderful land of democracy.[39]

The experiences of these two countries, Indonesia and Iraq, though located at opposite ends of Asia, portray the power which multinationals exercise on nations singled out for exploitation and economic control. No fancy phrases can hide the fact that the fate of these peoples is of no consequence when weighed against the interests of global corporations, whose goal is profit: no matter what the cost to the ecology, the environment, the climate, and the populations of the countries from which billions are siphoned off.

The uncaring ecological destruction of several Asian countries, through exploitative and wasteful concessions, is best illustrated by the decrease in forest cover of the Philippines from 44 per cent of the total land area in 1957 to 33 per cent in 1976, a fate that later befell Indonesia as well. The stripping of their mineral and timber wealth for the profit of US mining and logging companies is just one amongst many indignities weaker nations have had to suffer at the hands of the multinationals.

There are countless other such instances – in different settings and forms – which for want of space cannot be included. Even though the United Nations is being systematically downgraded, what one of its agencies has had to say on this subject will be appropriate as the last word: "Multinational corporations, through the variety of options available to them, can encroach at times upon national sovereignty by undermining the ability of nation-states to pursue their national and international objectives".[40]

The message of the Iraq war is clear: death from the skies will be the fate of those whose political leaderships dare to differ from America's view of the world, or whose national and development priorities are unacceptable to Washington.

§

Resentment at the subversion of their sovereignty is shared by countries increasingly alienated by Washington's oppressive dictates. The new phenomenon of international demonstrations against globalization indicates the increasing awareness of the many different forms of economic exploitation. The newest mantra of globalization is synonymous with a global economic strategy. Who formulates the strategies and for whose benefit?

The principal institutions responsible for the formulation and execution of global economic strategies are the International Monetary Fund and the World Bank, although others too with similar mandates have been established over the years, including the World Trade Organization and its many offshoots, such as the Trade-Related Intellectual Property Rights group (TRIPS) and Trade-Related Investment Measures (TRIMS). With the IMF formulating strategies for facilitating the entry of major financial institutions into emerging market economies, and with the US Treasury its largest shareholder – the only one with the power to veto any policy – the United States is in sole position to influence global economic policies for its own benefit.

There is little reason to doubt that the spirit in which the IMF and World Bank were conceived at Bretton Woods towards the end of World War II was entirely ecumenical. They were seen as catalysts for growth – providers of capital to war-damaged economies and governments which needed it for development, as also countries newly released from colonial bondage. The World Bank would help all these countries build their infrastructure, industries, and natural and human resources alongside post-war reconstruction, while the IMF would assist nations facing balance-of-payments deficits with hard currency loans. The two would help the world get off to an inspired new beginning after the trauma of World War II. But noble intentions often end up ignobly.

America's sense of 'manifest destiny' required not only military but financial dominance of the world as well. And what other instruments of control could be more appropriate than the IMF and World Bank? So their functioning gradually changed, reflecting Washington's growing global aspirations. Along with United States militarization, the contours of US financial strategy became more sharply defined after the election of President Ronald Reagan in 1980. His administration, ably assisted by Margaret Thatcher in the UK, propounded free market ideology with evangelical zeal, imposing on straitened economies – badly in need of development loans and grants – concepts and conditions which would push them further into an increasingly dependent and vulnerable state.

The change in the working of the two world financial institutions manifested itself in their increasingly aggressive style, with the IMF taking the lead because of its virtual control by the United States. At the beginning of the 1980s, caught between steeply rising oil prices and equally stiff increases in dollar interest payments, developing countries were forced to face the harsh realities of an unsympathetic IMF, which would provide a bail-out only if trade barriers were removed, social spending was cut, labour unions were brought to heel, and national assets sold to foreign investors.

Globalization, the current catch-phrase for development, was aimed at countries which were trying to exercise control over their own economic affairs, and which needed to be persuaded or pressurized into dismantling the safeguards they had established to ensure an even development of their economies. Globalization, a multi-faceted mega-process, would provide multinationals with greater access to the markets and resources of such countries, aided and abetted by the World Bank and IMF. Once their national assets had been sold to foreign investors and their industries' ability to develop along lines suited to their own nature crippled by the conditions and barriers placed in their way, these countries could be forced to give up their own paradigms of development. As most of them have had to.

The IMF and the World Bank fell into disfavour with the peoples they were created to help because of the Fund's heavy-handed dealings with countries precariously placed between the growing demands of their populations on the one hand and their already over-stretched financial resources on the other. In the words of Joseph Kahn in *The New York Times*, "The Treasury Department and the IMF, which follows the preferences of Washington, its largest shareholder, used huge loans to compel governments to sell off companies they controlled. Even some of the least developed nations were instructed to allow competition in their stock, bond and banking businesses immediately. Aid was withheld if governments spent too much money or protected key industries".[41] And how did this economic formula forced down the throats of poor countries actually work?

It didn't work. For many reasons. Where objectives differ, consensus is seldom possible, and where agreements are reached it is usually because the party with the upper hand has its way. The Fund, more often than not, has the upper hand, especially as it is untroubled by qualms about withholding funds at the most critical junctures. Or about suggesting reforms – based on insufficient knowledge – even where their implementation would do irreparable harm to vulnerable economies. Numerous instances show how its arrogant assertions about knowing what was best for other countries have landed them in a mess. Joseph E. Stiglitz, one-time chairman of President Clinton's Council of Economic Advisers and former chief economist of the World Bank, has provided a forthright critique of the IMF in his book *Globalization and Its Discontents* (2002).

He gives specific instances to illustrate how the Fund's insistence on its advice being followed not only created grave economic crises in many countries, but very nearly caused the meltdown of their economies. Describing the East Asian economic upheaval towards the end of the 1990s as "the greatest economic crisis since the Great Depression, one that would spread from Asia to Russia and Latin America and threaten the entire world", he shows how the IMF aggravated the crisis through its inability to grasp the ground realities in the countries concerned; and also, more importantly, because the interests of the lenders – the big American banks and financial institutions – came first. The result was:

> The unemployment rate was up fourfold in Korea, threefold in Thailand, tenfold in Indonesia. In Indonesia, almost 15 per cent of males working in 1997 had lost their jobs by August 1998, and the

economic devastation was even worse in the urban areas of the main island, Java. In South Korea, urban poverty almost tripled, with almost a quarter of the population falling into poverty; in Indonesia, poverty doubled ... In 1998, GDP in Indonesia fell by 13.1 per cent, in Korea by 6.7 per cent, and in Thailand by 10.8 per cent.[42]

Some idea has already been given of the abysmal working and living conditions of Indonesian workers who produce designer goods for the fashion houses of London, New York and elsewhere. It shouldn't be difficult to imagine how these new economic conditions will affect lives in countries whom international financial institutions have supposedly benefited.

Stiglitz was even more critical of the IMF a year after the publication of his book. When asked in an interview why the economic route which the Fund urged developing countries to take "often ended up causing more distress to those economies, especially for the poor there", his answer was forthright. "I think the IMF has little idea of the macro- and micro-economic picture in the countries it deals with. Often, such decisions were taken on the basis of ideology and politics. So its formulations for them tend to become lopsided and severely impact the countries ... for example, the currency crises in South-East Asia in 1997. I believe that attracting short-term capital is not a good idea, *though the international lending agencies were strong votaries of it.*" But when the currency crises hit the countries of this region, "the short-term capital fled these countries, leaving them in the lurch".[43]

Another commentator has written that to help the lenders of the capital rather than the countries it was lent to, "The IMF scrounged up tens of billions of dollars to save Indonesia's financiers and, by extension, the US and European banks from which they borrowed ... There are lots of losers in this system, but one clear winner: the Western banks and the US Treasury, making the big bucks from this crazy new international capital churn".[44] Significantly, bigger countries which preferred to develop without the IMF's assistance survived the upheavals that felled the economies of nations dependent on it. "It is no accident", writes Stiglitz, "that the two large developing countries spared the ravages of the global economic crises – India and China – both had capital controls. While developing world countries with liberalized capital markets actually saw their incomes decline, India grew at a rate in excess of 5 per cent and China at close to 8 per cent. This is all the more remarkable given overall slowdown in world growth, and in trade in particular, during that period".[45] Stiglitz elaborates in detail on the examples of Russia and China. In a well-reasoned analysis of the two economies, he shows how Russia – which gave in to the dictates of Washington and the IMF – paid a bitter price when the effect of the 1997–98 financial crises in East Asia was felt around the world. "It is no accident", Stiglitz reiterates, "that the only major East Asian country, China, to avert the crises, took a course directly opposite that advocated by the IMF".[46] The growth model Russia followed on the IMF's advice – stabilization, liberalization, privatization – worked in the short run but proved disastrous over time.

Once again the economic strategies prescribed for Russia were designed to suit the preferences of those who preached "the gospel of the market economy ... arguing for a new religion – market fundamentalism – as a substitute for the old ..."[47] But here too, as in other spheres of life, fundamentalism caused havoc. Privatization led not to creation of national wealth, but to the stripping of national assets for the benefit of a new breed of billionaires. "Though it had difficulty making budget ends meet, the government, pressured by the United States, the World Bank, and the IMF to privatize rapidly, had turned over its state assets for a pittance ... The government was borrowing billions from the IMF, becoming increasingly indebted, while the oligarchs, who had received such largesse from the governments, were taking billions out of the country. The IMF had encouraged them to open up its capital accounts, allowing a free flow of capital."[48] How else would foreign banks and financial institutions be able to bring money in and out with such ease?

The subversion of the founding principles of the IMF and World Bank by their main financier, the United States, is only part of the story. A number of other institutions created since, with the aim of promoting and regulating the development of worldwide trade and investment, face an equal risk. The World Trade Organization (WTO) is the most notorious of these.

The WTO's tentacles reach out in many directions. TRIPS (the agreement on Trade-Related Intellectual Property Rights) deals with the legal framework and supervision of patents and copyrights; TRIMS (the agreement on Trade-Related Investment Measures) with facilitating trade-related foreign direct investment. As the largest sources of both finance and intellectual property, the G7 countries are the principal beneficiaries, yet the US continues to weaken the WTO by evading its multilateral approach whenever possible in favour of bilateral agreements with often very unwilling partners.

GATS, the WTO's General Agreement on Trade in Services, facilitates the creation of worldwide markets in service sectors like education, welfare, private health care and pensions. For Asia, GATS is an altogether new trading concept, although it is a familiar one in the United States. What it means, quite simply, is trade in social services on a commercial basis.

GATS is a minefield. In the existing volatile political situation in most Asian countries, where the rising expectations of marginalized people require the state to provide practical solutions to perennial problems of poverty and disease, any moves to privatize the most basic human services to benefit those whose main motive is profit are sure to prove disastrous, to lead to social upheavals and bloody uprisings. People, including the very poor, are keenly aware of the contrast between their own degrading existence and the lifestyles of their leaders and privileged classes. To introduce, in this surcharged political and social atmosphere, market-driven services which are script-written by people ignorant of the wholly different conditions in other cultures is to court disaster on a scale to set the clock back for these countries for a long time.

If the IMF – through its ignorance of ground realities – destabilized countries by insisting on far-reaching policy changes, there seems scant reason for hope in a situation where the changes will be more radical and their ramifications far greater. To stand up to the domineering ways of a militarized, self-obsessed and arrogant American establishment requires incorruptible national leaders with backbone. As such leaders are anathema to the American administration, the challenge is that much greater. Even more so since the Bush administration's intense pressure made the World Bank propose private participation in social sectors. In much the same way as countries were coerced or induced to allow free entry and exit of financial service firms, so too would nations be forced to agree to the most fundamental changes in their social services sector to enable US companies to profit from the new market opened up for them.

Ironically, by all accounts, the US public is less than ecstatic about corporate control of medical and health care sectors in America. Nor is much confidence inspired by the fact that one-fifth of America's own children grow up in poverty.

§

Despite the difficulties, hope for Asian countries lies in collective resistance to Washington's inroads and heavy-handed methods, and alteration wherever necessary of its policies. This has been forcefully spelt out by President K. R. Narayanan, India's former head of state. Underscoring the dangers to Asia of a globalization "inspired by a single power to subjugate the world", he warned the Asian Social Forum (ASF) in India's southern city of Hyderabad in January 2003: "Globalization is a fact today, and it is also a fact that it is indiscriminately eating into the lives of people. It is a mindless imposition of policies irrespective of the conditions obtaining in each country. The whole world is caught in a debt trap from which no country can escape". Questioning the basic propositions of globalization, he said "reforms are necessary, but for whom and for what?" If they lead to exploiting still further those already deprived, then much more than mere catch-phrases is called for. "We believe the world is pluralistic with different religions and nationalities. We want it to remain so. We do not want globalization of a single power. We want it to be multipolar".[49] He urged the ASF to grow into a credible "counterblast" to the pressures being applied to developing countries and to "herald a new people's movement to fight globalization".

Aung San Suu Kyi, winner of the Nobel Peace Prize, who has for years led Myanmar's democratic struggle, expressed similar convictions in her message to the ASF, which she couldn't attend because her country's military rulers wouldn't let her.

> Not only should we believe another world is possible but we have to say that another world must be created in order that we may be able to live in dignity as human beings. Occasions like the Social Forum help all of us to focus on problems of this world. You talk about anti-neoliberalization. I think we have yet to get to the stage in Burma when there is such a thing as liberalism.[50]

What each speaker at the Hyderabad Forum of January 2003 reiterated was a desire for a life of dignity not servitude, for development priorities reflecting human concerns not corporate profits, for social and political systems accountable to people not to global cartels. The Asian

Social Forum, described as part of a new 'rainbow coalition' of social movements developing in India and other Asian countries, is inspired by the World Social Forum which has met regularly over the years in Porto Alegre, Brazil and in Mumbai, India, in January 2004. The ASF is committed to creating alternatives to globalization which are rooted in equitable and sustainable development appropriate for each Asian country or region. The wide appeal of the Hyderabad meeting, for instance, can be judged from the fact that over 15,000 participants, ranging from women's groups, peasant movements, trade unionists, non-governmental organizations and peoples' movements to artists, environmentalists and others, attended it. If, however, the ASF and other groupings like it are to coalesce not only into movements which oppose world dominance, but also into initiators of innovative strategies for growth, they will have to fight attempts to destroy them every step of the way. When the stakes are high, the game is seldom played by Queensberry Rules.

To get a sense of how that game will be played, an understanding of the players' mindset can help. Particularly players of seniority and proximity to the present centres of power like the hardline hawk R. James Woolsey. In the first two years of the George W. Bush administration this former chief of the CIA was a member of the New American Century Project and Defense Policy Board (these are discussed in Chapter 3) and an ardent advocate of the Iraq war, and many other wars he and his ilk would like the United States to launch in the coming years. Even for an unabashed advocate of imperial America, Woolsey's views are off-the-wall.

Woolsey told students at UCLA in April 2003 that World War IV had started; the Iraq war was only the first round. "This fourth world war [the Cold War being the third], I think, will last considerably longer than either World War I or II for us." Why would World War IV last so long? Because "I don't believe this terror war is ever really going to go away until we change the face of the Middle East".

If America's allies in the Middle East expect preferential treatment, they are in for a rude awakening. Woolsey admitted that American moves to support democratic movements throughout the Middle East "will make a lot of people very nervous", particularly Egyptian President Hosni Mubarak and the Saudi Arabian oligarchs. "We want you nervous", he declared. "We want you to realize now, for the fourth time in a hundred years, this country and its allies are on the march and that we are on the side of those whom you – the Mubaraks, the Saudi Royal family – most fear. We're on the side of your people."[51]

For Woolsey this means any country that needs to be brought under US hegemony, such as Syria, Iran or Libya, will be labelled a terrorist state and treated the same way as Iraq. Woolsey's thinking provides a chilling insight into the attitudes and illusions of those who fervently believe in America's unchallenged world supremacy. Supremacists like these, whose voices apparently carry weight in Washington, can no doubt mobilize the resources and military power to sabotage movements that oppose US designs on the wealth of other nations. But these movements too can exercise their right to strike back, if not with military power, then in other ways.

In economic terms, globalization means not only trade but also direct foreign investment, the bulk of which is controlled by a handful of transnational corporations, and financial flows, such as those from currency speculation, which are dominated by international banks. These elements of globalization, spurred on by the policies of the International Monetary Fund, World Bank and World Trade Organization, ran rampant in the 1980s and 1990s, profoundly affecting the economies, and peoples, of the world.

Globalization, however, is also a cultural phenomenon. Turn on a television set anywhere in the world and you will be able to watch the news as presented by CNN, or the latest programmes portraying the life styles of the rich, the famous and the sordid. Global culture cannot, obviously, be equated with what the US networks consider worth presenting. But today the influence of the few media conglomerates is indisputably shaping people's values and aspirations the world over. And the predominant values that the media portray and idealize are the fast buck, hedonism, and conspicuous consumption.

What, then, is the balance sheet of globalization?

I am not unaware of the statistics trumpeted by the IMF and other apostles of what Joseph Stiglitz scornfully describes as "market fundamentalism": a steady increase in the world's production, a decline in the numbers of the world's poor, the diffusion of technology to less developed countries, and so on. No doubt many Indians have benefited from globalization by finding jobs in the IT sector, ranging from college graduates who have become computer scientists to secondary school graduates in the call centres servicing multinationals.

But I am acutely aware of the debit side: the billion plus people in the world – a large proportion in India and elsewhere in Asia – with incomes of $1 or less a day, and the even larger numbers of people who do not have access to housing, medical care, clean water, sanitation, electricity, schools, and transportation. Has globalization helped these people? Ask the farmers who have been persuaded by Monsanto and other multinational seed companies to adopt high-cost genetically modified seed in order to increase yields, the fishing communities decimated by the fleets of immense trawlers owned by multinationals that devastate the seabeds and marine life, and the inhabitants of filthy slums ringing the cities of the developing world. No, if we take what seems a sensible yardstick – comparing the number of people who have benefited with the number who have been left behind or harmed by globalization, the balance sheet is globally negative.

Fortunately, there are Americans of intellect, integrity and moral authority who reject what these fundamentalists stand for, individuals like Bernard Lown, Howard Zinn, Barbara Ehrenreich, Susan Sontag, Noam Chomsky, Mark Kesselman, and many more from different walks of life who forcefully question their country's dangerously intensifying militaristic, authoritarian, monopolistic and exploitative tendencies.

So to end this chapter on a positive note, I will quote Howard Zinn:

> Our government has declared a military victory in Iraq. As a patriot, I will not celebrate. I will mourn the dead – the American GIs, and also the Iraqi dead, of which there have been many, many more … As a patriot, contemplating the dead GIs, should I comfort myself (as, understandably, their families do) with the thought: "They died for their country"? If so, I would be lying to myself. Those who die in this war will not die for their country … They will die for Bush and Cheney and Rumsfeld. And yes, they will die for the greed of the oil cartels, for the expansion of the American empire, for the political ambitions of the President. They will die to cover up the theft of the nation's wealth to pay for the machines of death … Should we not begin to redefine patriotism? … Should we not begin to consider all children, everywhere, as our own? In that case, war, which in our time is always an assault on children, would be unacceptable as a solution to the problems of the world.[52]

5

The Willing Media

The Decline of Journalistic Integrity

Once a newspaper touches a story, the facts are lost forever,
even to the protagonists.

NORMAN MAILER[1]

THE MAN WHO IS CREDITED WITH CREATING MODERN JOURNALISM, along with
Thomas Barnes of the London *Times*, was James Gordon Bennett
who founded the *New York Herald* in 1835. Bennett battled hard to build
public opinion so that it could influence government policies, and his
contribution towards making editorial independence matter is widely
acknowledged. His legacy has been honoured by journalistic enterprise
ever since, earning some of America's newspapers admiration around
the world for exposing misdoings at the highest levels.

The two investigative stories that most captured public imagination
in recent decades were publication of the Pentagon Papers, first by
The New York Times and then *The Washington Post*, and the *Post*'s
Watergate exposé two years later. These were milestones of profound
significance. The Pentagon Papers – a confidential study of the Vietnam
War prepared for Robert McNamara, the Defense Secretary – revealed
the extent to which John Kennedy and Lyndon Johnson consistently
lied to the American people about US policy and plans in Vietnam. The
study showed that even as plans to intensively bomb North Vietnam
by air were under way, Johnson fought the 1964 presidential campaign
against Barry Goldwater on a peace plank. Another disgraceful fact that
surfaced was the ignorance of the 'defense intellectuals', from Ivy League

universities like Harvard and Yale, about Vietnam and its people; the very same men who formulated policies and set successive administrations on their disastrous course in Vietnam.

Rattled by the "presidential and political perfidy" revealed in the first instalment of the papers on July 13, 1971, John Mitchell, the Attorney-General, asked the *Times* to stop further publication. When this was refused a court injunction was obtained, but the Supreme Court eventually ruled in favour of the *Times*. That ruling retains full pertinence today. Justice Hugo L. Black said in his concurring opinion:

> Only a free and unrestrained press can effectively expose deception in government. And paramount among the responsibilities of a free press is the duty to prevent any part of the government from deceiving the people and sending them off to distant lands to die of foreign fevers and foreign shot and shell. In my view, far from deserving condemnation for their courageous reporting, *The New York Times*, *The Washington Post* and other newspapers should be commended for serving the purpose that the Founding Fathers saw so clearly.[2]

The Watergate exposé represents a unique contest in which *The Washington Post* took on the formidable power of the American presidency – and won. This landmark victory was entirely due to the exceptional courage of Katherine Graham, the *Post*'s publisher, and Bill Bradlee, its executive editor. For at stake was not just the future of the paper but of Mrs Graham's publishing and television empire as well, since she was pitted against Richard Nixon, a man as ruthless as they come who was determined to emasculate the paper. But Graham and Bradlee's decision to back Carl Bernstein and Bob Woodward's investigations of the Watergate burglary to the hilt led to President Nixon's resignation. As one observer put it, "The rule of law was applied against the most powerful man in the world. The American system worked, but it was the *Post* that first sounded the alarm and produced the evidence which set the wheels in motion".[3]

§

If for the next thirty years the American investigative media achieved nothing comparable with the two historic campaigns of the early 1970s, at least the more prestigious newspapers and magazines maintained civilized standards. September 11, 2001 was the turning point. After that date, hysterical and xenophobic commentary and reporting became the order of the day for print media and even more so for television. American media seemed to feel it their patriotic duty, after the tragedy, to be entirely uncritical of the administration's over-wrought response to it. What was ignored was that their patriotism could never be in doubt, and that the tragedy did not absolve them of their professional responsibility to explain to the public the dangers underlying the administration's excessive reaction, and the hazards it might expose the nation to in the future.

To go back a bit. In her satire *The Worst Years of Our Lives* (1990), Barbara Ehrenreich brilliantly lampooned the Reagan-Bush era of the 1980s in her essay *The Unbearable Being of Whiteness*: "Yes, I know the conventional explanation – white people lack convincing role models. Consider President Reagan, whose own son grew up believing – hoping? – that his true parents were the black help. Or consider the vice president, George Bush, a man so bedeviled by bladder problems that he managed, for the last eight years, to be in the men's room whenever an important illegal decision was made …".[4]

George Bush Sr's son is obviously blessed with a healthier bladder. Manfully shunning the men's room, President George Bush Jr announces his administration's illegal decisions himself. His order to the US armed forces to produce Osama bin Laden "dead or alive" reflects a resoluteness which is undeterred by legalities or moral clarity. It also reflects an inexplicable squandering away of worldwide sympathy for Americans in the aftermath of the September 11 attacks. That goodwill ebbed as a horrified world watched the gruesome dance of death Washington choreographed in Afghanistan. These excesses give Barbara Ehrenreich's comments made in 1990 a prescient quality: "… our extreme isolation from people of alternative races meant there was never anyone to point out the self-destructive tendencies inherent in white behavior, which is still known collectively as Western Civilization".[5]

Civilized conduct, of course, has never been an identifying characteristic of civilizations.

American society has withstood many attempts in the past to derail its democratic institutions. The system has triumphed over the wilful efforts of those who found open governance galling. But the

September 11 attacks on American symbols of financial and military power put an end to all pretensions of civilized behaviour in the United States. The American public, unnerved by the suddenness of the September events, accepted the administration's every move to trample on its rights – as also the rights of Afghan citizens – with many of the media falling over themselves to perpetuate the myth of patriotism. As if patriotism required a people to give up their civil liberties, racial equality, a fair criminal justice system and freedom of expression, to accept the institution of military tribunals to try suspected terrorists, and to hold suspects indefinitely without trial.

Once renowned for their independence and investigative spirit, most American papers and television stations – with a few exceptions – abandoned their critical judgement after 9/11, dragged down by the unhealthy undercurrents gnawing at a society unable to cope with the trauma of terrorist strikes on its own soil.

"The question I have", said Hume of Fox News Channel's *Special Report* with Brit Hume, commenting on the bombing of Afghanistan, "is, civilian casualties are historically, by definition, a part of war, really. Should they be as big news as they've been?" CNN handled it a little more delicately by reminding its reporters to bear in mind while reporting civilian casualties that "the Pentagon repeatedly stressed that it is trying to minimize" such casualties, and that "the Taliban regime continues to harbor terrorists who are connected to the September 11 attacks that claimed thousands of innocent lives in the US". Maria Liasson of National Public Radio needed no reminding. "No. Look, war is about killing people. Civilian casualties are unavoidable." Michael Barone, columnist of *US News and World Report*, was equally direct. "Civilian casualties are not, as Maria says, news. The fact is that they accompany wars."

For that matter, why are terrorist strikes, which take their tragic toll of civilian deaths, and are part of the war various terrorist groups have declared against different states, so extensively reported?

Some mediamen, supposed defenders of peoples' freedoms, argued in favour of torture for getting suspects to talk. Jonathan Alter, a *Newsweek* columnist, said "even a liberal can find his thoughts turning to … torture". Shephard Smith, a Fox News anchor, innocently asked: "Should law enforcement be allowed to do anything, even terrible things, to make suspects spill the beans?" Conservative commentator Tucker

Carlson was more forthright on CNN: "Torture is bad. Keep in mind, some things are worse. And under certain circumstances, it may be the lesser of two evils". Whether upfront or between the lines, the drumbeat after 9/11 was the same: thousands of lives could be saved if some of the suspects are made to talk. Even this kind of 'collateral damage' to their justice system was acceptable to some Americans in the mistaken belief that their lives would be safer because of it.

Yet another form of 'collateral damage' was inflicted on the freedom of the media itself. Two members of the *Oneida Daily Dispatch*, an upstate New York newspaper, were fired for an editorial which some readers found offensive. It quoted a Pakistani who held that the Jews were responsible for the terrorist attacks since hatred of the United States in West Asia could be traced to Israel's creation. Confronted with cries of anti-Semitism, the paper's owners not only withdrew the editorial, they sacked the city editor for writing it, and the managing director for running it. As Rekha Basu, a columnist on the *Des Moines Register*, put it: "It's offensive to scapegoat a people, but if that view is out there it is not the paper's job to hide it. If publishers can't take a little heat in the interest of free speech, then democracy is on a shakier footing than we realize". Shakier or not, many media owners were quick to give in.

Not all papers and columnists felt threatened. At least not those like Charles Krauthammer, who occasionally writes for *Time* magazine. Chastising Colin Powell for his judicious answer to a question about whether Americans would suspend bombings in Afghanistan during Ramzan, he wrote: "Why such sensitivity? We were attacked. Our enemy chose the date. We have no choice but to fight back – on our timetable. The enemy cannot murder thousands of innocents and then call time out for piety … the enemy has declared total war. Yet we eschew all but limited war. The asymmetry is potentially suicidal".

Attitudes like his will prove suicidal for America.

In an equally unfortunate vein was a column by Thomas Friedman of *The New York Times*. Author of the splendid book *From Beirut to Jerusalem* (2001), Friedman seemed to have lost his cool after September 11. "These terrorists aren't out for a new kind of co-existence with us. They are out for our non-existence."[6] These comments were typical of those made by many others. Few of the high-flying hawks showed moral qualms about the genocidal bombings of Afghans. The extent and scale of firepower used in Afghanistan threatened not only their present but also their future existence. The deadly and destructive nature of the bombs used while targeting Osama bin Laden's hideouts also destroyed centuries-old tunnels, aqueducts, aquifers and reservoirs built into the mountains to store water and other supplies for people of a country which alternates between droughts and heavy snows. So while mourning the innocent victims of the September 11 attack, Krauthammer and those who think like him might also have spared a thought for those innocents the Americans murdered in Afghanistan in a manner no less repugnant.

As I write these lines the thought strikes me that just as there are double standards people live by, there are two worlds we live in – what are commonly called the 'real' and the 'unreal' worlds. In the 'real' world people are supposed to grieve over their own dead only and not to expend their emotions on others. Pragmatic people are supposed to feel a sense of personal outrage over a wrong inflicted on themselves, but not when inflicted on others. That is why, in the 'real' world, Donald Rumsfeld can announce with his unattractive smirk that no US combatants lost their lives in the Afghanistan war. How many innocent Afghan men, women and children were bombed out of existence was no concern of his. Howard Zinn gives a meaning to 'real' existence which is directly contrary to the cynicism and crassness of the Krauthammers and the Rumsfelds: "The much-heralded 'free press' of this country, by its failure to report fully on the terror visited daily on the people of Afghanistan, has become a handmaiden to the US government, and bears some responsibility for the continuation of this spurious 'war on terrorism', or the deaths and mutilations reported in this article". [7]

Zinn's article in the authoritative left-wing weekly *The Nation* of February 11, 2002 presented meticulously assembled accounts from various newspapers and agencies to give Americans glimpses of the tragedies inflicted on the innocents of Afghanistan:

> … for the Afghans we will have to imagine the hopes and dreams of those who died, especially the children, for whom 40 or 50 years of mornings, love, friendship, music, sunsets, and the sheer exhilaration of being alive were extinguished by monstrous machines sent over their land by men far away. My intention is not at all to diminish our compassion for the victims of the terrorism of September 11, but to enlarge that compassion to include the victims of all terrorism,

any place, any time, whether perpetrated by West Asian fanatics or American politicians.[8]

§

The US media debased themselves not only by their insensitive support of the savage bombings in Afghanistan, but also by their dishonest reporting of the Iraq war. Instead of denouncing the indiscriminate use of massive air power against the innocent populations of these Asian countries, the media – with a few honourable exceptions – loudly acclaimed Washington's unconscionable adventurism. Having in the past revelled in their role of keeping wayward administrations reminded of their constitutional responsibilities, the US media now allowed themselves to be induced or intimidated into a morally debased position. They failed to differentiate between nationalistic overdrive and national interest. This needs a free and unfettered press to alert the government – and the public – whenever it is in danger of being compromised by excessive nationalistic zeal. If the government is given carte blanche to determine what is in the public or national interest, the media have no role left to play. It is particularly degrading when the media forsake their honoured place in society to become an embedded adjunct of the defence establishment. Greg Dyke, Director-General of the BBC, made a serious point when he wanted to know "how can we guard against 'embeds' being seen as 'in bed' with their hosts?"[9]

Many explanations have been offered for declining journalistic standards. The most plausible of them relate to the changed nature of media ownership. This has resulted in a slanting of the content of newspapers and television and declining professional standards in favour of a money-is-what-matters-most approach. The media's new corporate owners are more concerned with profit and less with exposing the misdeeds of wilful governments than the independent 'newspaper barons' of past eras. According to an Indian commentator quoting Ted Turner, founder of CNN, Rupert Murdoch, owner of one of the biggest of all media organizations, is "a warmonger". "He promoted it [the 2003 Iraq war]", Turner is reported as saying, "because it's good for his newspapers and good for his television stations". Of Iraq's weapons of mass destruction Turner said he would have liked to see evidence of the Bush administration's justification of the war.

"I want to see the proof. I want to see what we went to war for."[10] Which, of course, Murdoch's media were, and are, *least* interested in seeing.

To Paul Krugman of *The New York Times*, the "China syndrome", that which was exhibited by Rupert Murdoch's News Corporation when dealing with the government of the People's Republic, is all too typical.

> In the United States Mr. Murdoch's media empire – which includes Fox News and *The New York Post* – is known for its flag-waving patriotism. But all that patriotism didn't stop him from, as a *Fortune* article put it, "pandering to China's repressive regime to get his programming into that vast market". The pandering included dropping the BBC's World Service – which reports news China's government doesn't want disseminated – from his satellite programming, and having his publishing company cancel the publication of a book critical of the Chinese regime.[11]

Krugman explained, in the article just quoted, the many ways in which government favours – and rewards – media companies which please it, and punishes those that fail to. He concluded with a damning indictment of the drift towards partisanship and quoted Fox News once again to illustrate his point:

> Meanwhile, both the formal rules and the codes of ethics that formerly prevented blatant partisanship are gone or ignored. Neil Cavuto of Fox News is an anchor, not a commentator. Yet after Baghdad's fall he told "those who opposed the liberation of Iraq" – a large minority – that "you were sickening then; you are sickening now". Fair and balanced. We don't have censorship in this country; it's still possible to find different points of view. But we do have a system in which major media companies have strong incentives to present the news in a way that pleases the party in power, and no incentive not to.[12]

If the present picture is gloomy, the future is worse. The US Federal Communications Commission (FCC), chaired by Secretary of State Colin Powell's son, Michael Powell, might effect far-reaching changes which will dramatically increase the reach of a handful of media corporations in the country.

By lifting existing regulatory restrictions on media ownership, it could allow just about every link in the crucial chain, from the local newspaper, radio stations and cable provider to TV channels, to be owned by a single corporation. This would remove every check and balance that exists at present in the highly competitive media market-place. It is conceivable that once the regulatory restrictions are lifted, NBC, ABC, CBS and Fox could end up owned by the same corporate parent: a concentration of ownership which could be deeply destructive to democracy.

These moves, which would vest unlimited media power in a few giant corporations in the USA, could have consequences of grave import for countries everywhere. Such concentration would futher multiply the number of tub-thumping, flag-waving patriots of the Brit Hume / Neil Cavuto variety, whose role would be to applaud each and every measure taken by an administration obsessed with the aim of global dominance. These 'patriots' would be embedded in the domestic theatre of war – in a battle for the hearts and minds of Americans undecided about the implications of America's new 'internationalism'.

The media scene was not very reassuring before the prospect of any such changes in the regulatory restrictions. It will be more dismal if they are carried out. According to Ted Turner, the big five in the broadcast business, News Corp/Fox, AOL/Time Warner/CNN, Disney Co/ABC, Viacom/CBS and General Electric/NBC, already control 99 per cent of what Americans are able to access on their television sets and radios.

Turner's comment has been borne out by Greg Dyke: "In the area of impartiality as in many other areas we [the BBC] must ensure that we don't become Americanised. We are still surprised when we see Fox News with such a committed political position ... This is particularly so since 9/11 when many US networks wrapped themselves in the American flag and swapped impartiality for patriotism ... commercial pressures may tempt others to follow the Fox News formula of gung-ho patriotism ... mixing patriotism and journalism is happening in the US and if it continues will undermine the credibility of the US electronic news media".[13]

The "gung-ho patriotism" was placed in perspective a few days after Dyke's speech by Michael Gillespie, a freelance journalist based in Ames, Iowa in a news release circulated to friends: "Fox News, headed by long-time Republican Party public relations mogul Roger Ailes, is viewed with growing alarm by many journalists as nothing more than the propaganda organ of the Bush administration and the Republican Party ... Fox reportage, which typically avoids any criticism of the Bush administration or its policies while it consistently dismisses, denigrates, or demonizes all who dare to be critical of the Bush administration, has pushed both the tone and content of reportage related to foreign policy well into the realm of xenophobia and warmongering".

On the very day Dyke was taking American TV and radio networks apart, Ashleigh Bashfield, a correspondent for both MSNBC and NBC News networks, revealed herself as one of the very few US journalists openly critical of US broadcast media's reporting of the war in Iraq. She pulled no punches while accusing mainstream broadcast organizations of emulating the mindless jingoism of Fox News.

Bashfield's employer, NBC News, huffily announced it was proud of its journalistic standards. Her colleague, MSNBC radio talk-show host Michael Savage, called her a "slut" after she reported a radical Arab point of view. Bashfield responded by ripping into NBC for putting Savage on the air. She also said: "He [Savage] was so taken aback by my daring to speak to martyrs … prepared to sacrifice themselves, he chose to label me a slut on the air, and that's not all, also a porn star and an accessory to the murder of Jewish children. These are the ramifications for simply bringing the message of the Arab world".[14]

To this extent jingoistic crudities have replaced civilized debate in the United States on matters of grave national importance.

§

The shared horror and deep sympathy which Asians felt for America after the 9/11 tragedy changed to disbelief at the administration's brash response in the following weeks and months. And then to anger as the government and media turned a national tragedy into a phobia against Islamic nations, against Afghanistan because Osama bin Laden lived there, even against co-Americans of different colour and religious per-suasion. Who or what whipped up this xenophobic frenzy, the religious and racial profiling, the public paranoia? The media played a major part in turning the debate away from a calm and clear analysis of events to an unabashed advocacy of military action which would "show heroic images of bang-bang and testosterone". The broadcasting industry did more than the newspapers to exacerbate the situation. While the deci-sion to retaliate with massive military strikes against entire countries was obviously government's, the media provided ample 'justification' for the administration's military and political moves. This in contrast to the past, when a confrontational press and television helped arouse American public opinion against the brutal engagement in Vietnam.

If the FCC opts for changes in the media's ownership in the United States there will be even less hope of it opposing government's intemperate actions. So far at least, conditions in the print media have been more encouraging. A number of editors, columnists and reporters have refused to march in step with the administration. If the media are deregulated, however, their numbers are likely to be reduced, and corporate owners like Murdoch's News Corporation would find it easier to manipulate news in the administration's favour.

Comments in the print media which have stood out for courageously unmasking the administration's falsehoods show that even in the oppressive atmosphere created by a handful of crazed empire-builders, traditions of a free press can be maintained by dedicated men and women. Here are two picked at random.

Robert Scheer, in an article in the *Los Angeles Times,* listed some of President George W. Bush's lies about the attack on Iraq:

> The first lie, claimed outright, was that Iraq aided and abetted the September 11 terrorists. There is no evidence at all for this claim. It is also interesting to note that not a single leading Al Qaeda operative has turned out to be an Iraqi ... The second lie was that Iraq's alleged weapons of mass destruction represent an imminent threat to US security. Despite the most hugely expensive but secret high-tech spy operation in human history ... we have not been able to find their supposed weapons. The third and most dangerous lie is that our mission now is to bring lasting peace to the Mideast by a devastating invasion of Iraq, which will end, as the president outlined last week, in US dominance over the structure of government and politics throughout the region.[15]

Scheer wrote this at the beginning of March 2003, in a column which had a prescient quality, especially his perceptive comments on "the third and most dangerous lie" of bringing lasting peace to the Middle East. What the Iraqi misadventure proved was that despite the hype and hypocrisy, the United States was unable to bring peace even to Iraq, let alone the entire Middle East. To assume that "US dominance over the structure of government and politics throughout the region" would bring "lasting" peace to a vast segment of Asia which is proud of its past and passionate about its future is to show either an abysmal ignorance of today's world or to mislead the American public by deliberate lying. This deliberateness is even more sinister since the quixotic aim of Bush's advisers – about which the American public has obviously not been fully informed – is to recast the very character of Islamic institutions throughout the Middle East to fit into the American ideal of this resource-rich region.

In an outstanding piece of reporting available on the web, Chalmers Johnson, author of *Blowback: The Cost and Consequences of American Empire* (2000), reveals the staggering toll depleted-uranium (DU) weapons, which the United States used in both the Iraq wars, took of its own forces. The havoc these weapons played with Iraqi lives after the 1991 Gulf War Is covered at length in Chapter 3 of the present book. Johnson details the casualty rate the US forces suffered at the hands of their own government. He writes that the casualty figures released after the first Gulf War in 1991 were: 148 killed in battle, 467 wounded in action, and 145 killed in accidents. Total 760. "However, as of May 2002, the Veterans administration (VA) reported that an additional 8,306 soldiers had died and 159,705 were injured or ill as a result of service-connected 'exposures' suffered during the war … After reviewing the cases, the agency has classified 168,011 applicants as 'disabled veterans'. In light of these deaths and disabilities, the casualty rate for the first Gulf War is actually a staggering 29.3 per cent."[16]

Whether these "deaths and disabilities" actually resulted from the use of DU ammunition has been hotly contested by apologists of the Pentagon. "Some researchers, often paid for by the Pentagon, argue that depleted uranium could not possibly be the cause of these war-related maladies … But the evidence – including abnormal clusters of childhood cancers and deformities in Iraq and also evidently in the areas of Kosovo where in 1999 we used depleted-uranium weapons in our war against the Serbians – points primarily toward DU."[17] What is perhaps not so well known is that by its insistence on using such weapons the Pentagon is ignoring a United Nations resolution of 1996 which has designated DU ammunition as an illegal weapon of mass destruction.

Johnson's conclusion is forthright: "The fact that the US High Command continues to rely on such weaponry for warfare is precisely why the world needs an International Criminal Court and why the United States should be liable under its jurisdiction … the use of DU ammunition should already be considered a war crime …"[18]

§

The US media's reporting of the 2003 war was entirely different from that of wars of the past. It had little connection with unfolding events. There are many reasons for the distorted coverage, but the two that contributed most to it were: 'embedding' of journalists with the troops, and the media owners' bias in the government's favour which correspondents could not – or would not – ignore. The effect of embedding reporters – for their own safety or whatever – is to undermine their objectivity, initiative, and an emotionally uncluttered approach to their job. These attributes are effectively subverted when they are embedded. Because 'embed' by definition means to fix into a surrounding mass: like embedding stones in cement. If that was the purpose of the exercise it worked admirably. The reporting of most of the 500 embeds was in marked contrast to those who worked independently – as many British, Arab and other correspondents did. No wonder 'embedded' emerged at the very top in a list compiled by *The Washington Post* of the most popular words of 2003. "'Embedded' suggested to many that news correspondents were in bed with the military!"[19]

In the Coalition Media Center at the Saliyah military base in Doha, Qatar, where over 700 journalists had registered, the questions European and Arab journalists asked during the 2003 war were more focused than those asked by most Americans. "The Europeans and Arabs would ask about the accuracy of US missiles, the use of weapons containing depleted uranium, the extent of civilian casualties. The Americans would ask questions such as: 'Why hasn't Iraqi broadcasting been taken out? Is Iraq using weapons prohibited by the UN? Can you offer more details on the rescue of Jessica Lynch?'", writes Michael Massing, an embed himself, in a nevertheless impressive account of this war's coverage in *The New York Review of Books*.

He describes the mobbing of the military press officer at the Center's briefings by ravenous reporters "desperately seeking to shake loose something even remotely newsworthy", the choice video clips showing 'precision-guided' missiles unfailingly hitting their targets, the grateful Iraqis receiving aid from American troops. "But remarkably few showed war's real-life effects, i.e., people getting killed and maimed … [because] television executives believe that when it comes to real war, Americans cannot bear to see bullet-ridden bodies and headless corpses. If they were shown, moreover, the effect might be to weaken support for the war. In the case of Iraq, the conflict Americans saw was highly sanitized … spared exposure to the victims of war, Americans had little idea of its human costs." [20]

Even the reports filed were often based on falsehoods fed by the officer conducting the briefings at the Coalition Media Center – usually Vincent Brooks, a polite and unflappable one-star general. The man chosen to manage the Center, Jim Wilkinson, was a protégé of Karen Hughes, President Bush's former adviser. He had worked hard during the 2000 presidential election and the Center too "had all the earmarks of a political campaign … Jim Wilkinson was known to rebuke reporters whose copy he deemed insufficiently supportive of the war; he darkly warned one correspondent that he was on a 'list' along with two other reporters at his paper".[21]

Massing was disenchanted with the reporting by his own countrymen. "After watching the British reports, I found the American ones jarring. In my hotel, MSNBC always seemed to be on, and I was shocked by its mawkishness and breathless boosterism. Its anchors mostly recounted tales of American bravery and derring-do. After the US attacks on the offices of Al-Jazeera and the Palestine Hotel in Baghdad, MSNBC brought on its resident terrorism expert, Steve Emerson, who insisted – before any of the facts were in – that the attacks were accidental. MSNBC's 'embedded' reporters, meanwhile, seemed utterly intoxicated by the war."[22]

Reporting of the Iraq 2003 war tended to resemble more a theatre of the absurd than a professionally sound coverage of a grave event. There is a story of a correspondent embedded with a marine unit moving across a bridge to Baghdad, excitedly telling someone over the phone, "We're about to cross the Ganges". When told he must mean the Tigris, he said, "Yeah, one of those biblical rivers or other". When Massing spoke to a reporter for USA Today about the problems of reporting on a region without much experience of it, she replied, "You can talk to any cabdriver and he'll tell you everything you need to know". As it happens, says Massing, most of the cabdrivers in Doha are from India and Pakistan.[23]

If British reporting was better it was for a good reason. There were more reporters, professionals and crew members sent out in the field; fewer embeds. The BBC deployed 200 reporters, producers and technicians in the area with experienced correspondents, anchors and commentators. An unusual aspect of CNN's coverage of the war was that what its international broadcasts showed was different from the coverage in its domestic channels. The international broadcasts were less frothy and self-congratulatory than the domestic ones, "a difference that showed just how market-driven were the tone and content of the broadcasts. For the most part, US news organizations gave Americans the war they thought Americans wanted to see".[24]

The reluctance of correspondents to file stories which would reflect adversely on Washington's lack of humanity in ordering unrelenting air strikes against Baghdad was evident in the sparse coverage of Baghdad's merciless pounding. A far cry from the objectivity with which Harrison Salisbury of *The New York Times* handled the USAF's bombing raids in the Vietnam War. Salisbury was one of a number of *Times* journalists who mistrusted government statements about the Vietnam war. He amply confirmed their disbelief when reporting that instead of confining their bombing to military targets as was publicly claimed, the US air force was dropping a huge number of bombs on civilian targets.[25]

An article that makes for harrowing reading, with its graphic descriptions of the punishment that Iraqis took, and the immensity of their pain at seeing their near ones torn apart in the brutal bombings, reveals realities rarely reported. It is a moving testament to the horrifying price ordinary Iraqis paid for their 'liberation' by US forces. Compiled by Marc W. Herold, Professor at the University of New Hampshire, Durham, it was published shortly after the war ended.

> A litany of lies has spewed forth from US and UK officialdom, whose intent appears to be to capture the headlines regardless of the substance said. The thinking is that the general public remembers mostly 'headlines', therefore priority must be to monopolise the headlines with claims [which later get retracted, but at no political cost]. The biggest official US lie remains the constantly repeated claim – one endlessly intoned by the solemn US corporate media choir with solos sung by 'defense intellectuals' – that unprecedented precision bombing is taking place in Iraq, bombing which largely spares civilians.[26]

How far mainstream corporate media bent over to accept blindly whatever the Pentagon and British commanders put out is revealed in a brief listing Herold provides of what actually transpired as against the military's claims. For instance, it was announced on March 23 that UK forces had taken the port of Umm Qasar; in actual fact fighting went on for weeks afterwards. On March 26 UK reports said 120 tanks were fleeing Basra; later reports placed the figure at three. On March 28, Prime Minister Blair announced at a news conference with President Bush that two UK soldiers had been executed; the UK government later retracted the story to say they had died in combat. On March 21 US defence officials announced the surrender of the Iraqi commander of 51st Division in Umm Qasar. He later appeared live on Al-Jazeera TV. On March 29 the US asserted that Iraqi anti-aircraft fire had destroyed al-Shu'la market, killing at least 62 civilians. Robert Fisk, the British war correspondent, reported that a US missile with Raytheon markings and produced in Texas had destroyed the market.

As for the "endlessly intoned claim" of unprecedented precision bombing in 2003 and in the Gulf War, well before the 2003 war veteran journalist Marvin Kalb had already effectively debunked the myths created around the accuracy of the smart bombs used in 1991: "80 per cent of the smart bombs missed their target but the press was told they were 100 per cent accurate".[27] Nor was the record any better in 2003, as is evident from the number of civilian lives lost and non-military buildings destroyed. Speaking of this war, Kalb was one of the very few to point out that "Patriotism is wonderful for the citizen but not for the journalist. Patriotism inhibits skepticism and a good journalist has to subject all statements and claims by the government to skeptical enquiry".[28]

As evidence of the administration's ill-advised actions after 9/11 mounted, some of the commentary and editorials in *The New York Times*, for instance, became more sceptical, more critical of the unfolding scenario, less prone to fall into line with the prevailing patriotic drum-beat. But the following lapse from objectivity remained typical of US journalism in general. In an article published on the front page of *The New York Times* on April 21, 2003, Judith Miller, its expert on chemical and biological weapons, tried to explain the administration's inability to find the offensive weapons over which the United States invaded Iraq. The mysterious source she cited for her scoop was an Iraqi scientist she had neither met nor interviewed, but who claimed his country had destroyed chemical and biological weapons shortly before the invasion. So how did she get the story? As an embed with the MET Alpha unit she was given the information by the military. "Those officials asked that details of what chemicals were uncovered be deleted. They said they feared that such information could jeopardize the scientist's safety by identifying the part of the weapons program where he worked", wrote Miller.[29] How could the scientist's safety, asked one critic, be in question with Saddam gone and the United States in control of Iraq? Miller's piece was met with "explosive disapproval" and a *Times* staffer called it "wacky-assed".

Another story that could have benefited from a healthy dose of scepticism was the rescue of Private Jessica Lynch of the US army. Described as "one of the most stunning pieces of news management ever conceived", it was a non-event painted as "one of the great patriotic moments of the conflict".[30] It involved the rescue of a nineteen-year-old army clerk captured in an ambush near Nasiriya. Taken to a hospital by her captors, she was under treatment for road accident injuries when US special forces stormed the hospital eight days later, faced – according to them – by fire from inside and outside the building. They dashed out with Jessica and whisked her away in a waiting helicopter, but not before recording the dramatic 'rescue' on a night vision camera so that Private Lynch could be made an icon of the war. In all the reports about the rescue it was claimed she had received bullet and stab wounds and had been slapped around in the hospital. General Vincent Brooks paid touching tribute to her rescuers: "Some brave souls put their lives on the line to make this happen, loyal to a creed that they know they'll never leave a fallen comrade".

Now for the facts. There were no bullets or stab wounds in Lynch's body according to Dr Harith a-Houssona, the Iraqi doctor who attended her. "I examined her. I saw she had a broken arm, a broken thigh and a dislocated ankle", he said – injuries sustained in the road accident. She was given the only specialist bed in the hospital, one of two nurses on the floor, and the best treatment that could be provided. "They want to distort the picture", he said, "I don't know why they think there is some benefit in saying she has a bullet injury". Another witness, Dr Anmar Uday, said of Private Lynch's rescue: "We were surprised. Why do this? There was no military, there were no soldiers in the hospital. It was like a Hollywood film. They cried 'go, go, go', with guns and blanks without bullets, blanks and the sound of explosions. They made a show for the American attack on the hospital – like Sylvester Stallone or Jackie Chan".

And to cap it all: "The special forces knew that the Iraqi military had fled a day before they swooped on the hospital". In the best traditions of American popular publishing, Knopf signed up nineteen-year-old Jessica Lynch in September 2003 in a million dollar book deal for her life story.[31]

While the US military and most of its media concocted a fraudulent tale of courage under fire, Lynch herself provided the final footnote on the web of lies woven around her. In a *Primetime* appearance with ABC's Diane Sawyer on November 11, 2003 she said the US military was wrong in manipulating and dramatizing the story of her capture and rescue. "It hurt in a way that people would make up stories that had no truth about them", like her fierce resistance when attacked until she ran out of ammunition. "I did not shoot, not a round, nothing … I went down praying to my knees. And that's the last I remember." As for her rescuers' courageously fighting their way in and out of the hospital to rescue her, Lynch says: "I don't think it quite happened like that".

Propaganda, since it thrives on lies, seldom resembles the truth.

§

How do Asians view the reconfigurations of power taking place on their continent? First, a look at some data on the people's mood in several countries, including the Muslim, from a survey conducted during April–May 2003 by the prestigious US-based Pew Research Center for People and the Press. It was released in June 2003 by Madeleine K. Albright, former Secretary of State who is chair of the global project. The survey covered 20 nations as also areas administered by the Palestinian Authority, and was part of an effort to assess changes in global attitudes. It found according to Andrew Kohut, the Center's director, that: "The [Iraq] war has widened the rift between Americans and Western Europeans, further inflamed the Muslim world, softened support for the war on terrorism, and significantly weakened global public support for the pillars of the post-World War II era – the UN and the North Atlantic alliance".[32]

The survey also revealed a decline in favourable views of the United States in almost all countries which favoured it in the past, with the steepest decline registered in Western Europe. The Russians, too, found by the Pew Research Center to have given the United States a 61 per cent favourable rating in the summer of 2002, dropped their support to 36 per cent in April–May 2003. As for Islamic countries, the most extreme shift was in Turkey where 83 per cent had an unfavourable opinion of it as against 55 per cent in 2002. "Dislike of the United States has spread in the Muslim world. Majorities in seven out of eight predominantly Muslim nations expressed a worry that their countries might be threatened by the United States. They voiced concern that Islam itself was in jeopardy."[33] Support for the war on terror was equally revealing. "Fewer than one in four in Indonesia, Pakistan, Turkey and Jordan support the war on terror. In Morocco, only one in ten backs the effort. There is considerable concern in several nations that the American policy of pre-emption could pose a threat against them, especially in Indonesia, with 74 per cent very worried or somewhat worried, and in Nigeria and Pakistan, at 72 per cent each."[34]

Egypt's *Al-Ahram*, in a lead article at the start of 2003, found it difficult to believe that except for a "few vague bleats of polite demurral", Arabs were doing nothing to oppose America's plan to redraw the map of the entire Arab world: "How can a region of almost 300 million Arabs wait passively for the blows to fall without attempting a collective roar of resistance and a loud proclamation of an alternative view. Has the Arab will completely dissolved?"[35]

Other voices have also tried to shake – and shame – West Asia's populations, if not the entire Muslim world of over a billion people, out of their inaction in the face of what Lebanon's Hezbollah-run news channel Al-Manar called a "War of American Aggression". The criticism was not only of American belligerence but of the violence it was beginning to spawn from Indonesia to Saudi Arabia and Morocco, with prospects of more to come. *Al-Ahram* was reported in May 2003 to have warned "that the US-led invasion and occupation of Iraq has boosted support for militant Islamists and extremists in the Arab and Muslim worlds … Anger and resentment in … [these] worlds will only subside with the resolution of the Arab-Israeli conflict".[36]

Equal concern at the increasing incidents of extremist violence has been expressed in other Arab countries. "Those who committed the crimes are not only the suicidal terrorists who perpetrated the act, but all those who have incited them and justified their actions, and all those who have described them as mujahiddin", wrote Jamal Ahmad

Khashoggi in the Saudi paper *Al-Watan*.[37] Which is ironic since Saudi Arabia was for years the major supporter of militancy in the region. The more recent acts of terror, however, it is widely believed are a blacklash against the assiduous targeting of Islamic people for almost every act of violence that takes place.

Al-Hayat, a Saudi daily, published a perceptive article by Dawood Al Shirian.

> There is no doubt that the explosions [terrorist bombings such as those in Casablanca and Riyadh] demand new solutions, the most important being monitoring religious institutions … The government has to address these events based on the conviction that they came as a result of an accumulation of several political, economic and religious factors. But the main factor that helped create an environment inciting terrorism is the intellectual factor … [it is] the preachers and educators who should move to reform their discourse …[38]

Al-Rai of Jordan felt: "The attacks in Riyadh were an appropriate response to the policy of the US which waged war against Iraq and supports Israel's attacks against the Palestinians".[39] Despite the authoritarian leaderships of some of these countries, many papers in West Asia were assertive and uninhibited in their comments in the aftermath of the 2003 war.

But credit for the most astonishing coverage of the war goes to Qatar's Al-Jazeera news channel and its broadcasts. Its emergence is a significant event because the Western networks, with their complete monopoly in this field, have influenced people around the world with slickly presented news and views, no matter how biased. Even before the invasion of Iraq in March 2003, Al-Jazeera had around 35 million viewers, and the figure was stated three months later to be over 55 million, with the number in Europe alone estimated to have gone up by 50 per cent. There are five other Arab channels, like the Saudi-backed Al-Arabiya and Abu Dhabi TV, but the pioneering Al-Jazeera is well ahead of them. Its central studios in Qatar with their advanced equipment – a large wall of monitors continuously provides worldwide satellite feed – and its skilled staff drawn from eighteen nationalities, does it proud. But its independence is not overly appreciated by the Americans. Which is understandable in view of the unvarnished reality shown by it. Michael Massing, a contributing editor of the *Columbia Journalism Review* who travelled to Qatar on behalf of the Committee to Protect Journalists, reported:

> Several times an hour, we saw footage of civilian casualties. Al-Jazeera took us to hospital wards to show us screaming children, women in pain, men without limbs. The camera lingered on stumps, head wounds, and tubes inserted in nostrils and chests. On gurneys in hallways lay bodies bandaged, bloodied, and burned. Doctors and nurses described how they were being overwhelmed by casualties and how they lacked the supplies needed to treat them ... the war has helped to solidify Islamist tendencies in the Middle East, and this development has been reflected in – and reinforced by – the Arab press and television.[40]

Paul Belden, reporting from Amman, also explained why the coverage by Al-Jazeera was causing such aggravation to the coalition forces invading Iraq:

> Before the day [March 23, 2003] was out, CNN's war coverage had been mocked and overtaken by images that showed the true face of war in all its madness and horror-images that almost invariably bore the label 'Al-Jazeera exclusive'. These were not scrolling maps or armchair generals – these were scenes of a 12-year-old child with half her head blown off in Basra. This was the sound and fury of the relatives of victims of Tomahawk cruise missile strikes in Northern Iraq loudly promising their revenge ... This was a guided tour of a roomful of US soldiers in a morgue. This was the fear in the eyes of a captured US soldier ...[41]

Washington reacted in anger to these images. Donald Rumsfeld said showing captured American troops could be considered a "war crime". President Bush told reporters: "I do know that we expect them [the US prisoners of war] to be treated humanely, just like we'll treat any prisoners of theirs that we capture – humanely".

The Arab media found this "new found affection for the Geneva Convention" laughable and immediately pointed to the prisoners being held at Guantanamo Bay whom their captors were not actually calling 'prisoners of war' under the Geneva Convention, but whom the Bush administration had shown to the world's media shackled and living in cages. Sarvsan-abu-Hamdeh, Al-Jazeera's news anchor, felt her station's coverage of dead American soldiers was "only the truth. I do not regret it [at] all. The [US] government might not like it, but there is a difference between the [US] government view of events and the local view of events. We try to portray what is really happening in the world". Belden's own concluding comment was that "if the true face of war is too much for American prime time television, then [it] ... should stick to covering the Oscars, and leave the war alone".

Had US discontent with Al-Jazeera ended there, it could have been overlooked. But reports that began circulating soon after the channel's correspondent was killed and his cameraman wounded in a missile attack on the channel's Baghdad office on April 8, 2003 were far more sinister. They accused the US military of deliberately bombing Al-Jazeera's office *after* it had been informed of its precise location. And many journalists recalled the US cruise missile attack on the Al-Jazeera office in Kabul in 2001, the night before the 'liberation' of the city – the very office that had broadcast the Osama bin Laden tapes around the world. Fortunately, Taiseer Alouri, Al-Jazeera's correspondent, had survived that attack. In Baghdad, less than three hours after the bombing of Al-Jazeera's office on April 8, an Abrams tank attacked the Palestine Hotel in Baghdad. Over 200 journalists were staying at the hotel and Reuters' TV bureau was also located there. The shell exploded in the Reuters office on the 15th floor, mortally wounding Taras Protsyuk, a Ukrainian cameraman, and injuring four others of the staff. José Couso, a cameraman for Spain's Tele 5 channel on the floor above, also died of his injuries after a leg amputation failed to save him.

Writing in London's *Independent* at the end of April 2003, veteran British journalist Robert Fisk reported that Mohamed Jassem al-Ali, the managing director of Al-Jazeera channel, had given him a copy of the letter he had written to an official in the Department of Defense in Washington, on February 24, giving the channel's exact location in Baghdad to avoid mishits. In addition to the address, in his letter al-Ali had also sent precise co-ordinates of the office: Lat: 33.19/29. 08, Lon: 44.24/03.63, and had emphasized that civilian journalists would be working in the building. In spite of this, on April 8 a US jet swooped low towards the building and "fired a single missile at the Al-Jazeera office – at those precise map co-ordinates Mr. Al-Ali had sent to [the official] – and killed the station's reporter Tareq Ayoub", who was on the roof filming a battle near the bureau.[42]

The question Fisk posed was: "Was it possible to believe this was an accident? Or was it possible that the right word for these killings – the first with a jet aircraft, the second with an M1A1 Abrams tank – was murder?" More damning still were some of the other questions raised by this journalist who is widely acknowledged as an outstanding war correspondent.

> Is there some message that we reporters are supposed to learn from all this? Is there some element in the American military that has come to hate the press and wants to take out journalists based in Baghdad, to hurt those whom our home secretary David Blunkett has maliciously claimed to be working "behind enemy lines"? Could it be that this claim that international correspondents are in effect collaborating with Mr Blunkett's enemy (most Britons having never supported this war in the first place), is turning into some kind of a death sentence?[43]

An already murky situation was rendered still murkier by evasive answers, contradictory statements and outright lies. General Vincent Brooks of the Coalition Media Center offered "outright misinformation", asserting that US forces had "come under fire" from the hotel, although this was denied both by journalists present at the time and by the commander responsible for the firing of the shell.[44]

The lies told to cover the attack on journalists in the Palestine Hotel were consistent. "General Buford Blount of the US 3rd Infantry Division, whose tanks were on the bridge, announced that his vehicles had come under rocket and rifle fire from snipers in the Palestine Hotel and that his tank had fired a single round at the hotel and that the gunfire had then ceased", Fisk reported.[45] Why was even a single round fired when there was no rocket or sniper fire from the hotel, because not one journalist present had heard any sound of firing? The four-minute videotape of the attack by the French television channel France 3 records absolute silence before the tank shelled the hotel – no sound of sniper or any other fire as claimed by General Blount. According to Fisk, "I was driving on a road between the tanks and the hotel at the moment the shell was fired – and heard no shooting".[46] General Blount had boasted a month earlier that his troops would be using DU munitions[47] which had already taken a deadly toll of Iraqi civilians – and US veterans – during and after the 1991 Gulf War.

During the bombings Indian columnist Seema Mustafa, whose incisive writings on the Bush administration's strategy to establish US hegemony over Asia have assured her a wide readership, had this to say:

The stories that are buried under the rubble of devastated Iraq will emerge. The truth, as they say, will come out with newspapers across the globe beginning to print reports and articles that draw attention to the most horrific human rights violations committed by the invading coalition troops as they sought to overturn a regime on the basis of falsehoods that are now being exposed by persistent journalists demanding answers. [48]

The Indian media have been ambivalent in their coverage of US foreign policy since the Republicans came to power in 2000. But despite the media's conservative bent, with their owners' political and business affiliations, there has been more criticism than support for the policy-makers in Washington. The Vajpayee government's views as usual were sanctimonious on the surface, but supportive of US actions underneath. A former editor and media specialist, Ajit Bhattacharjea, found this perfectly understandable. In a commentary on Iraq's occupation by American forces, he observed: "Every occupied country, including our own, has a long history of people at the upper and lower ends of society coming to terms with the occupying force for mutual benefit, and this being used to justify occupation".[49] This observation made in the context of the Iraq war and its supporters in India reveals the mindset of many of India's political leaders and opinion-makers, with the deep colonial imprint left on it by the British, and displaying a curious awe of power and its trappings. Thus the strange and convoluted justification sometimes advanced by the admirers of American muscle-flexing, of which this comment by a retired naval officer is typical:

> Should all nations be left to stew in their own anarchic despotic, genocidal juices? Shouldn't international relations have some kind of a levelling role in the world? … Maybe it is unjust that the 21st century will be America's but we cannot fail to see that American power comes not from its ships and aircraft but from the potentially unlimited capacities that their social system unleashes in any person who completes his schooling well … General Jay Garner may not be a world class statesman and may not set the Euphrates on fire but it is a safe wager that the General can easily do much better than Saddam Hussein for the people of Iraq. It must take extraordinary incompetence and stupidity to keep the Iraqi people poor.[50]

Unfortunately for this ardent admirer of America's capacity to better the lot of the Iraqi people, the General was sacked before he could unleash his "unlimited capacities" on Iraq. And it still remains to be seen how much more "incompetence and stupidity" it might take the Americans "to keep the Iraqi people poor" considering what that country has been subjected to for almost a year since the US and UK invaded it in March 2003. The continued presence of the occupation forces does not augur well for a proud and once prosperous people.

Fortunately for India, despite the prejudices, predilections and preferences of those who own most of its print media, its profusion of newspapers and periodicals ensures that a wide range of opinions and viewpoints are available to the reader, and especially on foreign affairs. On Washington's long-standing self-appointed global role Sashi Kumar was informative in *The Hindu* a month after the fall of the Iraqi regime: "From Truman to Bush, the US has pursued supremacy in the information sector as a conscious plank of its foreign policy, spending over three trillion dollars since World War II to achieve this".[51] Dominance in the information sphere, as in the military and economic spheres, is of vital importance to the United States if international public opinion is to be influenced in favour of an American-centric global agenda.

It is reassuring to read reactions such as the following – again in *The Hindu*:

> Last week [the end of March 2003] I almost threw a rock at my television set. Because I saw the elected head of a country telling such a blatant lie … I am referring to the live press conference by the Bush-Blair duo after their meeting at Camp David … Tony Blair talked about the death of over 400,000 Iraqi children over the last decade as an illustration of the villainy of Saddam Hussein … such a blatant lie when the world knows only too well that these Iraqi children died because Britain and the United States, amongst others, imposed economic sanctions on Iraq that denied its citizens basic medicines and its children adequate food.[52]

§

If international public opinion is to coalesce into an organized and coherent opposition to America's global agenda, then the media have to help pull people together on a platform of shared concerns. Crucial will be Asian countries' capability of establishing print and broadcast media to break the West's monopoly in this critical sector.

That the American and Western monopolies can be challenged has been brilliantly proved by tiny Qatar, smaller than Connecticut, but fortunate enough to have a ruler, Hamad bin Khalifa al-Thavi, whose vision and wealth helped establish Al-Jazeera. With a grant of $140 million from him, and an energetic and motivated staff in place, Al-Jazeera's central studio in Doha – aside from its own increasing network of correspondents – keeps getting continuous feedback from seven different time zones around the clock. The first Arabic channel to counter the oppressive monopoly of US and other networks, Al-Jazeera has proved it is possible to build up a multi-million worldwide audience in little more than a decade.

Of all the countries in Asia, India is ideally placed to establish an international TV presence. With its immense reservoir of technologically skilled and innovative young people, its facility with the English language, and its impressive financial resources, it has potential for spectacular successes in an area which offers great opportunities. But because of a strange amalgam of indifference, timidity, and lack of initiative and vision, it has refused to recognize the media's potential in this information age. It has instead allowed Rupert Murdoch to invidiously establish a major TV channel in India – thousands of miles away from his own home base, with official connivance and the help of self-seeking persons in public life.

Although Barbara Tuchman's artful dig in her book *Sand Against the Wing* (1970) was aimed at the British, it could easily be read as a commentary on America's current efforts to make its unsavoury interventions in the world look uniquely inspired:

> No nation has ever produced a military history of such verbal nobility as the British. Retreat or advance, win or lose, blunder or bravery, murderous folly or unyielding resolution, all emerge alike clothed in dignity and touched with glory … Whatever the fiasco, aplomb is unbroken. Mistakes, failures, stupidities or other causes of disaster mysteriously vanish. Disasters are recorded with care and pride and become transmuted into things of beauty. Official histories record every move in monumental and infinite detail but the details serve to obscure.[53]

Leave aside verbal nobility, even common decencies and a dignified treatment of the dead were brushed aside by the Americans in Iraq when they closed in on Saddam Hussein's two sons, and later him. The reporting of the US media fell from all civilized norms by taking, as did the military with which they were embedded, a ghoulish delight in publishing gruesome photographs of Uday and Qusay Husseins' corpses – and of Qusay's teenage son Mustafa – after the American forces killed them in northern Iraq on July 22, 2003.

The manner in which their killings were treated is exemplified by *Newsweek*'s cover story of August 4, 2003. "The first photos by US forces showed some bloody, bearded men who might have been almost anyone fished out of the morgue. So the next day, American officials summoned newsmen to videotape Uday and Qusay as they lay, groomed and shaved, stitched up and waxed, but still riddled with bullet holes, on a pair of gurneys at the Army-Air Force morgue at Baghdad International Airport." The magazine ran close-ups of the dead brothers before and after they were "shaved, stitched up and waxed", with the accompanying text: "So ended the reign of terror of two memorable monsters".

In an opening essay in the same issue of *Newsweek*, Anne-Marie Slaughter responded in similar vein to an Iraqi's suggestion that it would have been better to capture the two brothers alive and bring them to justice: "Perhaps in the best of worlds, this would be so. But in Iraq these days the best is often the enemy of the good. America is still at war; its soldiers die every day. And in war, you shoot first and ask questions later". Later in her essay, it must be said, she stepped back from her Wild West stance enough to concede that "simply shooting 'wanted men' is assassination, not justice".

The formidable firepower used to exterminate three men and a boy – Uday, Qusay, Qusay's fourteen-year-old son and a guard – came from tanks, armoured vehicles, fighter jets and helicopters, machine-guns and an assortment of other weapons, with air-to-ground missiles and much else. In distinction from the less than disapproving stance of most of the US media, the *Boston Globe* (July 25, 2003) did point out that "the killings of the sons looked ... like a zealous political assassination ...". Not inhibited by patriotic fervour, South Africa's *Mail and Guardian* of the same date felt that the killings were "thinly veiled extra-judicial executions, [which] are part of a growing pattern of American lawlessness in dealing with the world since 9/11". No satisfactory answer as to why Uday and Qusay were not taken alive has ever been provided.

The capture of Saddam Hussein on December 13, 2003 from Dawr not far from his hometown, Tikrit, showed even more graphically how a once vibrant US democracy has abandoned the most basic human decencies in the loutish belief that American military power gives it the right to trample on all civilized rules framed to regulate the conduct of nations. The manner in which Saddam was treated after his capture was as unsavoury as the way in which the bodies of his two sons and grandson were gloated over. *Time* magazine for December 22, 2003 reported his capture out of a chamber eight feet below the ground in these terms: "the palace monster of monuments and torture chambers had been reduced to the life of a bug. His captors picked through his shaggy hair, the raccoon beard. They scraped his throat, checked his teeth. 'Merry Christmas', said the soldiers to one another, and they lit cigars and took pictures and smiled".

Photographs of Saddam Hussein that started circulating after his capture in newspapers and magazines, on television and the internet by courtesy of the US military showed the degradation to which the former head of the Iraqi state was subjected by his captors. In some he is being dragged out of his place of capture and pinned to the ground by a burly, smirking GI; others show a DNA swab being taken from his mouth; in still others he is being examined for lice, and so on.

Cardinal Renato Martino, Head of the Vatican's Justice and Peace Department, voiced the feelings of millions across the globe when he said: "I felt pity to see this man destroyed, [the military] looking at his teeth as if he was a cow. They could have spared us these pictures. Seeing him like this, a man in his tragedy, despite all the heavy blame he bears, I had a sense of compassion for him". The Cardinal also added that it would be "illusory" to assume that Saddam's arrest would heal the damage caused by the war, which the Holy See had opposed.[54]

In a sharply focused article in New Delhi's *Hindustan Times* for January 13, 2004, the distinguished Indian jurist A. G. Noorani considered the possible fate that awaits Saddam Hussein. He dismissed the impartiality of Iraq's so-called Governing Council's (GC) statute establishing an Iraqi Special Tribunal for Crimes against Humanity because it was issued without involving the UN while its American provenance was obvious. International jurists have also criticized the statute. Noorani quotes Hanny Megally and Paul van Zyl, two directors of the International Centre for Transitional Justice, who are "not clear whether international humanitarian law authorizes an occupying power to establish such a tribunal. Justice dispersed by an occupying power will therefore be of dubious legality and questionable legitimacy".

While Donald Rumsfeld had announced on December 15, 2003 that the Geneva Convention would govern Hussein's treatment since he would be accorded the status of a prisoner of war, Noorani had his doubts. As he pointed out, "The Geneva Convention relating to the treatment of PoWs (1949) has been flouted brazenly by the US. Article 14 enjoins their protection 'against insult and public curiosity'. Saddam's confrontation with his opponents was arranged and publicized. It forbids 'medical or scientific experiments' which are not 'justified' in their interest. DNA tests were carried out. Article 14 says: 'Prisoners of war are entitled in all circumstances to respect for their persons and their honour'".

Noorani observed in conclusion that "Saddam Hussein deserves to be tried for the crimes he committed against his own people – apart from those against Iran and Kuwait. But a fair trial can be held only by an Iraqi government elected by a free vote, conducted by an impartial agency after foreign troops are withdrawn or by an impartial tribunal set up by the UN excluding judges from countries which lauded his capture. George W. Bush has demanded a death penalty. His captive can neither be let loose nor kept in detention for long. A murder has been arranged. How effectively, only time will tell".[55]

Whatever their reservations about Saddam Hussein, hundreds of Arab and international lawyers have volunteered to defend him – six hundred in Jordan alone. If Saddam Hussein were tried fairly in accordance with accepted international laws and by an impartial tribunal, the US would be in a strong position. If not, the impression of America as an unprincipled power bent on achieving its own arrogant and ambitious goals will continue to grow worldwide, leading to increasing anti-American sentiments, a rise in terrorist violence and a progressively less stable world order.

6

A Democracy's Imperial Burden

The Emergence of the Bush Doctrine

The Constitution provides for every accidental contingency
in the Executive, except for a vacancy in the mind of the
president.

SENATOR SHERMAN OF OHIO[1]

THE MOST IRRESPONSIBLE ASPECT of George Bush's presidency from the
Asian standpoint has been his obsessive urge to emasculate the
United Nations. This view is based on the Asian experience of colonial
powers during the heyday of empires. They trampled on the sovereignty
and rights of subject people and plundered their wealth to build their
own extravagant symbols of prosperity and greatness. There were no
international laws which recognized the rights of others. These were
first framed by the League of Nations formed at the end of World
War I, and then by the United Nations after World War II. Each attempted
to provide an ethical framework by which nations could, and should,
coexist in a world torn apart by devastating war.

Whatever their underlying motivations, and notwithstanding
the extent of their interference in its working ever since, the major
powers which promoted and helped establish the United Nations
deserve credit for it, and for helping it become – much more than the
League of Nations – an effective instrument for ensuring respect for
civilized norms in international relations. UN specialized agencies
have also contributed very significantly in critical areas of human
development.

For cynics, whose anti-UN stance is due to ignorance of its achievements, a few facts might throw more light on its special relevance for Asian, African and South American nations. Dag Hammarskjöld, its distinguished former Secretary-General (1953–61) and Nobel Peace Prize winner, summed up this relevance when he said the UN was not created for big powers but for smaller nations; to provide them with a platform from which to voice their views and concerns, a forum for negotiations, for consultations and consensus on common goals, and for defusing tensions.

The Bush administration's antipathy to the UN does not make it irrelevant or impotent. Even in the case of Iraq, the UN helped delay the March 2003 invasion and gave people around the world – including the United States and United Kingdom – time to protest the military action the Bush-Blair coalition had choreographed for Iraq. If the protests failed to deter the duo, they at least registered the degree of international outrage at the aggressors' arrogant and illegal use of military power. That the decision to invade Iraq rested on morally impaired and false assumptions was also revealed to the world by the UN chief weapons inspector, Hans Blix.

But the best way of judging the UN's relevance for the vast majority of the world's people is through its achievements. First, in its political initiatives, even if they have often been throttled when they clashed with big power interests, the UN has impressive gains to its credit: its work, for example, for the independence of countries such as Namibia, Angola, Mozambique and East Timor; its efforts to end apartheid in South Africa; and by allowing representatives of national liberation movements to participate in UN debates along with representatives of governments then in power in those countries, it created a new climate of negotiation and discussion. It has played an equally important role in containing conflicts between neighbouring countries, and prevented many conflicts from becoming major wars. Its peacekeeping role in conflict-prone societies has prevented escalation and bloodshed, and ensured peace. In post-war reconstruction work too, in the Balkans, East Timor and elsewhere, it has helped ravaged regions regain some semblance of normalcy.

But the most noteworthy of all the UN's contributions has been in alleviating disease and hunger, establishing universal norms and conventions for human rights and fundamental freedoms, furthering the advancement of women and the rights of children, fostering respect for the rule of law, undertaking population studies, promoting education, science and culture, protecting the environment, creating atomic safeguards, and much else. No other individual nation or organization in history has ever attempted social development on a global scale as the UN has done, through its specialized agencies and funds like the World Health Organization, Food and Agriculture Organization, International Court of Justice, International Labour Organization, United Nations Environment Programme, United Nations Educational, Scientific, and Cultural Organization, International Atomic Energy Agency, and others. It is a long list. What needs to be underscored for denigrators of the UN – mostly conscious of the Security Council's frequently warped decisions – is that the activities of the UN do not stop at the Security Council.

The Security Council is the mechanism through which powerful Western nations, who see themselves as the arbiters of the world's fate, exercise their power on global issues. It has been manipulated over the years to suit their goals. That is why for many it is tainted. The same Security Council that served these Western nations' interests well in the past is now seen as an irritant – especially by the world's only superpower. For that reason President Bush's advisers feel the UN, and all it stands for, is no longer needed in the world of the future as they envision it.

Between the Project for the New American Century (announced in September 2000), and the Bush administration's National Security Strategy (September 2002), the future that is conceived leaves little to doubt, embracing "permanent US military and economic domination of every region on the globe, unfettered by international treaty or concern". To remove any remaining doubts about American Internationalism, the name of America's new global strategy, it is made clear that the United States will ignore "international opinion if that suits US interests". Because what is visualized for the years ahead is the United States providing the world with "American political leadership rather than ... the United Nations". No wonder Washington, according to Hans Blix, regards the UN as an "alien power" which it hopes will "sink in the East River".[2]

The question UN member states must squarely face is: can Washington do what it wishes with the UN? Can the world permit, through ignorance, indifference or inertia, one of the most worthwhile collective initiatives in human history to be cynically discarded because of a single member state's insatiable appetite for global supremacy? Can this forum, which informs the world of the morbid and mindless violence with which men treat each other, be closed to them for good, and the world allowed to return to its old anarchic ways? Should the future of specialized UN agencies, whose brilliant and multi-faceted contributions in so many different areas have made a profound difference to the lives of countless people the world over, be jettisoned along with the hopes they inspire in underprivileged nations? There are many questions that need to be asked, each more disturbing than the other.

The above is not an idealized or romantic view of the UN. Far from it. The organization has in fact made grievous errors over the years. It has failed to measure up to enormous humanitarian challenges facing it. The extent to which one or two recalcitrant powers can derail or disrupt its key initiatives remains the UN's major flaw. The UN Sanctions Committee allowed US and British advisers to block life-saving drugs and vital medical equipment to Iraq for twelve years.

That the UN has been able to deliver so often, despite the power politics that continuously plague it from within, goes to its credit. But its future is uncertain because of the Bush administration's determination to do away with it. Worse than shutting it down altogether would be to surrender it to Washington's complete control in the service of the New American Century.

The mockery Washington has made of its commitment to the principles of the UN Charter was vividly brought home during the UN debates preceding the Iraq invasion. To begin with, the American delegation's contemptuous disregard for the UN Chief Weapons Inspector's interim report because it did not support the American position on Iraq's alleged weapons of mass destruction. Then the arrogant indifference to other member states' objections to military action against Iraq; the naked attempts to bribe, coerce or cajole countries into joining America's punitive action against it; the propaganda unleashed to influence public opinion in favour of an illegal invasion; the unconcern for the number of innocent people who would perish in a country pulverized by the most lethal weapons yet invented, despite the false claims about precision bombings and such.

Each aberration confirms the emergence of a different America. Instead of the nation that believed in justice, liberty and egalitarianism, there is now an arrogant, ambitious and self-absorbed military power, unable to contain its imperial ambitions, uninterested in views at variance with its own, indifferent even to the right of other states to exist. This moral coarseness is a far cry from the moral clarity that guided the United States through its most tumultuous years, from Abraham Lincoln's injunction at Gettysburg that America, "conceived in liberty, and dedicated to the proposition that all men are created equal", must revere the laws as "the political religion of the nation". The Bush administration however, has little concern for law, domestic or international.

It will be instructive to view the above against the backdrop of the aims and purposes of an organization the United States helped establish. The International Court of Justice at The Hague, which is the principal judicial arm of the United Nations, deals with matters concerning territorial sovereignty, non-interference in the internal affairs of states, the non-use of force, rights of passage and economic rights, and much more. Since 1946, the year the Court was established, it has delivered major judgements on disputes in these and other matters in accordance with international treaties and conventions and the general principles of law. In contrast, recent actions of the United States show the extent to which America has changed. Instead of a champion of the free, it has become a threat to the freedom of nations. Instead of a guarantor of the territorial sovereignty of countries, it now covets their territories and resources. Instead of rejecting the use of force, it revels in the use of its military power against the powerless.

What kind of contribution could a US-dominated UN, or any other organization it puts in its place, make to a world seeking a change from the barbaric ways of the past? It is sad to ask this question of a country whose presidents once pledged their nation, as Woodrow Wilson did, to resisting the violation of any country's borders or its sovereignty. Or as Franklin D. Roosevelt also pledged his country to "a world-wide reduction of armaments to such a point and in such a thorough fashion that no nation will be in a position to commit an act of physical aggression against any neighbour – anywhere in the world".[3]

§

President Bush has not only refused to honour those ideals, he has repudiated most of the goals his recent predecessors subscribed to in principle.

This is starkly evident in his administration's rejection of the International Criminal Court (ICC).

The United Nations recognized its need on December 9, 1948. It felt an independent and permanent court to investigate and prosecute persons charged with crimes against humanity, genocide and war crimes was necessary after the experience of the bloody wars and revolutions in the first half of the century. The ICC was not intended to replace but to complement national judicial systems, and to step in only if they proved "unwilling or unable to investigate or prosecute such crimes". But it wasn't until July 17, 1998 that the final Statute for the creation of the court was adopted at Rome, where 120 countries voted for it while seven voted against it. Those, ineffectively, against its creation included Israel, Iraq, India, China and the United States. By December 31, 2000, 139 states had signed the treaty, and after the final ratifications the court was established on July 1, 2002. Its governing body, called the Assembly of States Parties, elected the first 18 judges, including seven women, in February 2003, and The Hague was chosen as its seat.

The Bush administration has repudiated the ICC because it does not wish to surrender an American citizen to the ICC even if investigation or prosecution in the United States finds that citizen's behaviour to be contrary to US justice. It has instead tried to negotiate bilateral impunity agreements with as many nations world-wide as it can, in order to ensure immunity for US nationals despite their crimes and wherever they commit them. To India's shame, it joined the war against the ICC by entering into an agreement with the United States on December 26, 2002 by which the two agree not to extradite each other's nationals to an international tribunal without the other country's consent. But the ICC is opposed to such impunity agreements, because they not only gravely weaken respect for international laws and the International Criminal Court, but also create a two-track situation in which one rule of law applies to US nationals and another to all other citizens of the world.

The double standards observed by the United States are nowhere more obvious than in its illegal incarceration of detainees from Afghanistan, Iraq and other countries at Guantanamo Bay, outside US jurisdiction and in direct contravention of the Geneva Convention. But the contraventions at Guantanamo Bay do not end there. In complete disregard of all humanitarian conventions, the US is holding juveniles as terrorist suspects in this camp. According to a Human Rights Watch report dated January 30, 2004, this is a clear violation of an international treaty governing the rehabilitation of child soldiers. While three – between the ages of 13 and 15 – were released in January 2004, "other juveniles aged 16 and 17 are being held among the approximately 650 other detainees from about 40 countries ... At least 21 detainees have tried to kill themselves ... at the prison, showing signs of depression at their prolonged detentions".[4]

§

Another global initiative undertaken for a safer and saner world, but repudiated by the Bush administration, is the Kyoto Global Warming Treaty. Its aim is to limit global emissions of heat-trapping 'greenhouse gases', released into the air by burning oil, gas and coal, which are liable to cause dangerous climatic changes with far-reaching consequences. The damage that altered weather patterns can do to the earth by increasing temperatures, melting snows, floods, droughts, rising sea levels and tornadoes is already apparent in many parts of the globe, including India, where agricultural production and trade are being adversely affected and human existence itself seriously threatened in hot and arid zones as erratic climatic conditions force people to migrate at times of extreme distress. Forecasts for this century predict a rise in global temperatures from 2.5 to 10 degrees Fahrenheit. Unless something is done in time about global warming, falling subsoil water levels and aridity on the one hand and melting snows and flooding of coastal areas on the other will cause immeasurable havoc.

Fortunately, the potential for disastrous environmental developments facing the world was recognized in the early 1990s, and the text of the Protocol to the United Nations Framework Convention on Climate Change (UNFCCC) was adopted by participating states in Kyoto, Japan, on December 11, 1997. By May 15, 2003, 84 parties had signed and 109 had ratified or acceded to the Kyoto Protocol. Even though the United States refused to ratify it, the Protocol's wide acceptance was viewed as a historic first step towards addressing "the most urgent environmental challenge facing the world today".

Washington did not stop at refusing to ratify the agreement, but according to a June 2003 Associated Press report, "The White House directed a major rewrite of an assessment of climate change, removing references to health and environmental risks posed by rising global temperatures ... Democratic Senators Joe Lieberman of Connecticut and Bob Graham of Florida, both running for president, urged Bush to take action against 'those responsible for doctoring the report'".[5] What the White House required of the rewrite was so different from the original "scientific consensus on climate change" that even the Environmental Protection Agency (EPA) saw the revised draft as an embarrassment. Whether coincidentally or otherwise the departure of Christie Whitman, moderate Republican and former governor of New Jersey, as secretary of the EPA followed soon after.

One of the sentences removed from an EPA summary was: "Climate change has global consequences for human health and the environment". Another deletion was the finding of a 1999 study which showed how sharply global temperatures had risen in the past decade compared to the previous 1,000 years. James Connaughton, Chairman of the White House Council on Environment Quality, preferred a report partly sponsored by the American Petroleum Institute, which disputed the 1999 study's conclusions. More succinct than most was Mark Van Putten, president of the National Wildlife Federation, who felt the matter provided "disturbing evidence of the administration's readiness to reject or spin scientific findings on crucial environment issues that do not suit the White House's political agenda".[6]

It is ironic that the leading generator of greenhouse gases – responsible for 36 per cent of the emissions in 1990 – should refuse to ratify an agreement that could prevent the world's dangerous drift towards untold disasters. George Bush's declared reason for refusing to submit the Kyoto Protocol signed by former President Bill Clinton to Congress for ratification has been that the limits and restraints visualized in it would prove too costly for the oil-dependent economy of the United States and irksome for those whose lifestyles require ever-increasing quantities of fossil fuels. Another qualification advanced by Bush is that economically developing nations should also be called upon to make cuts for controlling emissions.

Industrialized countries with just 20 per cent of global population account for over 60 per cent of greenhouse gas emissions. Those most resistant to change are the United States, Japan, Australia, Canada and New Zealand. Equally opposed to reductions in emissions are oil- and coal-exporting countries, and, of course, energy giants whose profits would fall following cutbacks in fossil fuels. It has been estimated that emissions of carbon dioxide and other greenhouse gases from Europe, the United States, Japan and other industrialized countries could grow by 17 per cent from 2000 to 2010, and that emissions by developing countries too could reach similar levels. But before coming to the developing countries, let us first look at the developed.

The sectors held most responsible for rising emission levels are transport, industry and energy. A study 'Reducing Greenhouse Gas Emissions from US Transport' by the Pew Center on Global Climate Change cites a staggering statistic: "The US transportation system emits more CO_2 than any other nation's total economy, except that of China, and presently accounts for seven of ten barrels of oil this nation consumes", according to Eileen Claussen, president of the Center. She adds that "the United States is the owner of the world's largest transportation system, and reducing emissions from this system is critical to an effective GHG [greenhouse gas] reduction strategy".[7]

The study indicates that if the United States uses the technology and investments it already possesses, it will be able to cut emissions by 20 per cent by 2015 and by 50 per cent by 2030.

"Many of the actions that would reduce emissions from transportation would also address other national priorities, including US dependence on foreign oil", concludes Claussen.[8] Other findings of the study are that fuel economy for new cars could be improved 25 to 30 per cent in 10 to 15 years with the use of available technology, and that fuel cell and hydrogen technology also offer great promise for dealing effectively with GHG emissions from this sector. But for this to happen, an unambiguous policy directive from the government would be needed to point private investment in this direction. And there lies the crunch.

On the question of reduction of US dependence on foreign oil, if the Bush administration's key men, including the president himself, are creatures of US oil cartels, why would they want to curtail their business? Why did the United States invade Iraq if not for its oil? What has inspired its stepped-up rhetoric against Iran? And what lies behind its moves to establish better control over Saudi Arabia?

The influence of powerful oil and energy corporations on all arms of US government, and perhaps the legislature too, does not augur well for the future. The National Governors Association, which supports the

White House's stand and is against the Kyoto Protocol, also recommends that the United States should "not sign or ratify any agreement that would result in serious harm to the US economy".[9] What this makes clear is that hard-nosed policies in these matters leave no room for concern about economies much more vulnerable than America's and which global climatic changes would seriously endanger. US concern for its own economy cannot be faulted since each country's decisions are based on its perceived self-interest. But when a country like the United States, with its technological advances and wealth, refuses to join the rest of the world in facing up to a global problem involving the lives and livelihood of millions of people including its own, its claims to moral authority ring hollow.

Surprisingly, many influential senators, including Joe Lieberman who now wants to "move America back into the Kyoto Process", have been ambivalent about ratifying the Protocol. Senator John Kerry, like Lieberman, insists on including developing countries in the cuts and restrictions envisaged in the Protocol. Perhaps the only Democrat unreservedly in favour of ratification is Congressman Dennis Kucinich who has emphatically endorsed Kyoto.

Instead of scaling down the use of fossil fuels, however, the Bush administration has remained keen to subsidize the oil industry in the face of warnings from the Department of Energy that US dependence on oil imports is growing, and that oil imports are expected to grow by 13 per cent in relation to US petroleum demand by 2025.[10] Although the debate on alternative energy sources, changes in consumption patterns, increased fuel economy in cars, and renewable fuels continued unabated in the United States through 2003, the Bush administration persisted in trying to push through a $58 billion bill which would increase subsidies to the oil, coal and nuclear industries. So much for world opinion.

Friends of the Earth International, an Amsterdam-based organization, has – along with several other organizations – tirelessly campaigned for concerted action against greenhouse gases, while vigorously advocating sustainable development and equitable use of the atmosphere. It has argued for "the overwhelming majority of reductions to be made at home, in industrialized countries", and reiterated its stand that the Kyoto Protocol's measures are inadequate and called for "long-term targets based on equity, sustainability and equal rights for all". It believes that reducing fossil fuel emissions must be the main thrust of the treaty.

In the case of developing countries, FoEI's position is that some of them, "such as China and India, have tremendous levels of poverty. They have much lower per capita emissions than industrialized countries, and there is a huge ecological debt from industrialized countries in terms of past and present emissions. It is therefore important to acknowledge the legitimacy of the claims of the developing countries, that they cannot be expected to sacrifice economic growth to achieve the same levels of cuts in greenhouse gas emissions as industrialized countries. This position is supported by international principles, such as the 'polluter pays' and 'common but differentiated responsibilities'".[11] It seems clear that developing nations can – and should – do more than they are presently doing to develop alternative sources of energy. Weather conditions in India and China, where sunshine is available all round the year, are ideally placed to make spectacular uses of solar power for a great many of their needs. India has made some headway in this field, but is nowhere near tapping the sun's immense potential. However, the development of solar energy on an industrial scale is complex and will take time to achieve, whereas the pressing demands of the rapidly growing populations of both China and India require immediate measures. It is not surprising, therefore, that politicians greet with enthusiasm each new eruption from an offshore oil-well, and that both countries' dependence on fossil fuels keeps on growing.

The irony of the Indian situation is that since a high percentage of oil exploration and distribution is state-owned, more pragmatic conservation policies and development of sustainable energy sources are not difficult goals to achieve. But the mandarins of state-owned enterprises are as notorious for building barricades to protect their fiefdoms as are corporate interests in other countries. The government has still to deal in a convincing and responsible manner with the global problem of greenhouse gases.

It is best to remember that if global weather conditions are pushed beyond the point of no return, nature is unlikely to differentiate between developed and developing nations. The bell will toll for both.

Yet Russia too, which was expected to show more pragmatism than Washington, for a long time displayed the same wilful disregard for the Kyoto Protocol as the US. In December 2003 it dealt a near-fatal blow to the treaty by initially refusing to ratify it because, according to President Putin's remarks to a group of European businessmen, it ran counter to Russia's national interests. Given the complicated structure of the treaty, Russian participation was vital to its survival and its rejection was seen as mocking the concerns of nations suffering from the effects of climatic changes caused by the United States and Russia, the first and fourth largest emitters of heat-trapping green-house gases in the world, with 36.1 per cent and 17.4 per cent of emissions respectively.

Dyed-in-the-wool opponents of the treaty, like the US industry's Competitive Enterprise Institute which opposes attempts to regulate environmental degradation, simply do not take global warming seriously. Says Myron Ebell, a climate policy analyst with the Institute, "If global warming turns out to be a problem, which I doubt, it won't be solved by making ourselves poorer through energy rationing. It will be solved through building resiliency and capability into society …".[12] It is this sort of irresponsibility that obscures one of the most critical issues facing mankind today. Does "building resiliency and capability" mean that US business interests should have priority over the needs of people suffering as a result of changing weather conditions? Ebell's view may be compared with that of the British climate scientist Sir John Houghton: "I have no hesitation in describing [climate change] as a 'weapon of mass destruction'".[13] Or with that of *Science* magazine, which included the establishment of the facts of global warming in its list of ten top scientific breakthroughs in the year 2003, mentioning "Growing evidence that global warming is linked to ice melting, drought, falling plant production, changes in plant and animal behavior".[14]

An article in the *New Statesman* in December 2003 placed the entire debate in perspective: "Despite an innate selfishness, we have time and again been goaded into action by appeals to our sense of nationhood, responsibility to our children, or our ideas about historical destiny. People willingly lay down their lives to defend cultural identities and religious beliefs … Why, then, are we paralysed in the face of climate crisis?" The authors of the article provide several explanations for that paralysis, the most succinct of which is: "In the case of climate change, we are all simultaneously bystanders, perpetrators and victims … while we accept the evidence for climate change intellectually, we reject it emotionally".[15] The price of this continued denial of stark realities is the survival of mankind.

§

In order to expand its nuclear arsenal to equip itself for its self-appointed role of global policeman, bringing democracy's blessings to all nations, the United States has repudiated two other key treaties, the Anti-Ballistic Missile Treaty (ABM) and the Treaty on Non-Proliferation of Nuclear Weapons (NPT).

The International Atomic Energy Agency of the United Nations (IAEA) helped prepare the NPT which entered into force on March 5, 1970. Its broad aim, in accordance with the UN Charter, was a reiteration of the resolve by member states to refrain from the use of military power against the independence and territorial integrity of any country in a manner inconsistent with the purposes of the United Nations. Its more specific aim was to seek a ban on nuclear weapons tests in the atmosphere, outer space and underwater; to work, in effect, towards ending test explosions of nuclear weapons for all time, and ensuring the destruction of existing nuclear stockpiles and stopping their future manufacture as well.

Meeting at the United Nations headquarters in New York in April–May 2000, 155 states finally agreed, after extended negotiations, to an unequivocal undertaking by nuclear weapons states to achieve the total elimination of their nuclear arsenals. This undertaking was given on May 1, 2000 in a joint statement signed by the five declared nuclear weapon states (NWS), China, France, Russia, UK and USA, pledging their "unequivocal commitment to the ultimate goal of complete disarmament under strict and effective controls".[16] They also called for the early entry into force of the Comprehensive Test Ban Treaty (CTBT), the preservation of the 1972 Anti-Ballistic Missile Treaty (ABM), and the timely conclusion of safeguard agreements with the IAEA.

Within months of Bush becoming President, the US withdrew from the NPT. It not only repudiated its commitment to the elimination of nuclear weapons, but also announced their centrality to the Bush administration's national defence policy and its commitment to the nuclear doctrine revealed in the still-classified Nuclear Posture Review (NPR). A briefing on it by the US Department of Defense was given to reporters on January 9, 2002. While the NPR is partly discussed in Chapter 3, aspects of it are highlighted here to show the extent of US commitment to unilateral nuclear proliferation.

According to Assistant Secretary of Defense J. D. Crouch, the US in 2002 was "projecting to keep the nuclear forces that we have to 2020 and beyond – and longer, and beyond".[17] From Crouch's media briefing, it seemed that "An 'operationally deployed' force of nuclear weapons, intended to deal with 'immediate and unexpected contingencies', would contain between 1,700 and 2,000 warheads available for launch in time periods ranging from minutes to weeks. Additional warheads – presumably thousands of them, though the public explanation of the NPR is ambiguous on this point – were to be maintained in a 'responsive capability', ready to be re-deployed on demand".[18] Even more telling was the new strategic triad to be given shape and substance – nuclear weapons deployed on land-based missiles, submarines and bombers. In order to 'modernize' its nuclear forces by adding new types of warheads,

> The NPR calls on the Department of Energy (DOE) to accelerate its "test-readiness program", so that a resumption of nuclear tests could take place more rapidly than it presently could (two to three years) should the administration decide to abandon the [testing] moratorium. The DOE's Stockpile Stewardship Program will continue, with the goal of providing the Pentagon with "modifications and refurbishments ... of nuclear warhead systems", in particular, the W-76 (Trident) warhead, the W-80 warhead for air-launched cruise missiles, and the advanced cruise missile, and the B-61 and other air-dropped bombs. The DOE will [also] resume production of tritium, using commercial light-water reactors, by the end of the decade.[19]

Not only was the Non-Proliferation Treaty dead where the United States was concerned, but a new generation of nuclear weapons would now form the core element of the US military. The resumption of nuclear tests for the design of new warheads by the DOE weapons labs also became a foregone conclusion. "The administration has sought funds to 'enhance' test readiness and shorten the time required to prepare for the resumption of full-scale test explosions", reported Kathryn Crandall of the British American Security Information Council (BASIC) in January 2003.[20]

The adverse impact of the Bush administration's about-face on the NPT was hardly helped by George Bush's National Security President Directive 17 issued in the run-up to the Iraq invasion of March 2003:

"The United States will continue to make clear that it reserves the right to respond with overwhelming force – including potentially nuclear weapons – to the use of [weapons of mass destruction] against the United States …".[21] When 187 countries attended the Preparatory Committee (PrepCom) of the Nuclear Non-Proliferation Treaty meeting in Geneva on April 28, 2003, the general feeling was that "the risks of proliferation are worse now than for 50 years. In the past two years the multilateral effort to contain and reduce the nuclear risk has unraveled. At the last NPT review conference in 2000 all member states signed a 13-point programme, that included an undertaking by the five declared nuclear-weapons states to nuclear disarmament".[22] Referring to that undertaking, Dan Plesch, senior researcher at the Royal United Services Institute, stated: "That agreement is now gathering dust in some filing cabinet somewhere. For the first time since the 1950s there isn't a global framework … to get rid of nuclear weapons".[23]

North Korea's withdrawal from the global treaty was equally disturbing, as also was its announcement a week earlier about possessing the bomb. And with the United States no longer a party to the NPT, the 'negative security assurances' proposed in 1978 and further strengthened by a 1995 UN Security Council resolution no longer held any meaning. In fact, non-nuclear weapon states are now likely to develop their own weapons since assurances not to use nuclear weapons against non-nuclear weapon states have ceased to be binding on the United States.

The consequences of the Bush administration's refusal to ratify the Comprehensive Test Ban Treaty (CTBT) – which has an 'endangered' status in its policy projections – were spelt out by Kathryn Crandall in her above-cited bulletin of early 2003, and her fears of a new arms race are already being borne out:

> A test ban is a security and non-proliferation goal that the world com-
> munity has worked toward for over fifty years, primarily because
> prohibiting testing effectively curtails nuclear weapons programs. As
> the world frets over North Korea's weapons program, imagine several
> years down the road to North Korean nuclear tests. Also imagine
> China resuming tests to modernize and expand its arsenal, Russia test-
> ing to develop new nuclear capabilities and India and Pakistan testing
> again in the midst of escalating tensions. The unleashing of a new
> arms race is an all too real and devastating possibility.[24]

The purpose of the Comprehensive Test Ban Treaty was to end nuclear testing explosions forever, whether in the atmosphere or underground. The CTBT became a reality in 1996, with President Bill Clinton the first to sign it on behalf of the United States. A conference was held in Vienna three years later, in 1999, to ratify the treaty. Up till then 154 states had signed and 51 had ratified it. By August 2003 seven more countries had signed it and 36 ratified it. The hold-out countries who had signed but not ratified included the United States, China, Israel, Iran, Indonesia, Egypt, Algeria, Vietnam and the Democratic Republic of the Congo. India, Pakistan and North Korea had yet to sign. Fortunately, the moratorium on testing has not been broken since 1998 – the year India and Pakistan carried out their tests; before that as many as 2,050 nuclear tests were conducted worldwide between 1945 and 1998. Warning that delaying the CTBT's entry into force would increase the risk of resumed tests, Kofi Annan, the UN Secretary-General, said: "We have a precious but fleeting opportunity to render this troubled world a safer place, free of the threat of nuclear weapons". But in conformity with the prevailing mood in Washington, the US Senate for its part also eased restrictions in September 2003 on nuclear tests at the military's Nevada site – where the last tests were conducted in 1992.

Since the threat of nuclear weapons comes mainly from the United States, we may consider how the ratification process fared there. Within a week of the 1999 conference, the US Senate rejected ratification by a 51–48 vote *even though public opinion polls indicated 82 per cent of Americans in favour of the treaty*. Furthermore, *even US military leaders supported it*. "General John Shalikashivili, former Chairman of the Joint Chiefs of Staff, conducted a study and gave the CTBT his seal of approval, [but] the incoming Bush administration turned its back on the treaty. President Bush refused to resubmit it for ratification … [the administration] cut its share of contributions to the CTBT Organization … [and] since the US share of the $83.5-million budget for the CTBT Organization is 22 per cent, a US pull-out would devastate the regime."[25]

The US administration's announcement in 2001 of a cut in America's stockpile of strategic nuclear weapons must be seen in perspective. The President's offer to reduce the number of deployed nuclear warheads to between 1,700 and 2,200 over the next decade may have earned him enthusiastic headlines like "US Will Slash Nuclear Arsenal", but what it really meant was phasing out of ageing weapons and their replacement by more lethal new generation nuclear weapons whose destructive potential would depend on their killing capabilities and not their numerical count. The questions Canadian Senator Douglas Roche wanted answered were: "What is the real meaning of Bush's announcement when one considers that the United States, with its NATO allies, intends to maintain nuclear weapons as 'essential' to the core of their military doctrine? How effective are cuts by the United States and Russia in redundant weapons when they still keep 5,000 nuclear weapons on instant alert status? What real contribution to nuclear disarmament is made when the US pursues a missile defence system that will stimulate an offensive arms race?"[26]

These are valid questions. Even more pertinent is the point that while the Bush administration has been openly disdainful of UN member states and multilateral treaties, following the terrorist attacks of 9/11 the United States immediately asked the international community for help in putting together a coalition to combat terrorism. As Roche pointedly emphasized in his report:

> It is not unilateral acts, however entrancing, that will secure international peace and security; rather it is negotiations to build a body of law that cannot be changed by political caprice. The International Court of Justice has said that the legal provisions of the Non-Proliferation Treaty must be concluded. That means there is a legal obligation to negotiate the elimination of all nuclear weapons. That obligation cannot be papered over by a unilateral declaration to cut unneeded weapons while insisting on the retention of a base number as 'essential'.[27]

President Bush put paid to the Anti-Ballistic Missile Treaty on December 13, 2001 – exactly 29 years after President Richard Nixon and Soviet leader Leonid Brezhnev signed it in 1972; it had entered into force on October 3, 1972. The treaty was an outcome of the first Strategic Arms Limitation Talks (SALT 1), which aimed at first slowing and then reversing the nuclear arms race between the United States and the Soviet Union. The treaty's provisions, based on a lively awareness of the destructive capabilities of the respective arsenals of the two countries, prohibited the deployment of anti-ballistic missile systems for the defence of either nation's entire territory. But it allowed each side to deploy limited ABM systems around two locations: the country's capital, and where ICBM silo launchers were located.

A further protocol signed in 1974 limited each nation to just one ABM site: either at the national capital or at an ICBM deployment area. The treaty also specifically banned the development, or deployment, of all kinds of ABM systems whether sea-based, air-based, space-based, or mobile land-based.

Since these prohibitions were no longer in consonance with the Bush administration's nuclear agenda, itself an essential element in its goal of global dominance, the ABM treaty was disowned. The usual scapegoats for this repudiation, as of past commitment, were 'terrorists' and 'rogue-states' – the standard fare for securing domestic support for each broken pledge. Said the President, "I have concluded the ABM treaty hinders our government's ability to develop ways to protect our people from future terrorist or rogue-state missile attacks. Defending the American people is my highest priority as commander-in-chief and I cannot and will not allow the United States to remain in a treaty that prevents us from developing effective defenses".[28] What the President did not explain was exactly how development of newer and more sophisticated nuclear missiles would make America safe from terrorist attacks. The September 11 attacks took place despite America's formidable nuclear arsenal.

Since the ABM Treaty was signed during the Cold War, Mr Bush referred to the latter in his announcement of December 13, 2001. "The Cold War is long gone. Today we leave behind one of its last vestiges. But this is not a day for looking back. This is a day for looking forward with hope of greater prosperity and peace." [29] Once again, he did not elaborate on how a renewed nuclear arms race would ensure peace and prosperity. Now that Russia is no longer a threat as the Soviet Union once was, and with no other power to challenge its nuclear supremacy, the United States clearly believes its ability to dictate terms globally will increase its prosperity. But this could be a grievous misjudgement. Nuclear know-how is no longer the prerogative of the United States. The scientific communities of many nations, whose number keeps increasing, are bringing them closer to achieving nuclear power status. Others have already achieved it and there is no guarantee they will not sell or trade some of their assets for reasons of their own.

When on December 13, 2001 the US notified the Russian government of its withdrawal from the ABM treaty, it sent a similar notification to the governments of Ukraine, Kazakhstan and Belarus which, as parts of the former Soviet Union, had also signed the memorandum of understanding with the Clinton administration in 1997 which bound them to the terms of the ABM treaty. But they are no longer bound by it now, nor, for that matter, is any other aspiring or arriviste nuclear power. So it is difficult to look forward 'with hope of greater prosperity and peace' to a world which no longer agrees on the dangers of nuclear proliferation. Or to a world in which only one power threatens the rest with its nuclear weapons.

§

The New American Century visualized by Donald Rumsfeld, Paul Wolfowitz and their ilk is not a blueprint for a free and democratic world. It is their vision of an ascendant and imperial America. Since it is no longer politically incorrect to talk of the imperial concept, its ardent admirers are rallying in its support. When it was put to the test in Afghanistan and then Iraq, its cheerleaders, though disconcerted, were not unduly daunted by the results. In the age of spin, each setback was given a new slant, each fiasco a deceitful explanation. But no lies or delusions of imperial glory could justify the American lives lost in Iraq to their kin. Not the lives of remote people as in Afghanistan – or even Iraq – but one's own family, alive, energetic and eager one day, dead the next. Is it possible to console the families of those killed by explanations about acceptable 'collateral damage' in times of war?

The invasion of Iraq in 2003 was of course not a war; it was not a just cause which required human lives to be sacrificed. It was banditry, a raid on an oil-rich country undertaken at the behest of the corporations who covet its oil and whose writ runs in the White House. As author and essayist Eliot Weinberger has pointed out, "It [George Bush's] is the first administration to openly declare a policy of unilateral aggression, a 'Pax Americana' where the presence of allies (whether England or Bulgaria) is agreeable but unimportant; where international treaties no longer apply to the US; where – for the first time in history – this country reserves the right to non-defensive, 'pre-emptive' strikes against any nation on earth, for whatever reason it chooses ...".[30]

The 'Bush doctrine' rests on two main supports: unquestioned military supremacy and the right to pre-emptive action. These two principles have in turn redefined the concept of sovereignty – in the words of the banker George Soros: "American sovereignty, which takes precedence over international treaties; and the sovereignty of all other states which is subject to the Bush doctrine". The doctrine is grounded in "the belief that international relations are relations of power; legality and legitimacy are decorations".[31] The two things George Bush lacked at the start of his first term – a clear mandate and a well defined enemy – were provided by the September 11, 2001 attack. In Soros's words again: "Terrorism is the ideal enemy … An enemy that poses a genuine and recognized threat can effectively hold a nation together. That is particularly useful when the prevailing ideology is based on the unabashed pursuit of self-interest. Mr. Bush's administration deliberately fosters fear because it helps to keep the nation lined up behind the president".[32]

In the matter of legality and legitimacy, Dominique Moisi of the Paris-based Institut Français des Relations Internationales has stated that "The United States found a legal rationale for intervening in Iraq in the threat of WMD. But this increasingly flimsy rationale now hampers its ability to act with a sense of legitimacy". No wonder the Bush doctrine considers legality and legitimacy mere decorations. Moisi's observation on the UN is equally pertinent. "The most important prerequisite for reconciling legality and legitimacy is a stronger, more credible UN … If Europeans – and France in particular – take seriously the need for a multipolar international order to balance America's unilateral tendencies, a relegiti-mized UN is vital. Only then might the gap that yawns between what is legitimate and what is legal in international relations start to close."[33]

An increasing number of US authors, academics, professionals and politicians, however, are excited by the idea of an imperial America. Sebastian Mallaby of *The Washington Post* is gung-ho about it. "Failed states are increasingly trapped in a cycle of poverty and violence. The solution is for the United States and its allies to learn to love imperialism – again."[34] Warming to his subject, he argues that the disorderly state of the third world's bankrupt countries with their endless violence, social decay and exploding populations leaves the US with no alternative.

Robert Kaplan of the *Atlantic Monthly* agrees. "Some 200 countries, plus thousands of non-governmental organizations, represent a chaos of interests. Without the organizing force of a great and self-interested liberal power, they are unable to advance the interests of humanity as a whole."[35] Zbigniew Brzezinski, who was President Carter's National Security Advisor, has observed that in the preservation of its empire, the

United States will have "to prevent collusion and maintain dependence among the vassals, keep tributaries pliant and protected, and to keep the barbarians from coming together".[36] Couldn't be more explicit than that. But then Jimmy Carter was more adept at bringing his empire-builders to heel than George Bush. "This may come as a shock to Americans", wrote Michael Ignatieff, after the attack on Afghanistan, "who don't like to think of their country as an empire. But what else can you call America's legions of soldiers, spooks and special forces straddling the globe?"[37]

According to reports, thousands of operations are conducted every year by small detachments of US Special Forces in nearly 170 countries, and after 9/11 US personnel have become deeply entrenched in foreign armed forces, police units and intelligence agencies across the globe. The US Air Force has a presence on six of the world's seven continents, and the military has bases or base rights in 40 countries. The Bush presidency has expanded US military presence abroad with each passing year.

From Harvard and Johns Hopkins Universities to the Hoover Institution, the drum-beat of the imperial discourse is the same: as it once did for the ancient Romans and the British, America's time is seen to have come, its imperial destiny to beckon. Even as its unparalleled military supremacy continues to power its imperialist drive, the debate stresses the benevolent and benign nature of Americans while underscoring America's unique qualifications for the imperial role. Stephen Peter Rosen, who heads the Olin Institute for Strategic Studies at Harvard University, maintains that "A political unit that has overwhelming military power, and uses that power to influence the internal behavior of other states, is called an empire. Our goal is not combating a rival, but maintaining our imperial position and maintaining imperial order".[38] Joseph S. Nye Jr, dean of the Kennedy School of Government at Harvard University, concurs. "Not since Rome has one nation loomed so large above the others."[39]

While to Charles Fairbanks, a specialist in foreign policy at Johns Hopkins University, America is an "empire in formation", Paul Kennedy, professor of history at Yale University, perceives that it has arrived. "Nothing has ever existed like the [present] disparity of power [in the world]. The Pax Britannica was run on the cheap. Napoleon's France and Philip II's Spain had powerful foes and were part of a multipolar system. Charlemagne's empire was merely Western European in stretch. The Roman empire stretched further afield, but there was another great empire in Persia and a larger one in China. There is no comparison."[40] For Robert Kagan of the Carnegie Endowment, "The truth is that the benevolent hegemony exercised by the US is good for a vast portion of the world's population. It is certainly a better international arrangement than all realistic alternatives".[41]

For Dinesh D'Souza too, a researcher at the Hoover Institution, America has already "become an empire, the most magnanimous imperial power ever".[42] Robert Kaplan (quoted earlier in this chapter), described as "an international policy mentor to Bush", draws on the Punic Wars for inspiration. He believes that just as Rome became a "universal power" after defeating and annexing Carthage following those three wars (waged between 264 to 146 BC), American victories in World War II have made it a "universal power". Kaplan has explained his vision in a book, *Warrior Politics: Why Leadership Demands a Pagan Ethos* (2001). For useful insights on how to establish and run an empire he suggests, in addition to the Punic Wars, a study of the strategies adopted by Winston Churchill as also a sprinkling of other empire-builders.

"Remember that even Gladstone's vision was more effectively implemented by the realpolitik of statesmen such as Lord Palmerston, Benjamin Disraeli, and the Marquess of Salisbury, who kept illiberal empires like Germany and Russia at bay, sometimes through sheer deviousness ..." His philosophic musings do not end with his admiration for Victorian statesman and their "sheer deviousness". He speaks idealism as well. "Americans are truly idealistic by nature, but even if we weren't, our historical and geographical circumstances would necessitate that US foreign policy be robed in idealism, so as to garner public support and ultimately be effective."[43]

The Iraq invasion too was "robed" in appealing raiments. It proved to be an exercise in deception and bloodshed.

Four decades ago, in 1963, the Kennedy liberals too – although at the other end of the political spectrum from George Bush's advisers – tried regime change in Cuba, which is what the Bay of Pigs and the missile crisis which followed were all about, a crisis that pushed the world to the brink of nuclear war. Noam Chomsky and David Barsamian point out that when the Kennedy administration stepped up an international anti-terrorist campaign and economic warfare against Cuba, *after* the missile crisis, Dean Acheson, Kennedy's adviser, "informed the Society for International Law that we had the right of preventive war against a mere challenge to our position and prestige, not even a threat to our existence. His wording, in fact, was even more extreme than the Bush doctrine last September [the National Security Strategy document of September 2002]".[44] But the important distinction made here is that while Acheson's remarks were not a declaration of official policy, the Bush doctrine described in the National Security Strategy document is not a mere statement by an official, but a statement of government policy, affirming that a transformed America will be unfettered by international treaties or concerns and at liberty to disregard international opinion if it questions US actions or interests. The result of this indifference to international opinion is that "the United States is now regarded as the greatest threat to peace in the world by probably the vast majority of the population of the world. George Bush has succeeded within a year in converting the United States to a country that is greatly feared, disliked and even hated".[45]

Discussing what he calls "at least an honest statement", Chomsky cites an article in *Foreign Affairs* by Michael Glennon, a well-known specialist on international law, who according to Chomsky "argues that we should recognize that international law and international institutions are what he calls 'hot air'. They have proven their inapplicability by the fact that the United States disregards them, and he says it is right to disregard them, and the United States must maintain the right to use force as it chooses, independent of these institutions, which we simply have to dismiss and disregard". The net result of taking such positions, Chomsky concludes, is that "people are going to be frightened, and they'll do something about it. They'll try to find means of deterrence. The United States is calling on the world to proliferate weapons of mass destruction and terror, if only as a deterrent".[46]

Chomsky points to the Republicans' election-winning strategy of instilling – and sustaining – a sense of fear and panic in the American population and convincing them that only a strong and indomitable figure can protect them from the dangers that lurk in the world, waiting to hurt the United States. This sort of propaganda blitz worked in the case of Saddam Hussein, frightening the population into acceptance of the bombing and policy of 'regime change'. Chomsky observes that at the beginning of the new millennium the Republicans have simply been "rehearsing a script" used during the Reagan years in the 1980s, when they stayed in office by repeatedly pressing the panic button. "In 1981 Libya was going to attack us. In 1983 Grenada was going to set up an airbase from which the Russians would bomb us. In 1985 Reagan declared a national emergency because the security of the United States was threatened by the government of Nicaragua. Somebody watching from Mars would have collapsed in laughter."[47]

It worked. It may not say much for the maturity of the electorate in the world's oldest democracy, but it kept the Republicans in power.

The key difference between the Reagan and Bush eras is that the line between aspirations and actual annexation of resource-rich nations has been erased. For George Bush's aspiring new imperialists Iraq was the first stop, with greater tragedies still to come as the United States starts destabilizing the world for its own ends. Unless it learns some lessons from its misadventure in Iraq. The resentments and anger of Iraq's population, and the virtual impossibility of controlling a proud and vigorous people, indicate what lies ahead. If Washington has found the daily loss of American lives in keeping a nation of 22 million down too high, and mounted immense pressure on other countries for help in 'policing' it, how can it cope with the six billion other people of the world it wants to dominate?

This book has, I hope, shown that the growing dominance of the Pentagon over the White House – and American society – is not a recent phenomenon. Leaving aside any possible differences between the policies of Reagan and Bush, Bernard Lown, for example, finds very few between Clinton and Bush.

> Imperial hegemony did not begin with Bush II ... for the past half century the US military has been preparing for global domination. It has engaged in policies of provocation and confrontation largely hidden from public view ... President Clinton's subservience to the military was second to none. The national security apparat received a mighty boost from him and thereby hastened the emergence of the bold faced hegemonic unilateralism of Bush. Clinton gave free rein to the military. The massive military build-up that became evident in the wars of Afghanistan and Iraq occurred under Clinton's aegis. He increased military spending beyond what the Pentagon requested ... gave legitimacy to our permanent dependence on nuclear weapons as a means of projecting America's might globally. [48]

To be starry-eyed about empire-builders like the British is one thing. To try and recreate that era today is quite another. Sophisticated technological and scientific skills are no longer the preserve of Western nations, nor the advantages of the industrial revolution which gave them a head-start over non-industrial countries in the past. Large numbers of people in Asia and other parts of the world are better informed today, better equipped to deal with interlopers than their ancestors were. They are not so easily intimidated into accepting an inferior status by myths of other nations' invincibility and racial superiority.

§

Inevitably, the recent military actions undertaken by the Bush administration, and the crude and self-centred stance it has adopted, have turned large numbers of Islam's followers into implacable adversaries of the United States. This was achieved with amazing insensitivity, every nation the United States looked at with hostility through 2003 – with the exception of North Korea – being Islamic. When the follies of the Bush presidency are documented in detail, this monumental error alone will show how poorly Americans and their friends around the world were served by it during this period.

Washington's recent actions raise many questions. If the American military were to attack Iran, or Syria, or Libya, or all three, does it believe its moves would unite Islam's followers – around 1.2 billion of them – or divide them? Would it make them less or more antagonistic to America; less or more determined to avenge the assaults on their people and their faith? Would incidents of terrorist violence increase or decrease in retaliation against imperial violence? Would the United States be able to police the countries whose regimes it had destroyed?

Would the puppet governments, or councils, or whatever it set up be able to provide effective governance? How effective is President Karzai's government in Afghanistan, where even his personal security is provided by, of all things, US-based 'security companies', i.e. mercenaries, and where neither his writ nor his influence runs much beyond Kabul? If a majority of Iraqis resented the dictatorial ways of their previous ruler, will they be less or more averse to taking orders from imperial invaders?

Add to this potent mix of pride, nationalism and cultural dichotomy the explosive ingredient of religion, and you have the biggest powder keg known to human history. It has become a commonplace to brand people of other faiths fundamentalists. 'Islamic fundamentalism' is a highly favoured term because every excess can be attributed to it, with an uncritical audience willing to accept this sweeping generalization. In contrast, other sorts of extremism, for example Christian fundamentalism in the United States, are seldom talked about. Yet they are no less a threat to peaceful coexistence.

President Bush, writes Eliot Weinberger,

> is the first to actively subvert one of the pillars of American democracy: the separation of Church and State. There are now daily prayer meetings and Bible study groups in every branch of the government, and religious organizations are being given funds to take over education and welfare programmes that have always been the domain of the state. Bush is the first president to invoke specifically 'Jesus Christ' rather than an ecumenical 'God', and he has surrounded himself with evangelical Christians, including his Attorney General...[49]

The attitudes of these 60 million evangelical Christians in the United States are disturbing – and equally so the astonishing hold of a Benny Elon over them. Elon is head of Israel's far-right Moledet Party and is tourism minister in Ariel Sharon's coalition government. He ranks amongst the most radically right of Israel's politicians, with views more extreme than those of the most rabid members of Sharon's Likud Party. He believes in denying Israel's Muslims the vote, and solving the Palestine problem by 'transferring' the Palestinians to Jordan. "The Palestinian Arabs already have a state", says Elon. "It's Jordan." His plan is simple. "Give [the] Palestinians a state by granting them Jordanian citizenship. Solve the Palestinian problem by declaring there will be no separate Palestinian state at all. Make the West Bank and Gaza a part of Israel ..." What the Palestinians and Jordanians have to say about this doesn't concern him. His coup de grâce is a prediction that Islam will be wiped out in a few years by a Christian crusade.[50]

What exactly does Benny Elon, an Israeli of Jewish faith, have to do with growing evangelical fundamentalism in the United States? The answer is: a good deal. Elon has pushed his views persistently in Washington, both on Capitol Hill and in the evangelical Christian community with lobbying groups such as the Christian Coalition and Gary Bauer's American Values. He has carefully built up his influence not just with these two but also through several powerful Christian lobbying organizations like the Jerusalem Prayer Team in addition to preachers like Pat Robertson, notorious for his inflammatory anti-Muslim pronouncements. Among the legislators he has cultivated and seems to have won over are Dick Amery, former House Majority Leader, Tom DeLay, the present House Majority Leader, Lindsey Graham, Republican Senator from South Carolina, Max Burns, Republican Congressman from Georgia, and Steve King, Republican Congressman from Iowa. They belong to different Christian denominations, Methodist, Baptist, Catholic ...

These are true believers. King's remark to Elon during one of their meetings in Washington was, "As I watch the Arab world rise up, as I watch the murder of women and children, or any innocents, I have to say I don't know why you have the patience that you have". [51] Elon's single-minded wooing of the Christian lobbies in the United States may seem paradoxical when compared to the time he invests with America's Jewish groups. But it is a pragmatic decision in light of the numbers involved. The 60 million far right evangelical Christians almost vote in a bloc, making them, it is said, more potent allies of Israel than American Jews. Which is not an accurate statement. American Jews do not need to be lobbied in Israel's favour, since they are its most powerful supporters. But it is also worth remembering that some of the sharpest criticism of Israel under the Sharon government has come from liberal American Jews – in refreshing contrast to many Christian groups. Elon explains:

> [Christian fundamentalists] are people who are wild about Israel and believe in the annexation of Judea and Samaria and even the transfer of Palestinians from the soil of the land of Israel ... Compared to them, I am considered a dove. [52]

Fundamentalism is not confined to any single faith. Osama bin Laden and al-Qaida aren't a bigger threat to the security and peace of the world than the Benny Elons and Pat Robertsons. Or the fundamentalists of the Hindu religion in India who are trying to project a fraudulent interpretation of that compassionate faith. Increasing American antipathy to Islam is giving a sinister twist to a situation already fraught with danger. Imperial obsessions are bad enough; religious intolerance will make them infinitely worse. If religious fundamentalism is allowed to subvert the crucial separation of Church and State, or push societies into subverting themselves by pitting followers of different faiths against each other, then unending bloodshed awaits the world in the years ahead.

7

Pitfalls of Power

Making the World a Wasteland

A statesman is a politician who places himself at the service of the nation. A politician is a statesman who places the nation at his service.

PRESIDENT GEORGES POMPIDOU[1]

"THEY CREATE A WASTELAND AND THEY CALL IT PEACE", was how Tacitus described Rome's invasion of Scotland in the first century AD. The historian's words are also appropriate to what the Bush administration has done to Afghanistan and Iraq.

What is not so well known is the extent of the damage the violence unleashed there has done to American society. The final balance-sheet will show that when the state itself substitutes violence for statesmanship, violence becomes endemic in that culture. I am not referring to everyday murders, muggings and such which exist in all societies. My concern is with a growing contempt for the rule of law which is now increasingly evident in the United States, a disdain for statutes which ensure the right to life and property and which govern citizens' conduct towards their fellow-citizens. This disdain is an involuntary spin-off of external violence by the state against those weaker than it.

When the attacks against the symbols of American power took place on September 11, 2001, people reached out to America in sympathy and condemned the depravity of the attack on innocent people. But instead of reaping the benefit of this enormous international reservoir of goodwill, the United States squandered it by its wanton bombing of Afghanistan and incineration of innocent men, women and children who had never heard of the twin towers, who had no hand in their destruction, and whose only crime was that they were Afghans. Their guilt was decided by men sitting thousands of miles away, their death sentence pronounced as the price for the terror network based in their country.

Just as the attacks of September 11 led to similar attacks by the United States in Afghanistan, violent outbreaks within America against American citizens of Arab, Afghan, Indian, Persian and Pakistani origin reflected an upturn in the culture of vengeful violence. Looking and dressing differently and belonging to other faiths has never been a problem in the United States hitherto – other than between blacks and whites. This racial profiling, and the mindless violence flowing from it, is a direct result of a growing contempt for any distinction between innocence and guilt.

I remember more than one conversation with the distinguished social anthropologist Dipankar Gupta, who observed that to be so unnerved by terrorist attacks as to give up the fundamentals of what makes democracies strong and resilient should be seen as insulting and humiliating by all right-thinking Americans, in fact by all democratic citizens everywhere. In democratic societies institutions are deliberately crafted so that their laws are universal and the state is always under scrutiny. If social institutions are left unchecked, they sponsor people who are a stone's throw away from being red in tooth and claw.

According to Jonathan Simon, a former professor of political science at the University of Michigan, the so-called war on terrorism "should be carefully monitoring the people arrested, punished and deported … to make sure the government is targeting people who act like terrorists instead of look like them".[2] In his view, the Bush administration's misdirected actions are responsible for the growing feeling among Americans that the federal government is emerging as the proponent of violence inside the country too, with its assault on the civil liberties of citizens, residents and visitors to the United States.

In his paper 'The Land of the Free and the Home of the Fearful: Governing America through Fear of Crime before 9/11 and Since', delivered at the University of Michigan on October 9, 2002, Simon argues that fear of violent crime in America has been growing ever since President John F. Kennnedy's assassination in 1963, and that the collective lives of Americans and their institutions are being reshaped by this fear. "The fear of crime can have a more powerful effect on people and neighborhoods than crime itself. Fear of crime governs us in our choice of where to live, where to work, where to send our children to school. And those choices are made with increasing reference to crime."[3]

These statements are borne out by another contemporary fact of life in the United States, which is that the dream of living in a land of different cultures and faiths has soured for many who became Americans with great anticipation, but whose experience of being discriminated against has left them disenchanted. This is a victory of sorts for the perpetrators of 9/11 who have succeeded in undermining America's civil society and its decencies, tolerance and cohesiveness.

A leadership wedded to falsehoods and violence weakens the innate strength of the nation's secular traditions and democratic institutions. To the register of everyday incidents of violence, an increasing number of hate crimes is now being added. "Reported hate crimes against Arab-Americans and Muslims and their businesses, including restaurants, have reached a fever pitch since the September 11 terrorist attacks and subsequent US military retaliation. Some 800 possible hate crimes throughout the United States have been reported so far to the Council on American-Islamic Relations in Washington, D.C."[4] These hate crimes cover the entire range of assault and battery, shootings, murders, fire-bombings, arson attacks on homes and places of worship, threatening phone calls, abuse and harassment on the streets, hate mail, workplace discrimination and vandalism.

The rising graph of hate crimes is fanned by the policy of US Attorney General John Ashcroft, who considers it legitimate for a state threatened by terrorist attacks to be 'strong' and not handicapped by all the democratic niceties. The list of freedoms he has taken away from American citizens is included in the paranoic provisions of the Patriot Act which curtails civil liberties and due process in the name of homeland security. As Jonathan Turley put it in the *Los Angeles Times*, "Ashcroft appears to covet the authority to hold individuals indefinitely". He recently announced that even "legal immigrants would be held indefinitely based on a simple declaration that such confinement served national security". As for citizens, Ashcroft has previously claimed that he has the unilateral authority to declare US citizens to be 'enemy combatants' and to strip them of all constitutional rights – including access to the courts or counsel. Alternatively, Ashcroft is seeking new powers in Congress giving him the ability to strip people of citizenship, subjecting them to deportation or indefinite incarceration.[5]

Gupta is amazed that these moves did not draw the kind of citizenship censure they deserved. In Britain too there is a marked tendency among a section of the power-wielders to undermine democratic safeguards – like the abolition of the position of Lord Chancellor in June 2003. These invidious steps towards 'a strong state' are a cause for worry to all those who respect the sovereignty of democratic institutions in modern societies. Because if America and Britain can begin a radical refashioning of the very foundations of democracy, it gives dictatorial rulers across the globe legitimacy. The authoritarian trends within these two countries are particularly ironic in view of their professed aim of bringing democratic freedoms to nations under dictatorial rule.

The damage arrogant powers inflict on others, and on their own cherished institutions and social fabric, is a major pitfall of power, in which a variety of twentieth-century leaders unwittingly landed. They dug pits to trap the weak, but ended up falling into them themselves. This is a hazard the United States could also face if it allows an elective office to become an imperial presidency.

Senator J. William Fulbright, in his book *The Price of Empire* (1989), observed that there is "no greater folly than the attempt to impose the preference of a single society on an unwilling world".[6] He did not mention the social consequences American society would suffer if its leaders continued to prefer violent solutions to international problems: that the price of their folly in trying to impose their will on an unwilling world would be compounded by the damage inflicted by their actions on America's own social fabric.

"Violence has become the nation's leading industry", said the Senator. His observations, made fifteen years ago in the context of America's growing militarization, uncannily predict George W. Bush's America:

> To question this militarization is portrayed as an attack on our very
> security and survival … It has become integral to the American
> political culture that advocacy of a militant, assertive position in
> international relations, of big defense, and, as they say, of 'standing
> tough' is identified with patriotism, strength and virtue. Warnings
> against the danger of war, on the other hand, along with calls for
> compromise and negotiations, are, subliminally if not overtly, identified
> with effeminacy and weakness, cowardice and a lack of patriotism.

It is a political handicap and a mark of guileless innocence to be for conciliation and the use of the United Nations to achieve peace.[7]

§

In contrast to the moral vision and idealistic concerns of earlier American leaders, whether in or out of power, very few on the political landscape now stand out for their moral convictions. This becomes obvious when William Fulbright's intellectual and moral clarity is compared to the utterances of Defense Secretary Donald Rumsfeld on the threat small groups of terrorists pose with their highly destructive weapons, possibly biological, chemical and even nuclear:

> There are things we know that we know. There are known unknowns. That is to say, there are things that we know we don't know. But there are also unknown unknowns. There are things we don't know we don't know … Each year we discover a few more of those unknown unknowns.[8]

According to G. John Ikenberry, Professor of Geopolitics and Global Justice at Georgetown University – who quoted these words with admiration – Rumsfeld "has articulated this frightening view with elegance".[9] Irrespective of whether the Defense Secretary makes sense or not, he was pointing to the main goal the Bush administration aims to achieve: not only to reorganize the world to suit America's political-economic needs, but to insist on the unquestioning acceptance by every nation of Washington's right to do so. It could not be more ironical that the opportunity to change the world order according to US interests and values came with the September 11 attacks. International terrorism's destructive potential became the touchstone for all US actions after that fateful date. Other nations around the world were and are, of course, no less concerned about this threat. But the United States claims the absolute right to deal with it as it sees fit. According to the Bush security doctrine, the United States will need neither UN endorsement of its actions nor that of its allies in fighting a real or fake terrorist threat.

"Even without a clear threat, the United States now claims a right to use pre-emptive or preventive military force", announced Bush at West Point. "The military must be ready to strike at a moment's notice in any dark corner of the world. All nations that decide for aggression and terror will pay a price." The administration defends this new doctrine as a necessary response to a more uncertain and shifting threat environment. But this policy of no regrets can also easily become "national security by hunch or inference, leaving the world without clear-cut norms for justifying force."[10]

When a nation decides to take pre-emptive action "without a clear threat" or "norms for justifying force", its actions can hardly lead to a stable world order. In the new US-sponsored world order, a continuous cycle of violence and counter-violence after the gruesome events of September 11 has come to haunt the globe. When the President says the US military will strike at any dark corner of the world at a moment's notice he forgets that even dark corners are peopled by living, pulsating, hard-working human beings, most of whom would have nothing to do with terrorism. But these countries would certainly react in anger if large numbers of their citizens were killed without a second thought.

The Ashcroft argument, that in exchange for some democratic freedoms the state can guarantee its citizens greater safety, is unconvincing. The rights citizens enjoy are not luxuries bestowed by an indulgent regime, but are integral to the continuance of democratic governance; these freedoms of constitutional democracy make it possible for the functioning of public institutions to be publicly monitored. Such guaranteed freedoms lead to universal rules that separate liberty from licence, the central tenet of liberty being that norms are universal in character and ensure constant pressure on the state to deliver, which in turn makes the state more efficient. To trade liberty for security is to prefer strength over efficiency. What recent events have also shown, however, is that strong states are not necessarily efficient states. The 900-page Congressional report which was released towards the end of July 2003 and which lists the intelligence failures leading to 9/11 highlights the inefficiency of US intelligence agencies which, despite prior warnings of possible strikes, were unable to prevent it.[11]

Taking away citizens' freedoms under the pretext of strengthening the state to fight terrorism as proposed by John Ashcroft, or for that matter his counterparts in Delhi, is a spurious argument. Gupta points to the horrors of the McCarthy era to illustrate this. McCarthyism grew out of Harry Truman's National Security Council Document 84 which pressed for a strong state to protect Americans against the communist threat. But it went so out of control that even President Truman was asked to depose before the House Un-American Activities Committee.

§

When an established democracy deviates from its democratic norms, as the United States did after 9/11, and takes steps which violate constitutional principles, it encourages other democracies to do the same. As India has been prone to do with its inroads on the citizen's constitutional freedoms.

Noam Chomsky and Edward S. Herman's comment on US atrocities in Indo-China, made in 1979, applies with equal force to policies adopted by different Indian governments: "The beauty of nationalism is that whatever the means your state employs, since the leadership always proclaims noble objectives, and a nationalist can swallow these, wickedness is ruled out and stupidity explains all despicable behavior".[12] This is as accurate a description as any of the strategies governments employ to hoodwink people into accepting violations of their rights. In India's case – as in the case of the United States – even sections of the intelligentsia support such violations.

Constitutional democracies neither condone the violation of such rights by wilful state functionaries, nor bend laws to protect them, nor enact new ones to oppress citizens. So the Prevention of Terrorism Ordinance (POTO) – which like the Patriot Act in America was enacted by India in 2001 – can only be seen as a demolition of constitutional democracy. In the name of curbing terrorism, that mother of all rationales for every retrograde move, POTO was hurriedly introduced and brazenly used by government to justify violations of constitutional safeguards and the more squalid deeds of its security forces. "The whole exercise of issuing such an ordinance is to create psychological terror, so that the arbitrary actions of the government are glossed over and a climate is created wherein opposition to such actions may be considered anti-national", in the words of Justice Rajinder Sachar, former chief justice of the Delhi High Court.[13]

Jurists, constitutional experts and advocates of human rights all agree that whenever the state is allowed to increase its coercive capacities, it clears the way for constitutional violations and for transgressions by politicians and police officers who sanction atrocities in the name of combating terrorism. It also enables politicians in power to settle scores with their opponents. The United States may not have come to that pass as yet, though the new powers to arrest, detain, torture and terrorize are steps in that direction. India has resorted to them, ostensibly to fight terrorism. Fortunately, the integrity of the Indian judiciary – despite attempts to manipulate it – has helped steer the nation away from becoming an authoritarian state despite the many odious powers government has armed itself with to arrest, detain without trial, torture and even at times kill in the name of national security. It is not the politicians' but the courts' contribution which has kept the constitutional foundations of the Indian state intact.

There is no denying the complexity of terrorist crimes. Developing intelligence on them, from identifying, infiltrating and monitoring the movements of terrorist groups to anticipating their strikes, calls for very special skills. More often than not, physical evidence to link a crime with a specific group of terrorists is difficult to assemble. Where the terrorist's motivation is ideology and he is prepared to die for his cause, the problem becomes even more challenging. But despite these enormous difficulties, indiscriminate, vengeful and wholesale bombing of nations in retaliation is not the answer. If state terror becomes the preferred weapon for fighting terror, it will only spawn more terror.

§

Many concerned Americans are insistently questioning the mindlessness of increasing military expenditures at the cost of the nation's most pressing social needs which are being starved of funds. As Ruth Rosen of the *San Francisco Chronicle* puts it, even though national security for most Americans means protection from external enemies, in reality they can hardly feel secure if public schools – pushed to the very edge of financial insolvency – are cutting courses and laying off teachers, health care to the poor is being axed, and shelters for the homeless closed. She cites as an example Ann Crittendon's report in her best-selling book *The Price of Motherhood* (2002) that in just one county in Iowa in America's heartland, 18,320 children are living in poverty, 5,500 have no health insurance, and 680 children live in homeless shelters. "Though no foreign enemy has attacked Iowa, this sure seems like a threat to our national security to me."[14] She explains:

> Among other industrialized nations, we have the highest rates of maternal and child poverty. The mortality rate of our children under the age of 5 is shared by Croatia and Malaysia ... We are 54th when it

comes to access to health care for women and children ... The Bush administration's decision to beef up the military and enact tax cuts is shrinking our public institutions ... librarians all over the country are protesting local budget cuts that are closing the doors to the growing number of people who seek access to books, newspapers, magazines, and most important, the Internet ... Public education is suffering as well ... Behind the rhetoric of compassionate conservatism is a methodical plan to unravel the New Deal, the social contract forged 70 years ago that placed a safety net under mothers with small children, the infirm, the ill, the elderly and the unemployed.[15]

The huge tax cuts the Bush administration has introduced to benefit big business and the wealthy do not help ordinary middle-class working families. But the "brave voices" called for by Ann Crittendon "that will trumpet our need for a stronger domestic national security" are not to be heard from either House of Representatives or Senate, both sides seeming to be affected by a curious inertia in the face of insensitive decisions affecting the lives of hundreds of thousands of Americans across the country. Thoughtful persons in Asia and elsewhere who have looked for inspiration to the United States are beginning to see through the web which public relations campaigns have ingeniously woven around the Bush administration. With increasing awareness of what this administration is about, that admiration is lessening. Mounting federal deficits, staggering outlays for the military and the administration's new nuclear programmes, when set against increasing cuts in welfare schemes, do not add up to a very inspiring picture of a compassionate state.

After Iraq, the world needs to be even more wary of such aggressions. The United States will hardly wage 'wars' to bring the fruits of democracy to its victims. Nor will it pay for such wars itself. Its leaders, and its people, are likely to demand quicker and better returns from its future military adventures, as compared to its misadventure in Iraq. Even if the invasion of that country eventually turns out in favour of US corporate interests, the American public will need a more convincing scenario for any such future actions. The rest of the world, therefore, will need to be extra-wary in assessing the direction the Bush administration takes to satisfy its gluttony for the rich resources of other nations. To the *éminences grises* around the President, the Cheneys, Rumsfelds, Wolfowitzes and their kind, it will matter little what effect their imperial greed has on nations working hard to develop their economies. If they can starve their own social sectors to support an already bloated military establishment, they will not spend time worrying about the devastation their policies will visit on the people, priorities and policies of economically developing countries. It is up to these countries to start reading the writing on the wall before events overtake them.

§

The Bush administration's eagerness to lead the world into the second nuclear age could prove no less disastrous for the United States than for more vulnerable nations. Other proliferators, whose numbers will increase, will not be lagging behind. The Bush presidency's unilateral rejection of non-proliferation treaties and moves to develop a new generation of nuclear weapons have opened the way for similar moves by both existing and aspiring nuclear powers, including Russia.

When George W. Bush and Vladimir Putin signed the Strategic Offensive Reduction Treaty (SORT) in the Kremlin Palace on May 24, 2002, Bush announced that it "liquidates the Cold War legacy of nuclear hostility between our countries". But the treaty, a paper tiger, did not stipulate the destruction of nuclear arsenals; merely a reduction in the number of 'operationally deployed' strategic nuclear weapons. Nor did it make any mention of the large numbers of tactical weapons each country possessed. Nor would the treaty be fully effective until December 31, 2012. But even this treaty didn't last long. Just three weeks after Bush signed it, the United States let the ABM Treaty expire and did not renew it. The Kremlin's response was to announce that it was abandoning START II, the strategic arms reduction treaty signed in 1993.[16] Then General Andrey Nikolayev, head of the Duma's defence committee, disclosed that Russia's defence budget for 2003 was the equivalent of $10.9 billion of which 35 per cent was for weapons development and purchases. This percentage in future defence budgets, he said, would rise to 60 per cent. When it comes to rejecting international treaties, two or more can play the game.

In the words of one analyst:

> The world is actually a single, bizarrely interlocked nuclear system. If the Koreans go nuclear, then the Japanese go nuclear, then the Chinese upgrade their arsenal, then the Indians respond, which leads the threatened Pakistanis to do more of the same, and then the

knowledge – and possibly weaponry or crucial material – floating out there descends on some other would-be-nuclear power ... This interconnectedness of proliferators is the deepest truth of the second nuclear age, and there is no way the Bush administration can blast it into nonexistence, no matter the power of its weapons.[17]

Despite its bluster the Bush administration, it is to be hoped, is not unaware of these facts. Nor of what the Nuclear Non-Proliferation Treaty deserves credit for, despite the administration's withdrawal from it. It is worth recalling some of the treaty's achievements. In 1970 only the United States, Russia, France, Britain and China possessed nuclear weapons, although many other nations were close to becoming nuclear haves – as Israel, India and Pakistan would. But with the framing of the treaty a group of countries, South Africa, Taiwan, Argentina and Brazil, which had begun to develop their nuclear capabilities and weapons programmes, drew back from the nuclear threshold in deference to its aims.

No less creditable was the stand taken by Ukraine, Kazakhstan, Belarus and North Korea. The first three, which inherited the former Soviet Union's nuclear capacity and weapons, could have continued and expanded their production facilities but didn't because of the hope held out by the non-proliferation regime. North Korea, favourably reacting to US persuasion, actually halted its plutonium production in 1994, while South Korea decided against crossing the dividing line between the nuclear haves and have-nots. It was not long, however, before North Korea resumed its weapons programme, and in 1999 it fired a medium range missile into the Pacific Ocean. Many other countries possessing scientific skills and resources could also have become nuclear powers but didn't. They are unlikely to hold back now.

James Carroll of the *Boston Globe* summed up their stand:

The nations that renounced nuclear ambition, and the 167 nations that renewed the Non-Proliferation Treaty in 1995, have done this not out of a preference for powerlessness, but out of commitment to two foundational principles. The first is the ideal of ultimate nuclear disarmament. The cornerstone of the treaty is Article VI in which the five possessor states ... agree "to pursue negotiations in good faith on effective measures relating to cessation of the nuclear arms race at an early date, and to nuclear disarmament". The process has proceeded in fits and starts, but until now it has remained at the center of international hope.[18]

That hope – and that ideal – have now been trashed by Bush and his advisers.

It is worth recalling how President Bush's predecessors and the Soviet leaders actively created a nuclear culture during the competitive years of the Cold War by helping many countries build atomic facilities, acquire weapons, and develop nuclear technology. James Sterngold of the *San Francisco Chronicle* has explained how they did it:

> Each side rewarded its friends with [nuclear] research reactors – often easily adapted to bomb-making purposes – or commercial power reactors. In hindsight, states determined to develop weapons programmes secretly transformed the reactors into bomb factories or training grounds. Countries as disparate as the Congo, Ghana, Jamaica, Peru, Syria, Turkey, Bangladesh, Algeria and Colombia all got reactors. A university in Tehran received a research reactor from the United States. South Vietnam got an American reactor during the Vietnam War.[19]

How does the US view its magnanimity "in hindsight"? Fred C. Ikle, an expert on arms control and a senior government adviser, is most critical of it. "We sprinkled reactors all over the world. It was insane."[20] According to the Pentagon's own assessment, over 70 nations at the present time sit atop 1,400 command posts and sites for weapons of mass destruction and missiles.[21] These estimates might be of the same dubious provenance as that used for the propaganda against Iraq prior to the Allied invasion. But they could equally well be true, given the shadowy world in which exchanges of skills, materials, and crucial know-how are now taking place between those who have crossed the nuclear threshold and those waiting to do so.

All this adds up to some unpalatable truths. The first of these – a direct outcome of the second nuclear age – is that even Japan, the only country in the world to have had two of its cities obliterated by nuclear bombs, may opt for the very weapons which incinerated hundreds and thousands of its citizens. While at one time even talk of such a possibility was unacceptable in Japan, the situation has taken a 360 degree turn. William J. Broad of *The New York Times* has reported that "Japan is considered a likely flash point, despite its historic disdain for things nuclear after the bombings of Hiroshima and Nagasaki. Nisohachi Hyodo, once seen as part of the lunatic fringe for promoting a plan by which Japan would quickly acquire nuclear arms, now has his own radio program on a major Tokyo station and is a popular speaker on college campuses. And if Japan went nuclear, experts say, China might feel compelled to expand its own arsenal".[22]

But China will not wait for Japan to go nuclear before expanding its arsenal. George W. Bush's comments on the 'axis of evil' states, and his warnings to both China and Russia about 'irresponsible' sales of WMD technology, have not been lost on the Chinese. Even without that extraordinary statement, America's global ambitions would be unacceptable to the Chinese, who cannot be expected to remain indifferent to the need to counter any future nuclear blackmail by the aspiring hegemon. So Japan's entry into the nuclear club could be an added incentive – not the main reason – for China to adapt its nuclear plans to the changing world situation. Broad endorses Paul Bracken's argument, in his book *Fire in the East* (1999) on the second nuclear age, "that the danger lies not just in the spread of nuclear arms but in the culture of the second age ... In a crisis ... the military repercussions of that trend could erode the traditional restraints on nuclear arms".[23]

In the context of Washington's disregard of international efforts to control the dawn of the second nuclear age, some facts about China are worth noting. It has an army of 2.3 million; its defence spending was due to increase by a projected 10 per cent in 2004; with an economy expanding at a rate of 10 to 11 per cent per annum it will in all likelihood sustain its defence spending and nuclear programmes at present levels; its astronaut Yang Liwei orbited the earth 14 times in 21 hours in October 2003, making it one of only three powers, alongside America and Russia, to have succeeded in manned space exploration; it hopes to set up a base on the moon by 2010; its space programme is controlled by the People's Liberation Army. Given the US military's belief that space will become a battleground in the not too distant future, all these facts deserve sober consideration.

Such factors have led many analysts to predict that by mid-century China will replace the US as the world's leading power.

To assess the degree to which the United States should respond to perceived nuclear dangers – and the new generation of nuclear arms required to meet them – the US Strategic Command organized a top-level meeting at the Offutt air force base near Omaha, Nebraska at the beginning of August 2003. It was attended by key scientists from Los Alamos, Sandia and Livermore, the three main nuclear weapons laboratories, as well as senior air force officials and weapons contractors. "Determined to fight fire with fire, the Defense Department wants bomb makers to develop a class of relatively small nuclear arms – ranging from a fraction the size of the Hiroshima bomb to several times as large – that could pierce rock and reinforced concrete and turn strongholds into radioactive dust."[24]

This was just one of the many items on the agenda for the Offutt meeting. But the resolve to fight fire with fire seemed more for rhetorical effect since no nation has offered to match its nuclear fire power with America's. The much-touted North Korean threat – presumably the rationale to some extent for allocating almost $8 billion in the current year for a missile defence programme – is also more fiction than fact. It is doubtful if North Korea would ever launch, or be in a position to launch, a nuclear attack on the United States.

What astonished outside observers most of all was the manner in which a US Department of Energy's independent oversight panel of experts, which played a watchdog role in the development of the nation's nuclear arsenal, was quietly asked to pack up by the Bush administration just days before the closed-door meeting at Offutt. To add insult to injury, the disbanding of this national security administration advisory committee, which is required by law to look into nuclear weapons matters and issue public reports, was not effected by officially gazetting its dissolution in the federal register, but by a simple email to its members.

Ed Markey, a Democratic congressman and co-chair of a congressional taskforce on non-proliferation, wished to know why, "given the importance and sheer complexity of the issues raised ... was the only independent contemplative body studying nuclear weapons disbanded – and disbanded in such a surreptitious manner?"[25] Furthermore, the Pentagon barred congressional staff and dissenting scientists and officials from attending the Nebraska conference. Greg Mello, who heads the watchdog organization Los Alamos Study Group, has pointed to the effrontery of this decision: "There will be tonnes of contractors there from the weapons labs and the weapons plants. Contractors can come, but Congress can't".[26]

The Offutt conclave again highlighted the executive's increasing tendency to treat even congressional privileges in a cavalier manner. What is particularly surprising is that Congress should acquiesce in such questionable conduct. Authoritarian attitudes in established democracies seldom come in through the front door; they work their way surreptitiously into the system and invidiously erode democratic structures before the danger is fully recognized. Thus threats to the security of the homeland can never be viewed in isolation from the threat to democratic institutions and beliefs, whose sanctity is as important as national security.

The danger of nuclear proliferation to countries like India is not posed by the number of missiles currently in the arsenals of existing and would-be nuclear powers, but rather in these countries' leaders following the US example and launching their countries into a renewed nuclear race. It must be said to India's credit that after conducting the first nuclear test in 1974, it waited 24 years to explode the next three in May 1998. If it didn't identify itself with the non-proliferation treaty, it didn't reject it either, since it waited a quarter of a century before conducting its second round of tests. However, in the current climate of cynicism in which the ideals of a nuclear-free world find no place, it is conceivable that India too will step into the second nuclear age with plans of its own. These will also be justified in the name of 'homeland security', even as thirty per cent of India's people live below the poverty line and investments for their welfare are diverted to new-age nuclear programmes.

Obviously, if India opts for second generation nuclear technology, no other country can be blamed for its decision, the onus of which will lie on the leadership which is in political power at the time. The very fact that such a decision is taken, however, will show that its leaders have learnt nothing from US experience in Iraq, where the inescapable fact which stands out beyond any doubt is that no outside aggressor can enforce his writ on a resentful population without paying the price in blood and tears. Iraq's lesson for any would-be aggressor against India is that if the anger of a population of 22 million was difficult to control, how much more so would be the outrage of over a billion people?

A country like India with a population of that size does not need a nuclear deterrent against would-be aggressors. A population of a billion should potentially deter anyone. But the key to igniting people's involvement with their country is that they must feel inspired enough to die for it. That motivation and enthusiasm can only come if the state cares for the needs of all, and not just for society's privileged segments. If vast numbers of citizens are left out of the reckoning while national resources are invested in garish status symbols, nuclear weapons, and other extravagant trappings of military power, people will not willingly give their lives in the face of such callous indifference to their needs.

§

The excitement and hope as we reached the new millennium at the degree to which the world had become so accessible, are giving way to an increasing sense of unease; and to a distasteful feeling of being held to ransom by the whims and vagaries of a handful of people in a single country – just one out of 192 nations. What an irony that the anticipation and excitement generated by the promise of a world made accessible by the marvels of science and technology should be replaced by disgust at what this interconnectedness is doing to the integrity of our universe. To its humanity, and the ideals evolved over time through the ceaseless efforts of scholars and thinkers who strove for humane alternatives to despotism and abuse of authority.

Still more shameful is that this dominant country should set itself apart from all others in the matter of international crimes, and refuse to allow its citizens to be tried by any courts of justice in the world other than its own. Even as it proclaims its right to demand, 'dead or alive', men it has pronounced guilty, their guilt established not by a court of law but by fiat. This is not what we had expected of our world.

We had not expected or looked forward to a world in which the self-indulgent and wilful decrees of one nation would decide the sustainability of our planet – decrees which are in callous disregard of the environment, the deterioration of which poses a greater threat to mankind than all the evil regimes put together – for example, the falling ground-water levels which are placing drinking water beyond the reach of millions of people of India, Africa and elsewhere. The recurring tragedies in the Asian and African continents during the six decades after World War II have made fewer newspaper headlines than the unprecedented heat wave in Europe in the summer of 2003, which at least placed the Kyoto Protocol at the centre of every newspaper report, television and radio broadcast.

An editorial in *The Guardian* commented on the Bush administration's withdrawal from the Kyoto Protocol: "To gain some scale of how reckless this act of political vandalism was consider this: if US states were independent nations they would comprise 25 of the top 60 nations that emit greenhouse gases – Texas's emissions alone exceed France's ... America should realize that there are many ways to tackle climate change but ignoring it is not one of them".[27]

Some leading scientists have also taken serious note of what the extreme weather conditions witnessed around the world in the summer of 2003 signify. Professor John Schellnhuber, head of the UK's foremost group of climate scientists at the Tyndall Centre, feels that "What we are seeing is absolutely unusual. We know that global warming is proceeding apace, but most of us were thinking that in 20–30 years time we would be seeing hot spells [like this]. But it's happening now. Clearly extreme weather events will increase".[28] Michael Knobelsdorf of the German weather service says, "We've not seen such an extended period of dry weather [in Europe] since records began. What's remarkable is that these extremes of weather are happening at such short intervals, which suggests that climate is unbalanced. Last year in Germany, we were under water. Now we have one of the worst droughts in human memory".[29]

Comparing climate change to a weapon of mass destruction, Sir John Houghton, former head of the Meteorological Office in the UK, has written: "Like terrorism this weapon knows no boundaries. It can strike anywhere, in any form – a heatwave in one place, a drought or a flood or a storm surge in another".[30]

Professor F. Sherwood Rowland of the University of California, Irvine, and Nobel Prize winner, along with Mario Molina and Paul Crutzen, "for their work on atmospheric chemistry, particularly concerning the formation and decomposition of ozone", was the first to warn the global community that the chlorofluorocarbons (CFCs) released into the atmosphere by chemical manufacturers were depleting the Earth's critical ozone layer, which protects us from the sun's ultraviolet rays. Sherwood Rowland's work eventually led to legislation in many countries regulating the manufacture and use of CFCs. This in turn led to the United Nations Environment Programme's Montreal Protocol of 1987 – the first international agreement for controlling environmental damage to the global atmosphere. The Protocol, according to Rowland, "has been very effective". [31]

What the lists of national companies prepared by it revealed was that most of the emissions into the atmosphere came from developed and affluent countries – from their automobiles, refrigerators, air-conditioners, aerosol can sprays, and so on. Of the billions of aerosol sprays in use in the developed countries, over half are in the US alone.

Ozone is in effect a form of oxygen (O_3) which helps sustain life on this planet by blocking the sun's ultraviolet rays, exposure to which can cause human skin cancer and cataract. The only way to prevent the depletion of the ozone layer is by not putting compounds like the CFCs into the atmosphere. Before the CFCs break up, they contribute to the greenhouse effect, the trapping of solar radiation near the Earth's surface. The resultant global warming is believed by many responsible scientists already to be making the Earth 2^0 C warmer than it otherwise would be. Rowland's path-breaking work since 1978 on the impact of methane gas on the atmosphere has shown that over the past hundred years methane has been second only to carbon dioxide as a 'greenhouse gas' contributing to the global warming which has caused such cataclysmic changes in climatic patterns in recent years.

Now for the American politician's point of view as provided by a Democrat and a Republican. Democrat Representative Henry A. Waxman, of the House Government Reform Committee, states that "When President Bush rejected the Kyoto Protocol on greenhouse gas emissions, he promised the American people that 'my administration's climate change policy will be science-based'. In fact, however, the Bush administration has repeatedly manipulated scientific committees and suppressed science in this area".[32] Republican Senator James Inhofe of Oklahoma, on the other hand, has this to say about the debate on the world's drift towards ecological disasters: "Could it be that manmade global warming is the greatest hoax ever perpetrated on the American people? It sure sounds like it".[33]

A stark summing up was provided in August 2003 by Paul Krugman of *The New York Times*: "... on environmental issues – above all, global warming – America's ruling party is pursuing a strategy of denial and deception ... will we avoid the fate of past civilizations that destroyed their environments, and hence themselves? And the answer is: not if Mr. Bush can help it".[34]

Such, then, is the world we are creating for ourselves and the coming generations. A world threatened by nuclear destruction, inadequate legal safeguards, environmental disasters, an unrelenting arms race, and the fantasies of power-hungry, latter-day empire builders.

If, in order to celebrate the new millennium, you wished to visit some of the cradles of world civilization, Mesopotamia, perhaps, an inspiration for much of the world for centuries, what are the prospects of such a visit? You would be lucky to get there, and luckier still to get out alive. Assuming you were successful both ways, your luck would run out when you looked for past treasures in Baghdad's national museum. They were 'liberated' from it during the US-led 'war of liberation' in March–April 2003.

Try planning a visit to Afghanistan instead, to savour the unique heritage of the land through which the ancient Silk Route bore caravans from Alexandria to India and China and back to Alexandria – a major transhipment centre for commerce between Europe and Asia. Or try visiting the archaeological diggings that have unearthed valuable objects providing ample evidence of the two-way traffic of riches that traversed the forbidding mountain ranges of this ancient land.

In the lush green Bamiyan Valley which lies 250 kilometres north-west of Kabul at a height of 8,430 feet you will, alas, no longer see the two towering statues of Gautama Buddha carved out of the cliffs in the sixth and seventh centuries. When the Buddhas of Bamiyan, 175 feet and 120 feet high, were reverently carved almost 1,500 years ago, Bamiyan was a major Buddhist centre, home to more than 1,000 monks. During his visit there in the seventh century, the Chinese pilgrim Hsuan Tsang saw hundreds of caves carved out of cliffs by the devout Buddhists. The paintings of divine figures and decorative motifs on the ceilings and walls of the rock-walls where the Buddhas once stood were comparable with the cave paintings at Ajanta, Bagh and Badami, and interwoven with them were the influences of other great schools like the Hellenistic and Sassanian.

In March 2001 this priceless heritage was blown to bits by the Taliban regime – the same Taliban which the United States had helped create, arm and train to fight the Soviets. If in the process its fanatical followers pushed Afghan women back into the Middle Ages, brutally killed their opponents, and destroyed their country's cultural wealth, too bad. US brain and brawn had to be put to more worthwhile uses than conserving the world's cultural heritage.

Afghanistan is still worth a visit, however, if you are interested in experiencing the bucolic sight of endless illegal opium fields which are the local alternative to the failing security and reconstruction efforts of the victorious power. If there is anything that can be said in favour of the Taliban it is the complete ban it placed on the cultivation of opium poppies. But what American-style democracy has done for Afghanistan is to give it a thriving narcotics trade. In 2002 opium production in Afghanistan increased eighteenfold, giving a yield that was more than 75 per cent of the world's heroin (and accounting for 90 per cent of the UK's imports).[35] Antonio Maria Costa, the UN's anti-drugs chief, warns that "there is a palpable risk that Afghanistan will again turn into a failed state, this time in the hands of drugs cartels and narco-terrorists",[36] and this view is endorsed by Afghanistan's finance minister, Ashrafi Ghani, who feels that the country's opium fields are "among the greatest threats to its stability" and that it "could soon revert to a 'narco-mafia' state".[37]

As if all this weren't enough, "violence has increased in almost direct proportion to the efforts of the 11,000 American troops who are in southern and eastern Afghanistan, trying to 'eliminate al-Qaida'. Careless bombing and heavy-handed US tactics by ground troops when they search villages are making more enemies than friends".[38] In December 2003 the US military carried out two raids in eastern Afghanistan in which altogether 15 children were killed, and explained these actions as follows. One was a tragic military blunder, and the other occurred because "if non-combatants surround themselves with thousands of weapons and hundreds of rounds of ammunition and howitzers and mortars in a compound known to be used by a terrorist, we are not completely responsible for the consequences".[39] And that takes care of that.

First the rivalries of competing powers and now the ambitions of an aspiring global power have stamped this country of breathtaking beauty and unique history with their own brand of unending violence. So Afghanistan too ought to be struck off your itinerary.

§

Washington needs to reach beyond its own hooded hawks for voices of reason. Only then, perhaps, will it realize the folly of destabilizing countries and undermining institutions established to uphold decencies in international relations, including laws framed to prevent a repetition of the twentieth century's bloodiest excesses in human history. The world still remembers the principled stand taken by Americans of distinction at defining moments in history. But future generations will find nothing to praise in an America whose administration goes on dismantling the ideals on which the republic was founded. Let us consider some Asian views on the present situation.

In an article written in August 2003, the Pakistani historian F. S. Aijazuddin recalled a letter Robert J. Jackson, US Supreme Court Justice, wrote to President Roosevelt on June 7, 1945, after his appointment as chief US counsel at the Nuremberg trials of Nazi leaders. Jackson told his president that "undiscriminating executions or punishments without definite findings of guilt, fairly arrived at, would violate pledges repeatedly given, and would not sit easily on the American conscience or be remembered by our children with pride". His opening speech at the trial was consistent with his convictions. "We must never forget that the record on which we judge these defendants is the record on which history will judge us tomorrow ... We must summon such detachment and intellectual integrity to our task that this trial will commend itself to posterity as fulfilling humanity's aspirations to do justice."[40]

Aijazuddin then compared this striving for intellectual and moral integrity to meet the ends of justice with the savagery with which Saddam Hussein's sons Uday and Qusay were gunned down by US forces on July 21, 2003 in their house in Mosul in northern Iraq – and the American media's response. When the distinguished jurist emphatically drove home the point to Roosevelt that arbitrary executions or punishments were unacceptable, he couldn't have imagined how his countrymen would gloat over the Mosul killings. As if the murder of one's opponents were an enjoyable sport. According to *Time*: "The removal of two aces from the Pentagon's deck of the 55 most-wanted Iraqis provided a much-needed boost to a White House reeling from growing public suspicions that it stretched its case for the war, which has claimed more American lives than did the first Gulf War".[41] And to *Newsweek*: "American officials were deeply gratified to have bagged Saddam's two sons ... The hope is that the Iraqis will finally realize that the old regime is dead and gone, that Saddam and his spawn are never coming back, that resistance to the new order is futile".[42]

Aijazuddin reflects the view of a large number of thoughtful Asians: "Anyone who is still a friend of the United States (and there are yet many who are not paid to be) cannot but deplore the senseless brutality being perpetrated on the Iraqi people. The justification offered for this carnage is war. If the unprovoked attack on Iraq is a war, it is the most unorthodox of wars – a war without a lawful beginning, a one-sided war, a war without a foreseeable end".[43]

It may be worth pausing between Asian voices for a brief consideration of the rationale behind President Bush's demand for a 'dead' rather than an 'alive' Saddam Hussein.

The descent from the high ideals that distinguished early American thinking from the unreformed colonial powers is harshly brought home by President Bush's 'dead or alive' slogan. Whether the man in question is Osama bin Laden, Saddam Hussein, or his sons, proof of guilt and fair trial find no place in the White House's sense of justice. And for good reason, given the deals successive US administrations have struck with Saddam: the CIA's help in bringing the Ba'ath Party to power in 1958; Washington's instigation of Iraq's invasion of Iran in 1980 and its arms supplies to Iraq during the eight-year Iran-Iraq War – supplies that included biological, germ warfare and poison gas plants; turning a blind eye to Saddam's slaughter of the Kurds and Shias in 1991 after Bush Senior had called on them to revolt; and similar milestones in Washington's murky relationship with Saddam. So, "Better a bullet-riddled Saddam, or one executed by a military kangaroo court in Guantanamo, or hanged by the new American-installed 'Vichy' Iraqi regime in Baghdad", as Eric E. Margolis of the *Toronto Sun* aptly put it.[44]

Amitav Ghosh, a widely-admired Indian author who was educated at Delhi, Cairo and Oxford, commented in *The Hindu* in July 2003: "The very extremism of the Bush administration's stance, in economics as in foreign affairs, makes it certain that these policies will be forcefully repudiated … No matter what the polls may suggest, there is massive and growing opposition to the policies of the Bush administration: the millions of Americans who demonstrated against the war in Iraq on February 15 of this year [2003] have not disappeared and will soon be heard again". On the idea of responding to the United States' repeated request for India to send 'peace-keeping' forces to Iraq, Ghosh writes: "some policy-makers appear to believe that the rendering of certain services can gain India entry into the innermost circles of global power. Our history has truly been suffered in vain if it has failed to teach us that this is not how the world works".[45]

Reiterating his faith in the UN's relevance in today's world, Ghosh reminds us that even if some of the conventions governing it are not perfect, nevertheless "these conventions were brought into being in

the wake of decolonization, and they represent a genuine and serious attempt to imagine an alternative to a global system of empires.
India, of all countries, cannot assent to the undermining of this body
of law and convention: it would be a repudiation of the lessons of our
history and a betrayal of the ideals of our independence".[46]

All across the Arab world, sentiment is increasingly critical of the
United States. Even Egypt's President Hosni Mubarak, for long a close
US ally, was opposed to military action against Iraq, and openly critical of it when it began. "When it is over, if it is over, this war will have
horrible consequences. Instead of having one [Osama] bin Laden, we
will have 100 bin Ladens", he told Egyptian soldiers in Suez. Praising
Iraqi troops who were battling US and British forces, he said at the
height of the war that they were "guarding Iraq's lands and defending its national honour and nobility".[47] Though there is strong anti-US
sentiment throughout the Arab world, its deep-seated dilemma is underscored by Talal Salman, a prominent Lebanese writer and editor-in-chief
of *Assafir* newspaper. "They – the Arabs – are torn between despotic
regimes which lack the political power to express their national will
positively, and a superpower which wants to impose its imperial designs
on the region".[48]

Today the gap between Western views of what goes on in the Arab
world, for instance, and what the Arabs feel about the West, is at its
widest. While some Western commentators like to think of the Arab
world as divided, dispirited and paralysed with fear before President
George Bush's crusade against Iraq, others warn against humiliations
of the Arabs by superior Western armies.[49] The holders of both these
views would do well to understand that the people of the Arab world
are daily becoming more united in their growing resentment of the West,
especially of the US.

The ruling regimes, according to Salman, believe "they can buy
their survival from the United States by discreetly agreeing to American
plans, while publicly denouncing the United States and suppressing all
forms of public resentment. They [of all people] should know that by
remaining complacent and digging Saddam's grave, the likelihood of the
US interfering in their own regimes if they go against American plans
for the region is increased". Before the war ever began, Salman was
convinced that the Ba'ath Party, "a great political movement", would not
disappear after an American take-over of Baghdad, but would "appear

in different forms". And that the American presence would be a catalyst for change: "the challenge, the *agent provocateur*, which will give
ammunition to popular movements across the Arab world. Politics will
be radicalized even further and anti-American sentiments will grow
stronger. With all its military might, America will be seen as an occupying force which betrays the very ideals it claims to espouse".[50]

Khaled Al-Dakheel, a Saudi sociologist, agrees that the prevailing
regional order which has existed for the past 50 years will change
because it has exhausted its effectiveness, that new and more radical developments in inter-Arab relations and within organizations like
the Arab League will impart a new thrust to Arab self-assertiveness.
According to him, the key difference between the showdown in 1990–91
and the recent one in 2003 is that while the former was between Iraq
and the United States, this time the face-off pitted the Arabs against the
United States. "We have reached a point where the US and Arabs fail
to agree on a single key Arab issue, be it the Arab-Israeli conflict, Iraq,
democracy, or the education curriculum."[51]

While agreeing with Al-Dakheel on some of these points, the
Moroccan history professor Abdel-Salam Al-Sheddadi believes West
Asia is moving more towards 'fundamentalism' than pan-Arabism. "No
matter what the consequences of the war on Iraq might be, throughout
the Arab world it will always be seen as an exercise in American power
and hegemony. It will be a living example and reminder of an act of
humiliation, just as Palestine is today."[52]

Whether fundamentalism or pan-Arabism, both are born out of
shared beliefs, concerns and experiences. And as the United States
throws its weight around, shared resentments too now figure on the
list. Anti-Americanism, or for that matter, anti-anything, is a unifying
experience. Anti-British feeling among Indians, in the years before independence, unified them and created a consciousness of their right to
determine their own destiny. The same is increasingly evident in the
Arab view of America.

Anti-American feelings are on the boil all across Asia: in the Far
East, in South Asia, in the Middle East. If they were simmering before
the invasion of Iraq, they are spilling over now into acts of violence, of
terror. US bombings of civilian populations in Afghanistan and Iraq, as
decades ago in Korea, Vietnam, Laos and Cambodia, and US instigation
of violence and bloodshed in Iran and Indonesia, are seen by Asians as

the worst forms of terror, representing the cold, calculated and pitiless destruction of human life, of large segments of populations and their villages and cities and means of survival.

This brings to mind some haunting words from Mario Puzo's novel *The Fourth K* which capture with uncanny accuracy the inexorable dynamics of terrorism. In this passage Yabril, an Arab terrorist, tells the American president: "If I highjack a plane, I am a monster. If the Israelis bomb a helpless Arab town and kill hundreds they are striking a blow for freedom ... Does the world expect us not to fight? What can we use except terror? ... What about your bomber pilots who rain down destruction as if the people below them were mere ants? ... I think I am no different ... You are my fellow terrorist".[53]

US bombings of Asia already span half a century, and none is likely to be forgotten or forgiven for a good deal longer still by those who have experienced their horror, or even by those who watched from a distance the mass killings of hapless men, women and children, either in furtherance of America's ideological goals, or in revenge and retaliation in more recent times. But this violence, no matter how sophisticated the weapons, will not work in the long run. The odds are weighted against America – in terms of numbers, logistics, economics, the scale of the world we live in, and the limits to which America can impose its will globally through violence and genocide.

The world has undergone critical change since the years of communist ascendancy and the Cold War in that many Asian nations have now come into their own. They have huge industrial plants, diverse technological skills, access to natural resources, scientific and military potential, and – most of all – a sense of self-esteem and national pride. Pride is not the exclusive prerogative of the privileged nations. This has still to dawn on the West. Pride is fuelling the drive of Asian nations to find a place in the sun. And why shouldn't they find it?

8

Epilogue

Cooperation or Confrontation?

"And while I am talking to you mothers and fathers, I give you one more assurance. I have said this before, but I shall say it again and again and again: your boys are not going to be sent into any foreign wars."[1]
FRANKLIN DELANO ROOSEVELT, 32nd President of the United States

TODAY, THE US MILITARY HAS 700 BASES or base rights in 130 countries, and the US Air Force has a presence on six of the world's seven continents. Detachments of US Special Forces conduct thousands of operations every year in 170 countries, while US personnel – over half a million soldiers, technicians, teachers, contractors, civilians and dependants – are very much a part of many foreign lands and their military and paramilitary forces, not to mention those fielded by US intelligence agencies, or attached to their counterparts in other nations. Thirteen naval task forces built around aircraft carriers cruise the world's oceans and seas. And US troops are engaged in the messy aftermath of two "foreign wars" – in Iraq and Afghanistan.

When the American people elected George Bush as their 43rd President in November 2004 – if, indeed, he did come to office by majority vote – they put at risk their own safety and stability as much as that of the wider world. Ample evidence of this was provided by the Bush administration's first term as it laid countries waste and appropriated their natural resources; by its pre-emptive strikes and regime changes; its contemptuous disregard for institutions and treaties which protect the rights of nations; by its development of nuclear arsenals which can destroy the world many times over while compelling others to sign non-proliferation treaties. What all this earned the US was worldwide hatred for its policies and unilateralism.

Despite its massive display of military power around the globe, the new administration's vision of America as the sole planetary policeman and arbiter of international relations cannot succeed. If Vietnam was not proof enough, America's Iraqi misadventure has shown that a nation of less than 25 million can stop the world's most heavily armed nation from having its way. Iraqi will and national pride, and its anger at being forcibly dispossessed of its self-esteem and national resources, have fuelled the continuing resistance. Even more significant is the degree to which the US, blinded by its own short-term interests, has inadvertently helped rally the countries of West Asia – and further afield – around the banner of shared resentments.

The arbitrary actions of the administration have also entailed onslaughts on the rights and freedoms of its own people, deep divisions in a society with a record of cohesiveness, and the parading of out-dated doctrines of intolerance and religious fundamentalism in the run-up to the presidential election. Perhaps for the first time in America, a large number of conservative religious leaders urged their parishioners to vote Republican: an extraordinary rejection of the principle that separates the church from the state. And that too by a nation currently at war with another to teach it the virtues of democracy.

The threat to constitutional decencies in the US has been evident in other areas as well. The designation of prisoners detained in the American Naval Base at Guantanamo Bay in Cuba as "enemy combatants" denied them all the safeguards prisoners of war are entitled to. According to the former US Attorney General John Ashcroft,[2] moves were afoot in late 2004 to detain American citizens in camps built on US soil. Their inmates, also designated "enemy combatants", would be held without charges, with no constitutional rights nor access to courts, their incarceration to last as long as it might please the state.

The prospect of these detention camps is already generating bitter hostility abroad because of the racial and religious profiling they underscore. After September 11, 2001 the US administration singled out Arabs, South Asians and Muslims for particularly harsh treatment on the assumption that they were more inclined than other groups to terrorism. The extraordinary typecasting of 1.2 billion persons of Islamic faith was breathtaking. Over 13,000 immigrants in these categories – out of the 80,000 asked to register with the government – were deported from the US. Many, though not charged with any crime, were deported as "potential terrorists" while still others were subjected to indefinite detention, inhuman treatment, and denial of access to family and lawyers.[3] If families were torn asunder, jobs lost and the sanity of those affected destroyed, it seemed to matter little as long as it was in the name of "national security".

As a result, the lines between the terrorist and terrorized have become increasingly blurred, making it difficult to distinguish between a state which terrorizes its own and other citizens and those who seek to avenge those wrongs. In the minds and hearts of people whose lives are shattered forever there is little difference. How the US treats its citizens is its own affair – although it has brazenly gone into other countries with the avowed purpose of ensuring justice for their people – but the humiliation and mistreatment of its citizens on the basis of their colour and religious beliefs become a matter of global concern when the simmering, spreading, all-consuming and explosive anger everywhere at such discrimination eventually translates into large-scale acts of retributive terror. A far-sighted and statesmanlike strategy for dealing with this, however, is still not evident in the war against terror.

A widely-shared assumption repeatedly voiced is that the undeclared war between Islamic fundamentalism and the West goes a long way back – to their shared history which spans several centuries. This is far from the truth. The dramatic growth of Muslim fundamentalism as it is presently understood was fuelled by aggressive US interventions during the last century in Muslim states like Iran in the 1950s, Indonesia in the 1960s, Afghanistan in the 1970s-1980s, and Iraq through the 1990s and up to the present time. Some of these countries were working their way towards modernity when the process was pre-empted by the arrogance and aggressiveness of Washington's policies and its indifference to the rights and sufferings of the Palestinian people. Until then the liberalism of most Arab states had been self-evident in the education of their young in schools and universities abroad (not least in America itself), the role of women in public life, inter-marriages, and fairly open borders. About Turkey, Egypt, Lebanon, Morocco, Jordan, Iraq, the Emirates and many other Muslim countries there was very little that could be called fundamentalist, whereas now even in a country like Malaysia fundamentalism is surfacing, as it is in America among evangelical Christians.

Washington's unprincipled and inconsistent changes of course have also contributed to the appeal of Islamic fundamentalism. Like its active support of Saddam Hussein in his war against Iran, before branding him America's enemy no. 1. Or extending massive help to Osama bin Laden in Afghanistan, then mercilessly bombing that country to flush him out. And, above all, the growing anti-Americanism around the world is due to the treatment of the Palestinians by the Israelis, who have the full backing of the US. Even in some Islamic countries where the governments are with the US, the people are not. This explosive situation will continue unless the US helps end the indignities inflicted on the Palestinian people – a key cause of the widening divide between the US and the Islamic world. As Sir Ivor Roberts, the British ambassador to Italy, aptly pointed out in September 2004: "If anyone is ready to celebrate the eventual re-election of Bush, it's al Qaida ... Bush is al Qaida's best recruiting sergeant."[4]

A comment on King Abdullah of Jordan by former UK Defence Minister Michael Portillo will also be à propos. He wondered how this "highly intelligent man keeps his patience as his country reaps the baleful consequences of the West's ill-informed meddling in this region ... whose [own] country is now surrounded by terror and war, its population driven from its pro-western outlook to an unprecedented level of anti-American fury".[5]

A telling account of the widening gulf between Islam and Christianity in the US is provided by the Boston Globe columnist James Carroll in the introduction to his book *Crusade, Chronicles of an Unjust War*.[6] In it he looks perceptively at how words become templates for creating a climate of alienation and separatism and gives as a prime example Bush's use, soon after 9/11, of the phrase "this crusade, this war on terrorism". Carroll is troubled by its "outrageous ineptitude ... religious war is the danger here and it is more serious than Americans realize ... the Jesus of this evangelical President is not 'turn the other cheek', Bush's saviour is the Jesus whose cross is wielded as a sword". And that is what religious extremism – or fundamentalism, is about.

In retracing fundamentalism's intolerances, Carroll finds sinister parallels in the cult of martyrdom and suicidal valour demonstrated by the crusaders and the present-day acts of self-destruction favoured by Muslims. Each received its dynamic from the theology of sacred violence. For the European crusaders, even though the infidel was an external enemy, the momentum of hate once generated soon discovered an "infidel near at hand" – the Jews.

Carroll believes that "The same dynamic – war against an enemy outside leading to war against an enemy inside – can be seen at work today. It is a more complex dynamic now, with immigrant Muslims and people of Arabic descent coming under heavy pressure in the West. In Europe, Muslims are routinely demonized. In America they are 'profiled', even to the point of being deprived of basic rights". But in an inexorable and ironic turn of events, "at the same time, once again, Jews are targeted. The broad resurgence of anti-Semitism [in both Europe and America] and the tendency to scapegoat Israel as the primary source of the new discord, reflects an old tidal pull".

§

Washington's distaste for international institutions and multilateral treaties is not new. It dates back at least to the League of Nations, an American creation which the US Congress nevertheless refused to join or support. During its first term the George W. Bush administration contemptuously brushed aside the authority and dignity of the United Nations, and then tried to block the creation of the International Criminal Court before ending up repudiating its jurisdiction over US citizens. It committed other such transgressions, but let us look at these two first.

The UN was scorned when a majority of members did not vote for the use of military power against Iraq after Hans Blix, the UN chief weapons inspector, had reported that, in the absence of any weapons of mass destruction there, a military offensive against Iraq would lack legal and moral justification. His recommendations cut no ice with Washington, which invaded the country in March 2003, creating another killing field to satisfy America's appetite for oil and global hegemony.

A year-and-a-half after that ill-fated invasion, UN Secretary-General Kofi Annan belatedly – though this time bluntly – told the 64 presidents, 25 prime ministers and 86 foreign ministers assembled for the UN General Assembly session in New York on September 21, 2004 that "those who seek to bestow legitimacy must themselves embody it, and those who invoke international law must themselves submit to it", adding that democracy could not be delivered through force nor "fundamental laws shamelessly disregarded". Speaking of "Iraqi prisoners who were disgracefully abused", he was equally and rightly unsparing of those who "massacred civilians in cold blood while relief workers, journalists and other non-combatants are taken hostage and put to death in the most barbarous fashion".

These acts of savage and senseless retaliation, mostly against innocents, certainly diminished the groundswell of sympathy for the Iraqis bombed, strafed, shelled and mercilessly killed by sophisticated weapons in the name of democracy. Washington's disregard for international laws and the hypocrisy with which members of the administration denounced the crimes committed by the Iraqis whilst ignoring the excesses of its key officials was astonishing. In his book *Chain of Command: The Road from 9/11 to Abu Ghraib*[7], Seymour Hersh reveals in graphic detail how the Abu Ghraib prison in Iraq, already notorious under Saddam Hussein, was taken over by the US forces with presidential authority, and placed under the direct responsibility of Donald Rumsfeld – the same Rumsfeld who had "repeatedly made public his disdain for the Geneva Convention". Both National Security Advisor Condoleezza Rice and Defense Secretary Donald Rumsfeld were fully protected by a top-secret presidential order signed at the end of 2001 or early 2002, "authorizing the defence department to set up a specially recruited clandestine team of special forces operatives and others who would defy diplomatic niceties and international law and snatch – or assassinate, if necessary – 'high-value' al Qaida operatives anywhere in the world. Equally secret interrogation centers would be set up in allied countries where harsh treatments were meted out, unconstrained by legal limits …".[8]

The contempt for all constraints became obvious when the gross abuse of prisoners in Abu Ghraib was revealed in the world press from mid-2004. The depravity of the interrogation methods used alone go a long way to explain why Asians are concerned over another four years of a Bush administration.

The experience of Vietnam, Afghanistan and Iraq should have proved to the American people that it is much easier today to claim "mission accomplished" before TV cameras – on the safe and secure deck of a national aircraft carrier, than to achieve dominance on the ground. But it didn't, and a declared majority of the American electorate clearly did not hold George W. Bush responsible for the bloody wars Washington is waging abroad. He had also emphatically declared that, if re-elected, he would continue with his Iraq and Afghanistan policies and had every intention of "staying the course".[9] Even so, Asian nations should not lose sight of the fact that many enlightened Americans are deeply opposed to using their military superiority to force political and cultural change on peoples of different religions and ideological persuasions abroad, as also to their own gradual repression at home.

§

The developing countries are determined to prevent the subversion of the United Nations. While the Security Council has all too frequently been used to promote the interests of its most powerful member states, the UN was created primarily to establish a just world order in which the concerns of less-developed nations would be conscientiously addressed. These concerns have often been admirably met by the UN and its specialized agencies. But some crucial decisions, even when supported by previous US administrations, have been summarily rejected by the Bush presidency. Among these is the treaty to establish the International Criminal Court (ICC).

The ICC is independent of the UN but draws on it for judicial assistance, information-sharing and ways to help its development. This relationship was sealed by an agreement adopted by the ICC Assembly of State Parties in The Hague on September 7 and the UN General Assembly in New York on September 13, 2004, and signed by UN Secretary-General Kofi Annan and Judge Philipe Kirsch, the court's president, on October 4, 2004.

Why, then, do the Republican administration and Congress continue to repudiate the ICC? According to Bush (in the first September 2004 debate with John Kerry on television), he would not sign a treaty to win a global popularity contest as he was not elected president to allow American troops and others to be prosecuted abroad as war criminals. He claimed he would protect US interests, not sign them away! As Newsweek's Fareed Zakaria put it, "Bush chose to mention his opposition to the International Criminal Court because he thought that would please the crowd. He mocked the idea of 'foreign judges' trying American soldiers".[10] Are US interests really best served by protecting American citizens accused of crimes abroad? Or does the US attitude spring from the fact that some of these crimes will be committed on Washington's instructions by its Delta Units, Special Forces, and other shadowy killer groups trained to protect "US interests"? Or the possibility that US forces personnel may be tried for "foreign wars"? The ICC, which holds the promise of providing equitable international justice, is unacceptable to Washington precisely because the Court would have the authority to hold American citizens accountable for crimes committed in other countries on US government orders.

Just as an overwhelming number of nations are interested in preventing subversion of the UN, so they are equally keen to save the ICC from a similar fate. The court's appeal to even the world's remotest corners is revealed by the response of sub-Saharan Africa where countries have witnessed savage atrocities against their civilian populations. Of forty-eight countries in the sub-Saharan region of the African continent, twenty-six signed up to the treaty because it has a particular appeal for countries which have suffered "devastating civil wars and human rights abuses in recent years". As Nicolas Michel, UN legal counsel, remarked of the ratification of the Rome Statute by Liberia: "This is a truly meaningful gesture from a state coming out of a very tragic situation, showing a real commitment to the need to build a momentum for international justice".[11]

§

Norman Cousins, the distinguished American editor, once said Nixon's motto was: "If two wrongs don't make a right, try three". George Bush did better than that - he trashed the UN and the ICC then took the count from two to five by repudiating the Treaty on Non-proliferation of Nuclear Weapons (NPT), the Anti-Ballistic Missile Treaty (ABM), and the Kyoto Protocol on Greenhouse Gases and Global Warming.

The United States and Russia between them possess 95 percent of the world's nuclear arsenal. The US has 6000 nuclear weapons operationally deployed, of which 3500 are submarine launched ballistic missiles, 2000 are intercontinental ballistic missiles, and the rest carried by bomber aircraft. This is only the beginning; weapons are now being developed with "global reach capability" that can strike a target 9000 nautical miles away in less than two hours. And the United States Space Command's doctrine of "full-spectrum" dominance promises a combination of global surveillance, missile defense, and space-based weapons systems to enable the US to strike pre-emptively anywhere in the world. Since all these and a range of other genocidal weapons come at a cost, the military budget request for fiscal year 2005 was $420.7 billion which, along with other appropriations, works out at a sum of over $1.30 billion every day of the year – exceeding the daily military expenditure of the rest of the world combined. The message these US defence appropriations convey to the world is that American military power can now obliterate any country it wants to without crossing that country's borders.

Russia's Achilles heel is that in addition to its arsenal of operational nuclear weapons it has stockpiles of over 600 tons of enriched uranium and plutonium, which are indifferently secured and could fall into the hands of terrorists or their sponsors. The destructive potential of these nuclear arsenals makes the existence of institutions, treaties and safeguards designed to prevent proliferation and stop the drift towards self-annihilation even more crucial.

The biggest danger may be to the US itself. Bernard Lown, Nobel Peace Prize winner, placed it in a compelling perspective in letters to the author when he pointed out how nuclear bombs, paradoxically, enable the weak to inflict incalculable damage on the strong:

> Few societies are more susceptible to the nuclear bombs' malevolent consequences than the rich, urbanized, highly developed industrialized North, foremost the United States. It is already the object of growing global resentment, envy, anger, fear and hatred. One may surmise that the US will increasingly be the target for terrorist acts. It is therefore only a matter of time before rogue states and fanatics avail themselves of these infernal weapons.[12]

Here is a timely reminder to the Pentagon's praetorians that the trillions of dollars of taxpayers' money wantonly spent on nuclear weapons will not stop those determined to settle scores with the US. Not so long ago the US was admired for its democratic decencies, the moral clarity of its Constitution, its openness, the opportunities it offered those who sought refuge there, the resolve with which it tried to put right its racial wrongs, the freedom of speech and accountability of those in public office, and its generousness. That moral grandeur has been tarnished, those admirable qualities eroded. More than fifty years of US unilateralist policies, culminating in the present administration's cynical disregard of hard-won international agreements, have changed the way much of the world now thinks of America.

Another reason for resentment is nuclear double-talk; the unquestioned presumption that only Western powers have the right to develop weapons of mass destruction. Is this neo-colonialist presumption based on race? Or the power of the haves over the have-nots? Investing in such weapons is rarely a priority for developing countries. Their peoples' social needs preclude that luxury. Why, then, do so many countries spend staggering sums they cannot afford on developing nuclear capabilities?

Of course there are the usual justifications: the threat posed by hostile neighbours; the spectre of a nuclear power menacing non-nuclear states, as Israel does Arab nations; the desire to acquire nuclear know-how for development purposes. But beneath these obvious arguments lie more complex, unspoken compulsions. Foremost among these may be the satisfaction of defying the racially arrogant Western nuclear states – principally America – who believe they alone can belong to the nuclear club. What gives the US the sole right to become a global threat with its own weapons of mass destruction? For Asians it is disturbing that five out of six countries Bush has classified as rogue states and shortlisted for "large scale nuclear attack", in the Pentagon's contingency plan, are Asian (Iraq, Iran, North Korea, Libya and Syria). Many Asian and African countries, for their part, would pick the US as the world's most dangerous regime today. Polarizing the world around colour, race and religion may be the most dangerous legacy of the Bush years.

§

Not content with invading Iraq without UN authority, Washington now threatens the planet's ecological balance by repudiating the Kyoto Protocol on global warming, which required ratification by either the US or Russia to take effect. Both originally refused to sign on grounds of national interest. Both argued that the scientific case is unproven in that, though global warming is a generally accepted fact, whether it is man-made is open to question. However, Russia yielded to pressure from the European Union and against expectation, President Putin signed, and Russia's State Duma duly approved, the Protocol on October 22, 2004. As a result, the Protocol came into force in February, even without US participation. Said Paul Prestrud, head of Oslo's Center for International Climate and Environmental Research, "The big challenge will be to get involvement by the United States, [and] big developing countries like China, India, Brazil, and Indonesia". As of November 2004 China, India and Brazil had all ratified the protocol.

George Bush claims that the non-participation of developing countries is a key reason for the US refusal to ratify the Kyoto Protocol, and these nations certainly cannot be indifferent to the consequences of their inaction. But they account for only a fraction of worldwide per capita emissions, and resent the hypocrisy of the world's foremost generator of greenhouse gases in pointing an accusing finger at them.

Widespread extreme poverty and growing populations in both India and China call for dramatic economic growth to avoid severe social unrest, and they may not be able to avoid appreciable increases in fossil fuel consumption for their development needs. The Protocol allows some headroom by setting emissions targets for developing countries above their present emissions levels. Even so, pragmatism and imaginative planning must produce, and are already producing, alternative energy strategies in many countries. In June 2001 the US Natural Resources Defense Council reported that "By switching from coal to cleaner energy sources, initiating energy efficiency programs, and restructuring its economy, China has reduced its carbon dioxide emissions 17 percent since 1997". The Chinese are also accepting great hardships, including widespread forcible resettlement, as China implements the world's largest hydroelectricity programme. In India, the eminent scientist Dr K. P. Prabhakaran Nair proposes an afforestation programme for the 50 percent of India's arable land that is uncultivated in order to create 'carbon sinks'. By reducing its emissions in this way still further below its quota, under the Kyoto provisions India would gain significant additional 'emissions credits' which it could sell to industrialized countries to balance their excess emissions. He explains that "although there is no 'carbon market' yet, contracts are being negotiated ahead of 2008 when industrialized countries will be obliged by the Kyoto Protocol to begin significant reductions of harmful greenhouse gases like carbon dioxide". Nair also suggests that India could reduce its dependence on fossil fuels by following other countries and using its vast wastelands to grow crops like Jatropha, that can be used to develop biodiesel fuel. His own contribution to soil technology is a revolutionary soil management concept known as "The Nutrient Buffer Power Concept".

§

It is disturbing for a citizen of democratic India, where great civilizations flourished for millennia, to see fascism, bigotry and religious fanaticism surfacing in another great democracy – as they almost did in ours recently. The outlines of a police state with intolerance and fear as its hallmark are now emerging in the US, an intolerance which finds all other countries inferior, no matter how ancient their lineage. It is becoming obvious that America's supremacists are doing as much harm to their own country as to the rest of the world.

This was coarsely underscored by Richard Nixon when he told his National Security Advisor Henry Kissinger to bomb North Vietnam "to smithereens [...with the] nuclear bomb, does that bother you? I just want you to think big, Henry, for Chrissakes ... we're gonna bomb those bastards all over the place ... we've got to use the maximum power of this country against this shit-ass little country".[13] When the end came it was not the Vietnamese who were bombed out of Vietnam but the power that wanted to show that 'shit-ass little country' its place – a country, as it happens, of great cultural traditions.

Asian antipathy to what was once seen as the colonial west is almost entirely focused on America – for its lack of statesmanship, especially in West Asia; for its disrespect for other cultures, traditions and beliefs; for its unconcern for Asian lives; for its messianic faith in military power; for its self-indulgence in the face of the everyday struggle for survival in four-fifths of the world; and for its increasing espousal of Christian fundamentalism.

All these are bound to intensify terrorism around the world. And the targets will be not only innocent Americans – the culpable are well-guarded – but citizens of many nations. When passions reach a pitch, distinctions blur and the primal urge to destroy takes over.

This indifference to distinctions will be increasingly evident in the coming months and years if an unrepentant Republican administration continues to make the world an unsafe place for innocent and guilty alike. I am, however, convinced that the humane and humanitarian traditions of the US are too strong to be so easily trampled upon. And if sagacity, statesmanship, and even common-sense prevail, if the US can, as Bush has hinted and Kerry clearly promised, learn to cooperate with other nations, rather than exploit or dominate them, then Asians can be won over. They can neither hold grudges for long, nor wish to. They want to get on with their lives, to better their lot, to live by their faith and beliefs, to celebrate their festivals with dance, music, prayer and rejoicing, in peace and without being told what to do. If that is what Americans and other nations aspire to as well, then Asians will not be found wanting. They will make great travelling companions.

As Mahatma Gandhi once said: "If I should now allow the West in its boyishly confident rowdyism utterly to crush out an opposing system of life and ideals through political power and material influence, would I not be playing traitor not only to my own people but to you very Westerners as well?".

□ □

References

Preface

Asians killed as a result of direct and indirect US action, 1950–2003

Scholars and researchers have put a great deal of work into compiling death tolls in the wars and armed conflicts in Asia between 1950 and 2003, in which the US military played a key part. The chief sources I have drawn upon for my estimate of Asian casualties in this period are William Blum's book *Rogue State* (2000), Jon Halliday and Bruce Cumings' *Korea: The Unknown War* (1988), and research by Professor Marc W. Herold, University of New Hampshire, and by Matthew White, especially his *Historical Atlas of the Twentieth Century*. Numerous other books, encyclopedias and newspaper articles were also consulted.

Two other figures which weigh heavily in Asian perceptions of US intervention but which fall outside the period under review here have not been included. These are: the number of Chinese killed in 1945–49 in the civil war between Chiang Kai-shek's Nationalists, supported with US ships, marines and huge quantities of arms, and Mao Tse-tung's communist forces; and the massive death toll from the atom bombs dropped on Japan in August 1945.

Vietnam, 1945–73	3,800,000
Korea, 1950–53	300,000
Iran, 1953	10,000
Cambodia, 1955–73	
US bombing	600,000
Khmer Rouge	800,000
Laos, 1957–73	350,000
Indonesia, 1965	1,000,000
Afghanistan, 1979–92	1,500,000
Philippines, 1970s–1990	175,000
Iraq, 1990–2004	1,678,000
TOTAL	10,213,000

1 The Long Shadow

1 *Partisan Review,* Winter 1967, p.57.
2 Patwant Singh, *India and the Future of Asia* (New York, Alfred A. Knopf, 1966), pp.18–19.
3 H. G. Rawlinson, *India: A Short Cultural History* (London, The Cresset Press, 1954), pp.211–12.
4 For an account of Sikh traditions and history see my book *The Sikhs* (London, John Murray, 1999).
5 Joseph Davey Cunningham, *A History of the Sikhs* (New Delhi, Rupa, 2002), pp.266–67.
6 Ibid., p.267.
7 Donald Featherstone, *At Them With the Bayonet: The First Sikh War* (London, Jarrolds, 1968), p.116.
8 Bikrama Jit Hasrat, *Anglo-Sikh Relations, 1799–1849* (Hoshiarpur, V. V. Research Institute, 1968), p.282.
9 Ibid., p.382.
10 Featherstone, p.162.
11 Barbara W. Tuchman, *The March of Folly: From Troy to Vietnam* (New York, Alfred A. Knopf, 1984), p.231.
12 Patwant Singh, *Of Dreams and Demons – An Indian Memoir* (London, Duckworth, 1994), p.13.
13 Anthony Read and David Fisher, *The Proudest Day* (London, Jonathan Cape, 1997), p.9.
14 United States, Great Britain, France, Japan, Italy, Portugal, Belgium, Netherlands and China.
15 Sergei I. Witte, *The Memoirs of Count Witte* (New York, Garden City, 1921), pp.121–22.
16 David J. Dallin, *The Rise of Russia in Asia* (New Haven, Yale University Press, 1949), p.26.
17 Ivan Barsukev, *Muaraviev-Asastiv* (Moscow, 1981), pp.321–23.
18 Dallin, p.20.
19 Tso Tsung-tang, Tsan Kao, *Compiled Petitions to the Throne* (Vol. 55), p.35.
20 Speech on September 17, 1920 to the Petrograd Soviet.
21 At the Second All-Russian Congress of Soviets of Workers' and Soldiers' Deputies, Petrograd, November 8, 1917.

22 Basil Dmytryshyn, *USSR – A Concise History* (New York, Charles Scribner's Sons, 1971), p.123.

23 Bruce Grant, *Indonesia* (Melbourne, Melbourne University Press, 1964), p.2.

24 Ibid., p.3.

25 Ibid., pp.16–17.

26 Ibid., pp.22.

27 Richard J. Barnet, *Intervention and Revolution* (New York, Meridian Books, 1968), p.228.

28 David Wise and Thomas B. Rose, *The Invisible Government* (New York, Vintage Books, 1974), p.111.

29 Manfred Halpern, 'Middle East and North Africa', in *Communism and Revolution*, edited by Cyril E. Black and Thomas P. Thorton (Princeton University Press, 1964), p.318.

2 Between Rhetoric and Reality

1 George Orwell, 'Politics and the English Language' in *Shooting an Elephant* (1950).

2 Carl Berger, *The Korea Knot* (Philadelphia, University of Pennsylvania Press, 1957/1964), p.41.

3 Ibid., p.41.

4 *The New York Times*, September 30, 1945.

5 Harold R. Isaacs, *No Peace for Asia* (New York, The MacMillan Company, 1947), p.87.

6 Berger, p.106.

7 Ibid.

8 Adam B. Ulam, *Expansionism & Coexistence* (New York, Frederick A. Praeger, 1968), p.519.

9 Morton H. Halperin, 'The Korean War' in *Case Studies in the Use of Force*, edited by Robert J. Art and Kenneth N. Waltz (Boston, Little Brown, 1971), pp.230–32.

10 *The New York Times*, January 8, 2003.

11 Ibid.

12 Ibid.

13 Bob Woodward, *Bush at War* (New York, Simon & Schuster, 2002), p.340.

14 *Time*, January 13, 2003 p.20.

15 Neil Sheehan, *The Pentagon Papers* (New York, Bantam Books, 1971), p.8.

16 Ibid., p.8.

17 Harold Isaacs, 'Independence for Vietnam', in *VietNam*, edited by Marvin E. Gettleman (New York, Fawcett World Library, 1965), p.55.

18 Ibid., p.55.

19 Donald Lancaster, 'Power Politics at the Geneva Conference 1954', in *VietNam*, p.135.

20 Roscoe Drummond and Gaston Coblentz, *Duel at the Brink* (New York, 1960), p.26.

21 *The Vietnam Hearings* (New York, Random House, 1966), pp.172–83.

22 *Ecological Effects of the Vietnam War*, Concerned Architects and Planners, UCLA.

23 William R. Corson, *The Betrayal* (New York, Norton, 1968), pp.48–71.

24 *Ecological Effects of the Vietnam War.*

25 Noam Chomsky, *At War With Asia* (New York, Vintage Books, 1970), p.99.

26 Orville and Jonathan Schell in a letter to *The New York Times*, November 26, 1969.

27 American Friends Service Committee, Vietnam 1969 (May 5, 1969).

28 Noam Chomsky, pp.298–99.

29 Ibid.

30 Ibid.

31 Ibid., p.297.

32 Christopher Hitchens, *The Trial of Henry Kissinger* (New York, Verso, 2001), p.33.

33 Ibid., pp.34–35.

34 Ibid., pp.40–41.

35 Ibid., pp.35.

36 William Shawcross, *Sideshow: Kissinger, Nixon and the Destruction of Cambodia* (New York, Simon & Schuster, 1979), pp.11–14.

37 Ibid., p.21.

38 Ibid., p.22.

39 Ibid., p.33.

40 Ibid., p.147.

41 Ibid., p.145.

42 Samantha Power, *A Problem from Hell: America and the Age of Genocide* (London, Flamingo, 2003), p.92.

43 Victor Marchetti and John D. Marks, *The CIA and the Cult of Intelligence* (New York, Alfred A. Knopf, 1974), p.32.

44 Nayan Chanda, 'Lao-Thai Gulf is Still Wide,' *Far Eastern Economic Review*, August 26, 1977.

45 Hitchens, p.39.

46 Ibid., p.39.

47 Nayan Chanda, 'Laos Gears up for Rural Progress', *Far Eastern Economic Review*, April 8, 1977.

48 Noam Chomsky and Edward S. Herman, *After the Cataclysm* (Montreal, Black Rose Books, 1979), p.127.

49 Ibid., p.120.

50 Address to the Conference of the Peoples of Indo-China, 1963.

51 Victor Marchetti and John O. Marks, *The CIA and the Cult of Intelligence* (New York, Alfred A. Knopf, 1974), p.29.

52 David Wise and Thomas B. Ross, *The Invisible Government* (New York, Vintage Books, 1974), pp.140–141.

53 Marchetti and Marks, p.114.

54 Quoted by John Pilger, *The New Rulers of the World* (London, Verso, 2003), p.32.

55 Peter Dale Scott, 'The Vietnam War and the CIA Financial Establishment,' in *Remaking Asia*, edited by Mark Selden (New York, Pantheon Books/Random House, 1974), p.121.

56 Pilger, p.39.

57 Ibid., p.41.

3 American Internationalism

1 Statement made on March 4, 1917. *The New York Times*, March 5, 1917.

2 Trumbull Higgins, *Korea and the Fall of MacArthur* (New York, Oxford University Press, 1960), p.27.

3 Alfonso A. Narvaez, 'Gen. Curtis LeMay, an Architect of Strategic Air Power, Dies at 83,' *The New York Times*, October 2, 1990, B6.

4 Ira Chernus, 'Shock & Awe: Is Baghdad the Next Hiroshima?', CommonDreams. org, February 27, 2003.

5 Ibid.

6 Ibid.

7 *A Statement of Conscience: Not in Our Name*, 158 Church Street, PMB 9, New York, N. Y10007–2204.

8 *The Progressive*, February 2003.

9 Edward Said, 'A Monument to Hypocrisy', *Al-Ahram*, February 14, 2003.

10 Arianna Huffington, 'The Bottom Line on Iraq: It's the Bottom Line', http://www.ariannaonline. com, February 19, 2003.

11 Jay Bookman, 'The President's Real Goal in Iraq', *The Atlanta Journal Constitution*, September 29, 2002.

12 Ibid.

13 Ibid.

14 James Carroll, 'The President's Nuclear Threat', *Boston Globe*, October 1, 2002.

15 William M. Arkin, 'Secret Plan Outlines the Unthinkable', *Los Angeles Times*, March 10, 2002.

16 In a debate on 'American Power and the World Order', www. openDemocracy.net on November 7, 2002.

17 William M. Arkin, March 10, 2002.

18 Ibid.

19 *Speeches and Lectures, Nobel Peace Prize* [1985], International Physicians for the Prevention of Nuclear War.

20 Ibid.

21 Bernard Lown to the author, March 2003.

22 Ibid.

23 Felicity Arbuthnot, 'Depleted Uranium: My Battle for the Truth', *Sunday Herald*, January 14, 2001.

24 Ibid.

25 Siegwart-Horst Gunther, 'Depleted Uranium and the Gulf War Syndrome', *Covert Action Quarterly,* Spring-Summer 2000 (No. 69).

26 Felicity Arbuthnot, 'Lie of the Millennium?', *Al-Ahram Weekly On-Line*, March 15–21, 2001, Issue no. 525.

27 Charlie Clements to the author, March 2003.

28 Felicity Arbuthnot, loc. cit.

29 John Pilger, 'Focus: Inside Iraq – The Tragedy of a People Betrayed', *The Independent*, February 23, 2003.

30 Susan Taylor Martin, 'Is Depleted Uranium Hurting the Health of Iraqis and US Gulf War Veterans?', *St Petersburg Times*, June 5, 2000.

31 Ibid.

32 Robert Fisk, 'The Truth About Depleted Uranium', *The Independent*, January 8, 2001.

33 Siegwart-Horst Gunther, loc. cit.

34 Ibid.

35 John Pilger, loc. cit.

36 *British Medical Journal*, January 16, 1999.

37 John Pilger, loc. cit.

38 P. Sainath, 'Coalition of the Killing', *The Hindu*, April 13, 2003.

39 John Pilger, loc. cit.

40 Ibid.

41 Ibid.
42 Ibid.
43 Ibid.
44 Seymour Melman, 'In the Grip of a Permanent War Economy', www.bear-left.com, March 9, 2003.
45 James Risen, 'CIA Aides Feel Pressure in Preparing Iraqi Reports', *The New York Times*, March 23, 2003.
46 In a letter to the President, March 17, 2003.
47 Ira Chernus, February 27, 2003.
48 John Pilger, extract from British ITV Archives.
49 Ibid.
50 George W. Bush, address to a Joint Session of Congress and the American People, September 20, 2001.
51 In a conversation with the author, summer 2003.

4 New Tools of Dominance

1 Farewell broadcast, January 17, 1961, *The New York Times*, January 18, 1961.
2 'World Armaments and Disarmament', *Stockholm International Peace Research Institute Yearbook 1981* (London, Taylor & Francis, 1981), p.15.
3 'Arms Sales Up, Security Down', Congressional Record – Senate, April 3, 1981.
4 Gene I. Rochlin, 'Arms Sales to Whom?', *The New York Times*, June 30, 1981.
5 Geoff Simons, *Iraq from Sumer to Sudan* (London, St Martin's Press, 1994), pp.179–81.
6 Ibid.
7 Richard Norton-Taylor, 'UK is Selling Bombs to India', *The Guardian*, June 20, 2002.
8 Ibid.
9 Ibid.
10 Ibid.
11 BBC News, June 20, 2002.
12 BBC News, July 9, 2002.
13 Paul Eavis, Director of Safeworld, quoted by Richard Norton-Taylor, June 20, 2002.
14 BBC News, July 9, 2002.
15 John Pilger, *The New Rulers of the World* (London, Verso, 2003), pp.23–24.
16 Ibid., p.27.
17 James Fallows, *National Defense* (New York, Random House, 1981), p.67.
18 Ibid., p.10.
19 Michael Moore, *Stupid White Men* (New York, Reagan Books/HarperCollins, 2001), pp.19–20.
20 Joseph Wilson, 'Republic or Empire', *The Nation*, March 3, 2003.
21 The figures for arms sales and some of the other details regarding trends in weapons transfers given in this chapter are taken from *The Military Balance 2002–2003* (London, The International Institute for Strategic Studies, 2002).
22 Anthony Sampson, *The Arms Bazaar* (London, Hodder & Stoughton, 1977), p.31.
23 *The Military Balance 2002–2003* (London, The International Institute for Strategic Studies, 2002), p.295.
24 Felix Greene, *The Enemy* (London, Jonathan Cape, 1970), p.15.
25 *The New York Times*, September 18, 1963.
26 Ibid., February 6, 1969.
27 Greene, p.126.
28 Charles Wolfe Jr, *Foreign Aid: Theory and Practice in Southern Asia* (Princeton University Press, 1960), pp.264–65.
29 Bill Moyers on 'Privatising Democracy', www.pbs.org/now, April 18, 2003.
30 Greene, p.139.
31 Pilger, p.101.
32 James A. Linen, 'An International Meeting to Establish a Creative Dialogue for Future Commentators', *Proceedings of the Indonesian Investment Conference* Report, November 2–4, 1967, Geneva.
33 Pilger, pp.17–18.
34 Ibid., p.19.
35 Moyers, April 18, 2003.
36 Bob Herbert, 'Spoils of War', *The New York Times*, April 10, 2003.
37 Ibid.
38 Oliver Morgan and Ed Vulliamy, 'Cronies Set to Make a Killing', *The Observer*, April 6, 2003.
39 Naomi Klein, 'Privatization in Disguise', *The Nation*, April 28, 2003.
40 United Nations: Department of Economic and Social Affairs, *Multinational Corporations in World Development* (New York, United Nations, 1973), p.2.
41 Joseph Kahn, 'A Disaffected Insider Surveys *Globalization and Its Discontents*', *The New York Times*, June 23, 2002.

42 Joseph E. Stiglitz, *Globalization and Its Discontents* (New York, W. W. Norton, 2002), pp.89–97.

43 Shaukat H. Mohammed, 'Development Rather than Privatization', *The Asian Age*, April 29, 2003.

44 Greg Palast, *The Best Democracy Money Can Buy* (London, Pluto Press, 2002), p.52.

45 Stiglitz, p.125.

46 Ibid., p.126.

47 Ibid., p.134.

48 Ibid., pp.144–45.

49 'Asia Must Fight Globalization', *The Hindu*, January 8, 2003.

50 Ibid.

51 David Corn, 'The Pentagon's (CIA) Man in Iraq', www.thenation.com/capitalgames, April 4, 2003.

52 Howard Zinn, 'My Country: The World', www.tompaine.com.

5 The Willing Media

1 *Esquire*, June 1960.

2 Neil Sheehan and others, *The Pentagon Papers* (New York, Bantam Books, 1971), p.663.

3 Ibid., p.150.

4 Barbara Ehrenreich, 'The Unbearable Being of Whiteness', *The Worst Years of Our Lives* (New York, Pantheon Books, 1990), p.42.

5 Ibid., p.43.

6 Thomas L. Friedman, 'Yes, But What,' *The New York Times*, October 5, 2001.

7 Howard Zinn, *The Nation*, February 11, 2002.

8 Ibid.

9 Greg Dyke, at a journalism symposium held at Goldsmiths College, University of London, on April 24, 2003.

10 C. P. Chandrasekhar, 'The Cost of Media Consolidation', *Frontline*, May 23, 2003.

11 Paul Krugman, 'The China Syndrome', *The New York Times*, May 13, 2003.

12 Ibid.

13 Greg Dyke, loc. cit.

14 Andrew Grossman, 'Bashfield Lashes Out at Own Network', *Hollywood Reporter*, April 28, 2003.

15 Robert Scheer, 'Bush Pushes the Big Lie Towards the Brink', *Los Angeles Times*, March 5, 2003.

16 Chalmers Johnson, 'The Real Casualty from America's Iraq Wars', www.tomdispatch.com.

17 Ibid.

18 Ibid.

19 *The Times of India*, January 6, 2004.

20 Michael Massing, 'The Unseen War', *The New York Review of Books*, May 29, 2003.

21 Ibid.

22 Ibid.

23 Ibid.

24 Ibid.

25 Louis Herren, p.132.

26 Marc W. Herold, 'The evil, the grotesque and US official lies', *Frontline*, May 9, 2003.

27 Marvin Kalb, at a Seminar in the Shorenstein Center, Kennedy School of Government, Harvard University, October 2001.

28 Ibid.

29 Russ Baker, 'News Without a Compass', www.tompaine.com, May 13, 2003.

30 John Kampfner, 'Saving Private Lynch Story Flawed', http://news.bbc.co.uk All quotations that follow on this story are from this source.

31 Information Clearing House, emailtom@cox.net, September 2, 2003.

32 Christopher Marquis, 'World turned against US after War on Iraq', *The New York Times* News Service/*The Asian Age*, June 5, 2003.

33 Ibid.

34 Ibid.

35 Edward Said, 'An Unacceptable Helplessness', *Al-Ahram*, January 17, 2003.

36 Raghav Gupta, 'Fear, Anger on Arab Street,' *The Indian Express*, May 29, 2003.

37 Ibid.

38 Ibid.

39 Ibid.

40 Michael Massing, May 29, 2003.

41 Paul Belden, 'Free Press and the Face of War', *Asia Times*, http://www.atimes.com, March 25, 2003.

42 Robert Fisk, 'Did the US Murder these Journalists?', *The Independent*, April 26, 2003.

43 Robert Fisk, 'Is there some element in the US military that wants to take out journalists?' *The Independent*, April 9, 2003.

44 Michael Massing, May 29, 2003.

45 Robert Fisk, April 9, 2003.

46 Ibid.

47 Ibid.

48 Seema Mustafa, 'Journalists Still Question US Attack on Hotel', *The Asian Age*, April 17, 2003.

49 Ajit Bhattacharjea, 'The Images Are at War', *The Asian Age*, April 15, 2003.

50 Raja Menon, 'In Defence of the Iraq Offensive', *The Indian Express*, May 3, 2003.

51 Sashi Kumar, 'The Medium's Temptations', *The Hindu*, June 1, 2003.

52 Kalpana Sharma, 'True Lies and War', *The Hindu*, April 6, 2003.

53 Barbara Tuchman, *Sand Against the Wind: Stilwell and the American Experience in China, 1911–45* (London, Macmillan, 1970), p.436.

54 *The Times of India*/Reuters, December 17, 2003.

55 A. G. Noorani, 'A Murder's Been Arranged', *The Hindustan Times*, January 13, 2004.

6 A Democracy's Imperial Burden

1 Senator Sherman on James Buchanan (15th President of the United States), *Barbed Quotes*, compiled by Colin M. Jarman (Lincolnwood / Chicago, Contemporary Books, 1999), p.343.

2 John O'Farrell, 'Hans Off the UN', *The Guardian*, June 13, 2003.

3 Message to Congress, January 6, 1941, in *Public Papers* (1941), vol. 9, p.672.

4 *The Hindu*/AP, February 1, 2004.

5 'White House Edits Global Warning Report', Associated Press, Washington, June 19, 2003.

6 Ibid.

7 'Transportation in US Largest Generator of CO_2 Emissions', Agence France Presse, Washington, May 30, 2003.

8 Ibid.

9 Katherine Stapp, 'Presidential Hopefuls Push Energy Alternatives, Pax Kyoto', Inter Press Service, www.commondreams.org, June 10, 2003.

10 Ibid.

11 Climate Change Campaign, http://www.foei.org/climate/faq.html, Friends of the Earth International, Secretariat P. O. Box 19199, 1000 GD Amsterdam, The Netherlands.

12 Andrew C. Revkin, 'Divisions over emissions', *The Hindu*, December 5, 2003.

13 George Marshall and Mark Lynas, 'Why we don't give a damn', *New Statesman*, December 1, 2003.

14 *The Times of India*/AP, December 19, 2003.

15 George Marshall and Mark Lynas, loc. cit.

16 'NPT 2000 Review Conference', April 24–May 19, 2000, UN Department for Disarmament Affairs, New York.

17 Bernard Lown MD, Ronald S. McCoy MD, Joanna Santa Barbara MD, 'The US Nuclear Posture Review: How the NPR Repudiates the NPT', International Physicians for the Prevention of Nuclear War, March 14, 2002.

18 Ibid.

19 Ibid.

20 Kathryn Crandall, 'Test Ban AWOL from Washington's WMD Strategy', British American Security Information Council, Washington, January 24, 2003.

21 Peter Popham, 'Nuclear War Risk Grows as States Race to Acquire Bomb', *The Independent*, April 29, 2003.

22 Ibid.

23 Ibid.

24 Katherine Crandall, loc. cit.

25 Senator Douglas Roche, OC, 'Precious But Fleeting', *Report on the November 2001 Conference on Facilitating the Entry-into-Force of the CTBT*, Ploughshares Working Paper 01–6.

26 Ibid.

27 Ibid.

28 Quoted in Merle D. Kellerhals Jr, 'US Will Withdraw From 1972 Anti-Ballistic Missile Treaty', US Department of State's Office of International Information Programmes, December 13, 2001.

29 Ibid.

30 Eliot Weinberger, 'What's Happening in America?', *The Hindu*, India, July 6, 2003.

31 George Soros, 'Bush's Inflated Sense of Supremacy', *The Financial Times*, March 12, 2003.

32 Ibid.

33 Dominique Moisi, 'The World Order Needs New Rules', *The Financial Times*, June 30, 2003.

34 Sebastian Mallaby, 'The Reluctant Imperialist, Terrorism, Failed States, and the Case for American Empire', *Foreign Affairs*, New York, March–April 2002.

35 Robert D. Kaplan, 'Supremacy by Stealth: Ten Rules for Managing the World', *The Atlantic Monthly*, July–August, 2003.

36 Quoted by Philip S. Golub, 'The Dynamics of World Disorder: Westward the Course of Empire', *Le Monde Diplomatique*, September 2002.

37 Michael Ignatieff, 'Nation-Building Lite', *The New York Times Magazine*, July 28, 2002.

38 Stephen Peter Rosen, 'The Future of War and the American Military', *Harvard Review*, May–June 2002, vol. 104, no. 5.

39 Joseph S. Nye Jr, *The Paradox of American Power* (New York, Oxford University Press, 2002).

40 Paul Kennedy, 'The Greatest Superpower Ever', *New Perspectives Quarterly*, Washington, Winter 2002.

41 Robert Kagan, 'The Benevolent Empire', *Foreign Policy*, Washington, Summer 1998.

42 Dinesh D'Souza, 'In Praise of Empire', *Christian Science Monitor*, April 26, 2002.

43 Robert D. Kaplan, loc. cit.

44 Noam Chomsky and David Barsamian, 'Imperial Ambition', *Monthly Review*, May 16, 2003.

45 Ibid.

46 Noam Chomsky, 'Does the USA Intend to Dominate the Whole World by Force?' Interview on Amsterdam Forum, Radio Netherlands' Interactive Discussion Programme, June 2, 2003. Michael J. Glennon's article 'Why the Security Council Failed' appeared in *Foreign Affairs*, May/June 2003.

47 Ibid.

48 From a letter to the author.

49 Eliot Weinberger, loc. cit.

50 Claire Tristram, 'Benny Elon's Long, Strange Trip', *Salon Magazine* and www.clairetristram.com, May 2003.

51 Ibid.

52 Ibid.

7 Pitfalls of Power

1 *The Observer*, December 30, 1973.

2 Kevin Berqquist, 'War on Crime Adversely Affects War on Terrorism, Professor says', The University of Michigan News Service, www.umich.edu, October 14, 2002.

3 Ibid.

4 Carolyn Walkup, 'Anti-Arab Bias, Hate Crimes Hit Operators', *Nations Restaurant News*, October 22, 2001.

5 Jonathan Turley, 'Appetite for Authoritarianism Spawned an American Gulag', *Los Angeles Times*, May 2, 2003.

6 J. William Fulbright, *The Price of Empire* (New York, Pantheon Books, 1989), p.128.

7 Ibid.

8 G. John Ikenberry, 'America's Imperial Ambition', *Foreign Affairs* (Council on Foreign Relations, New York), September–October, 2002.

9 Ibid.

10 Ibid.

11 The argument set out in this paragraph was put to me by Dipankar Gupta in private conversation.

12 Noam Chomsky and Edward S. Herman, *After the Cataclysm* (Montreal, Black Rose, 1979), p.15.

13 Conversation with the author.

14 Ruth Rosen, 'At Home, No Superpower', *San Francisco Chronicle*, April 28, 2003.

15 Ibid.

16 Paul Webster, 'Just Like Old Times', *The Bulletin of Atomic Scientists*, August 2003.

17 'A Nuclear Pandora's Box (Part I)', Tomeditor@aol.com, August 5, 2003.

18 James Carroll, 'The President's Nuclear Threat', *Boston Globe*, October 1, 2002.

19 James Sterngold, 'Beyond North Korea: A New Nuclear Threat', *San Francisco Chronicle*, August 3, 2003.

20 Ibid.

21 William J. Broad, 'Facing a Second Nuclear Age', *The New York Times*, August 3, 2003.

22 Ibid.

23 Ibid.

24 Ibid.

25 Julian Borger, 'US Scraps Nuclear Weapons Watchdog', *The Guardian*, July 31, 2003.

26 Julian Borger, 'Dr Strangeloves Meet to Plan New Nuclear Era', *The Guardian*, August 7, 2003.

27 Editorial, 'The Climate Must Change, and Reform Must Start With America', *The Guardian*, August 6, 2003.

28 John Vidal, 'Global Warming May Be Speeding Up, Warns Scientist', *The Guardian*, August 6, 2003.

29 Ibid.

30 Editorial, *The Guardian*, August 6, 2003.

31 F. Sherwood Rowland, in conversation with the author, February 2004.

32 http://www.house.gov

33 Paul Krugman, 'Salt of the Earth', *The New York Times*, August 8, 2003.

34 Ibid.

35 Michael Scherer, 'The Return of the Poppy Fields', MotherJones.com, May 19, 2003.

36 Tom Parfitt, 'On Europe's new drugs border, a tide of heroin floods through Tajikistan', *Sunday Telegraph*, November 2, 2003.

37 Michael Scherer, loc. sit.

38 Jonathan Steele, 'Time to talk to the Taliban', *The Guardian*, January 7, 2004.

39 '6 Afghan children die in US raid', *The Hindu*, December 11, 2003.

40 F. S. Aijazuddin, 'Judgement at Mosul', *Dawn*, August 4, 2003.

41 'And Then There Was One', *Time* (Asia), August 4, 2003.

42 'See How They Ran', *Newsweek*, August 4, 2003.

43 F. S. Aijazuddin, loc. cit.

44 Eric Margolis, 'US Wants Saddam, But Dead – Not Alive', *The Toronto Sun*, August 3, 2003.

45 Amitav Ghosh, 'Lessons of Empire', *The Hindu*, July 24, 2003.

46 Ibid.

47 'Mubarak says Iraq War Will Produce "100 bin Ladens"', www.commondreams.org, March 31, 2003.

48 'Arab Apathy', *Al-Ahram Weekly Online*, February 27–March 5, 2003.

49 Ibid.

50 Ibid

51 Ibid.

52 Ibid.

53 Mario Puzo, *The Fourth K* (London, Pan Books, 1991), pp.393, 396, 397.

8 Epilogue

1 Speech in Boston, October 30, 1940, in *Public Papers* (1941), Vol. 9 pages 643.

2 Jonathan Turley, 'Attorney general shows himself as a menace to liberty', *Los Angeles Times*, September 3, 2004.

3 Travis Morales, 'The challenge before us – stopping the repression against Muslim, Arab and South Asian immigrants', www.notinourname.net, July 2003.

4 At an annual Anglo-Italian gathering in Tuscany according to a Reuter report in *The Times of India*, September 21, 2004.

5 Michael Portillo, 'A Sage King teaches us how to be Middle East wise men', *The Sunday Times*, London, November 28, 2004.

6 James Carroll, *Crusade: Chronicles of an Unjust War* (Metropolitan Books, 2004)

7 Seymour M. Hersh, *Chain of Command: The Road from 9/11 to Abu Ghraib* (New York, Harper Collins, 2004).

8 Ibid., 16.

9 In a 90 minutes television debate with John Kerry at the end of September 2004.

10 Fareed Zakaria, 'Americans eat cheese too', *Newsweek*, reproduced by *The Asian Age*, October 9, 2004.

11 'Burundi & Liberia to Ratify International Criminal Court', http://www.scoop.co, September 23, 2004.

12 In letters to the author.

13 Greg King, 'Daniel Ellsberg's crusade against the abuse of presidential power, from Nixon to Bush', *The Sun*, October 2004

Select Bibliography

Robert J. Art and Kenneth N. Waltz (editors), *Case Studies in the Use of Force*, Little, Brown, Boston, 1971.

Richard J. Barnet, *Intervention and Revolution*, Meridian, New York, 1968.

Ivan Barsukev, *Muaraviev-Asastiv*, Moscow, 1981.

Carl Berger, *The Korean Knot*, University of Pennsylvania Press, Philadelphia, 1957/1964.

Cyril E. Black and Thomas P. Thorton (editors), *Communism and Revolution*, Princeton University Press, Princeton, 1964.

Noam Chomsky, *At War With Asia*, Vintage Books, New York, 1970.

Noam Chomsky and Edward S. Herman, *After the Cataclysm*, Black Rose, Montreal, 1979.

Andrew Cockburn, *The Threat*, Random House, New York, 1983.

William R. Corson, *The Betrayal*, W. W. Norton, New York, 1968.

Joseph Davey Cunningham, *A History of the Sikhs*, Rupa, New Delhi, 2002 (first published 1849).

David J. Dallin, *The Rise of Russia in Asia*, Yale University Press, New Haven, 1949.

Basil Dmytryshyn, *USSR: A Concise History*, Charles Scribner's Sons, 1971.

Roscoe Drummond and Gaston Coblentz, *Duel at the Brink*, New York, 1960.

Barbara Ehrenreich, *The Worst Years of Our Lives*, Pantheon Books, New York, 1990.

James Fallows, *National Defense*, Random House, New York, 1981.

Donald Featherstone, *At Them with the Bayonet: The First Sikh War*, Jarrolds, London, 1968.

Frances Fitzgerald, *Fire in the Lake*, Little, Brown, New York, 1972.

J. William Fulbright, *The Price of Power*, Pantheon Books, New York, 1989.

Marvin E. Gettleman (editor), *VietNam*, Fawcett World Library, New York, 1965.

Bruce Grant, *Indonesia*, Melbourne University Press, Melbourne, 1964.

Felix Greene, *The Enemy*, Jonathan Cape, London, 1970.

Roy Gutman and David Rieff (editors), *Crimes of War: What the Public Should Know*, W. W. Norton, New York, 1999.

Bikrama Jit Hasrat, *Anglo-Sikh Relations*, 1799–1849, V. V. Research Institute, Hoshiarpur, 1968.

Louis Herren, *The Power of the Press?*, Orbis, London, 1985.

Trumbull Higgins, *Korea and the Fall of MacArthur*, Oxford University Press, New York, 1960.

Christopher Hitchens, *The Trial of Henry Kissinger*, Verso, New York, 2001.

Harold R. Isaacs, *No Peace for Asia*, The Macmillan Company, New York, 1947.

Chalmers Johnson, *Blowback: The Cost and Consequences of American Empire*, Henry Holt (Owl Books edition), New York, 2001.

Robert Jay Lifton, *The Nazi Doctors: Medical Killing and the Psychology of Genocide*, Basic Books, New York, 1986.

Victor Marchetti and John D. Marks, *The CIA and the Cult of Intelligence*, Alfred A. Knopf, New York, 1974.

The Military Balance 2002–2003, The International Institute for Strategic Studies, London, 2002.

Michael Moore, *Stupid White Men*, Reagan Books/HarperCollins, New York, 2001.

Joseph S. Nye Jr, *The Paradox of American Power*, Oxford University Press, New York, 2002.

Greg Palast, *The Best Democracy Money Can Buy*, Pluto Press, London, 2002.

John Pilger, *The New Rulers of the World*, Verso, London, 2003.

Samantha Power, *Problem From Hell: America and the Age of Genocide*, Flamingo, London, 2002.

Ahmed Rashid, *Taliban*, Yale University Press/I. B. Tauris, New York and London, 2000.

H. G. Rawlinson, *India: A Short Cultural History*, Cresset Press, London, 1945.

Anthony Read and David Fisher, *The Proudest Day*, Jonathan Cape, London, 1997.

Edward W. Said, *Covering Islam*, Vintage, London, 1997.

– *Culture and Imperialism*, Vintage, London, 1994.

– *Orientalism*, Vintage, London, 1978.

Anthony Sampson, *The Arms Bazaar*, Hodder & Stoughton, London, 1977.

Ziauddin Sardar and Merryl Wyn Davies, *Why Do People Hate America?*, Icon Books, Cambridge, 2002.

Mark Seldon (editor), *Remaking Asia*, Pantheon Books, New York, 1974.

William Shawcross, *Sideshow: Kissinger, Nixon and the Destruction of Cambodia*, Simon & Schuster, New York, 1979.

Neil Sheehan, *The Pentagon Papers*, Bantam Books, New York, 1971.

Geoff Simons, *Iraq from Sumer to Sudan*, St Martin's Press, London, 1994.

Patwant Singh, *India and the Future of Asia*, Alfred A. Knopf, New York, 1966.

– *Of Dreams and Demons: An Indian Memoir*, Duckworth, London, 1994.

Joseph E. Stiglitz, *Globalization and its Discontents*, W. W. Norton, New York, 2002.

I. F. Stone, *The Trial of Socrates*, Anchor Books/Doubleday, New York, 1989.

James C. Thompson, *Sentimental Imperialists*, Harper & Row, New York, 1981.

Barbara W. Tuchman, *Sand Against the Wind: Stilwell and the American Experience in China, 1911–45*, Macmillan, London, 1970.

– *The March of Folly: From Troy to Vietnam*, Alfred A. Knopf, New York, 1984.

Adam B. Ulam, *Expansion and Coexistence*, Frederick A. Praeger, New York, 1968.

United Nations: Department of Economic and Social Affairs, *Multinational Corporations in World Development*, United Nations, New York, 1973.

Gore Vidal, *Perpetual War for Perpetual Peace*, Thunder's Mouth Press/Nation Books, New York, 2002.

The Vietnam Hearings, Random House, New York, 1966.

David Wise and Thomas B. Rose, *The Invisible Government*, Vintage Books, New York, 1974.

Sergei I. Witte, *The Memoirs of Count Witte*, Garden City, New York, 1921.

Charles Wolfe Jr, *Foreign Aid: Theory and Practice in Southern Asia*, Princeton University Press, Princeton, 1960.

Bob Woodward, *Bush at War*, Simon & Schuster, New York, 2002.

World Armaments and Disarmament: SIPRI Yearbook 1981, Taylor & Francis, London, 1981.

Howard Zinn, *A People's History of the United States, 1492 – Present*, HarperPerennial, New York, 1995.

– *Terrorism and War*, Seven Stories Press, New York, 2002.

Index

Copyright Acknowledgments

The author and publisher thank the following copyright owners for permission to quote from the articles listed. All other sources of quotations are identified in 'References'.

© *The Atlantic Monthly*
Robert D. Kaplan, 'Supremacy by Stealth: Ten Rules for Managing the World', July–August, 2003.

© *Boston Globe*
James Carroll, 'The President's Nuclear Threat', October 1, 2002.

© *Foreign Affairs*
G. John Ikenberry, 'America's Imperial Ambition' (Council on Foreign Relations, New York), September–October, 2002.

© *The Guardian*
Julian Borger, 'US Scraps Nuclear Weapons Watchdog', July 31, 2003.
– 'Dr Strangeloves Meet to Plan New Nuclear Era', August 7, 2003.
Richard Norton-Taylor, 'UK is Selling Bombs to India', June 20, 2002.
John O'Farrell, 'Hans Off the UN', June 13, 2003.
Editorial, 'The Climate Must Change, and Reform Must Start With America', August 6, 2003.

© *The Hindu*, Kasturi and Sons Ltd
Amitav Ghosh, 'Lessons of Empire', July 24, 2003.
P. Sainath, 'Coalition of the Killing', April 13, 2003.
Kalpana Sharma, 'True Lies and War', April 6, 2003.
Eliot Weinberger, 'What's Happening in America?', July 6, 2003.

© *The Hindustan Times*
A. G. Noorani, 'A Murder's Been Arranged', January 13, 2004.

© *The Independent*
Robert Fisk, 'The Truth About Depleted Uranium', January 8, 2001.
– 'Did the US Murder these Journalists?', April 26, 2003.
– 'Is there some element in the US military that wants to take out journalists?' April 9, 2003.

John Pilger, 'Focus: Inside Iraq – The Tragedy of a People Betrayed', February 23, 2003.
Peter Popham, 'Nuclear War Risk Grows as States Race to Acquire Bomb', April 29, 2003.

© *The Indian Express*
Raghav Gupta, 'Fear, Anger on Arab Street', May 29, 2003.
Raja Menon, 'In Defence of the Iraq Offensive', May 3, 2003.

© Naomi Klein
'Privatization in Disguise', *The Nation*, April 28, 2003.

© *Los Angeles Times*
William M. Arkin, 'Secret Plan Outlines the Unthinkable', March 10, 2002.
Robert Scheer, 'Bush Pushes the Big Lie Towards the Brink', March 5, 2003.
Jonathan Turley, 'Appetite for Authoritarianism Spawned an American Gulag', May 2, 2003.

© *The Nation*
Joseph Wilson, 'Republic or Empire', March 3, 2003.
Howard Zinn, February 11, 2002.

© *The New York Times*
William J. Broad, 'Facing a Second Nuclear Age', August 3, 2003.
Bob Herbert, 'Spoils of War', April 10, 2003.
Dispatch by Richard J. H. Johnston, September 30, 1945.
Joseph Kahn, 'A Disaffected Insider Surveys *Globalization and Its Discontents*', June 23, 2002.
Paul Krugman, 'The China Syndrome', May 13, 2003.
Gene I. Rochlin, 'Arms Sales to Whom?', June 30, 1981.

© *San Francisco Chronicle*
Ruth Rosen, 'At Home, No Superpower', April 28, 2003.
James Sterngold, 'Beyond North Korea: A New Nuclear Threat', August 3, 2003.